F. S. SCHWARZBACH

Dickens and the City

UNIVERSITY OF LONDON
THE ATHLONE PRESS
1979

Published by
THE ATHLONE PRESS
UNIVERSITY OF LONDON
at 4 Gower Street London WC1

Distributed by Tiptree Book Services Ltd
Tiptree, Essex

USA and Canada
Humanities Press Inc
New Jersey

British Library Cataloguing in Publication Data
Schwarzbach, F. S.
    Dickens and the City.
    1. Dickens, Charles—Knowledge—England—
    London   2. London in literature
    I. Title
    823'.8   PR4592.L5/
    ISBN 0 485 11174 8

Printed in Great Britain by
WESTERN PRINTING SERVICES LTD
Bristol

To Michele

Preface

This study is a development of research begun for a Master of Arts thesis at Columbia University, and continued as a Ph.D. dissertation at University College London. I am profoundly grateful to the many friends and colleagues at both of these institutions who have helped me with it, but I owe far too much to far too many to be able to acknowledge adequately all my debts. I beg forgiveness in advance from those I have forgotten to mention.

By far my greatest debt is to John Sutherland, to whose patient midwifery of this work from initial conception to final product, I owe its very existence. I also owe much to Steven Marcus, for inspiring and guiding my first study of Dickens, and for the continuing inspiration of his writings on Dickens and many other subjects; to Michael Slater, for generous advice and encouragement, especially on Chapter One; to K. J. Fielding, for correcting many errors of fact in the typescript; to the librarians and staffs of the British Library, the Victoria and Albert Museum, the University College Library, the London Library, the New York Public Library, and the Pierpont Morgan Library; and to Michele Krause, for too willing and selfless assistance in researching, editing and typing this study. I should also like to thank the Dickens Society of America and the Dickens Fellowship, London, for allowing me to reprint in slightly altered form material which first appeared in these publications: *The Dickensian* (Chapter One) and *Dickens Studies Newsletter* (Chapter Six). I am grateful to the British Library Board for permission to reproduce Plates 1, 2 and 8; the Trustees of the British Museum for permission to reproduce Plates 3, 4, 6, 7 and 9, and the Trustees of the Victoria and Albert Museum for permission to reproduce Plate 5. I am also indebted to the Trustees of the Pierpont Morgan Library and the Trustees of the New York Public Library for permission to publish brief extracts from manuscript material in their holdings. My last but by no means least debt is to the Dean's Travel Fund and Chambers' Fund of University College for generous financial assistance toward research expenses which helped speed completion of this work.

I would also like to beg pardon for the many omissions that will be evident in a study which purports to be a developmental, chronological examination of Dickens' work. I must plead in my defence that I have tried to keep before me the main concern, Dickens and the city, and rigorously to exclude everything that did not illuminate it. The most serious omission is the failure to discuss at length *David Copperfield*; I have not done so because its inspiration and subject, at least in its early pages, are so directly autobiographical that my discussion of it has been subsumed indirectly by the sections of the Introduction below that deal with Dickens' early life.

London, March 1977   F. S. S.

Contents

List of Plates

Plates 1, 2 and 8, The British Library Board;
plates 3, 4, 6, 7, and 9, The British Museum;
plate 5, Victoria and Albert Museum

A Note on References

All references to Dickens' novels, and to most of the minor writings, are to volumes of the *Oxford Illustrated Dickens* (London: Oxford, 1947–58). Those volumes of the *Clarendon Dickens* that have appeared to date have been consulted, but to avoid confusion have not been cited in the text. Those of Dickens' works not included in the *Oxford Dickens* are cited from the following: *Miscellaneous Papers*, ed. B. W. Matz, Biographical Edition (London: Chapman and Hall, 1908); *Collected Papers*, ed. Walter Dexter *et al.* (London: Nonesuch, 1938); *The Speeches of Charles Dickens*, ed. K. J. Fielding (London: Oxford, 1960); *Charles Dickens: The Public Readings*, ed. Philip Collins (Oxford: Clarendon, 1975); the Nonesuch and Pilgrim editions of Dickens' letters, ed. Walter Dexter (London: Nonesuch, 1938), and Madeline House and Graham Storey *et al.* (Oxford: Clarendon, 1965ff.), respectively; *Letters from Charles Dickens to Angela Burdett-Coutts*, ed. Edgar Johnson (London: Cape, 1953), and *Uncollected Writings*, ed. Harry Stone (London: Allen Lane, 1969). References to all of these works, and to the revised Everyman edition of John Forster's *Life of Charles Dickens* (London: Dent, 1969), will be made parenthetically in the body of the text.

A number of manuscript sources have been consulted, and references to them will also be made parenthetically in the text, using the following abbreviations:

Berg   Berg Collection, New York Public Library
V&A   Forster Collection, Victoria and Albert Museum
PML   Pierpont Morgan Library

The following standard abbreviations of Dickens' works have been used in the text when the source of a quotation is not obvious:

SB	*Sketches by Boz*	AN	*American Notes*
PP	*Pickwick Papers*	MC	*Martin Chuzzlewit*
OT	*Oliver Twist*	CB	*Christmas Books*
NN	*Nicholas Nickleby*	CS	*Christmas Stories*
OCS	*The Old Curiosity Shop*	PI	*Pictures from Italy*
BR	*Barnaby Rudge*	DS	*Dombey and Son*
MHC	*Master Humphrey's Clock*	DC	*David Copperfield*
		BH	*Bleak House*

HT	Hard Times	OMF	Our Mutual Friend
LD	Little Dorrit	ED	The Mystery of
RP	Reprinted Pieces		Edwin Drood
TTC	A Tale of Two Cities	HW	Household Words
UT	The Uncommercial	AYR	All the Year Round
	Traveller	MP	Miscellaneous Papers
GE	Great Expectations		

Certain other abbreviations have been used:

Life	Forster's Life of Charles Dickens
PL	Pilgrim Letters
NL	Nonesuch Letters
PR	Public Readings
Coutts	Letters . . . to Angela Burdett-Coutts
Speeches	Speeches of Charles Dickens

References to other works have been made in the following manner: to books—the first citation in each chapter will give author, title, place publication and publisher, and successive citations, author and title; to periodicals—each citation will give author, title, the name of the periodical, the volume number and the date of publication.

The Genesis of a Myth

It may be said that Mr. Dickens's genius is especially suited to the delineation of city life. . . . He describes London like a special correspondent for posterity.

Walter Bagehot

Modern life is city life. There can be little doubt that one of the most important and far reaching of all changes in the development of human societies over the past two hundred years has been the exponential growth of large cities. An ever increasing proportion of the world's population has become concentrated in urban areas. This has happened with astonishing speed. Even as recently as 1800, it is estimated that only 2.4 per cent of the world's people lived in cities of greater than 20,000; by 1970, the ratio was 28.1 per cent. If one uses a somewhat looser definition of urban, the proportion in 1970 was 37.1 per cent, and growing rapidly. Nor, as one might expect, is this primarily a North American and European phenomenon: the countries of the world which experienced the highest rates of urban concentration between 1940 and 1960 were Venezuela, Uruguay, Mexico, Colombia, Chile, Korea and New Zealand.[1]

Yet, impressive though they are, these statistics alone do not accurately reflect the impact of urbanisation on the world. Given the traditional dominance of town over country, augmented considerably by modern communications and technology, the degree of urbanisation of a given society invariably is far in advance of the numerical proportion of its people living in cities.[2] In this sense, the world we inhabit is already an urban one.

The implications of this global change in the nature of human society are monumental, and clearly involve far more than merely a shift in geographical patterns of residence. Human nature has been, and is being, transformed. Urbanisation has meant the development of a new way of life, an urban culture and an urban sensibility, that which we call quintessentially 'modern'. To study and by doing so to come to understand this transformation, is one of the great intellectual projects of our age.

For a variety of reasons, the study of urbanisation has been carried out most systematically and in the greatest detail upon England. For one thing, England was among the first, if not the very first, of modern countries to become urbanised: more people in England lived in towns than in the country as early as 1850. England has also been examined so extensively simply because reliable, documented sources of statistical information for most of the nineteenth century (and often earlier) exist and are readily available. It is therefore not surprising that the process of urbanisation in England has been studied in great detail from many points of view: historical, sociological, technological, economic, and so on. Yet, oddly enough, literary studies have been slow to recognise the importance of the broad cultural impact of the growth of urban living.[3]

This book is an attempt to begin to redress that imbalance. It examines one aspect of the cultural impact of urbanisation in nineteenth-century England, as it affected the life and literary work of one man, Charles Dickens. There are several important reasons for concentrating such a study upon Dickens. Walter Bagehot's magnificently apt remark, that Dickens described his city 'like a special correspondent for posterity',[4] is one which all subsequent readers would endorse. Indeed, as any student of the social history of the Victorian period knows, when one turns to specialised studies to check the accuracy of Dickens' observations, as often as not, Dickens is quoted as the leading witness on that very matter. What was the criminal underworld like in early Victorian London? Turn to *Oliver Twist*, we are told. What was it like to experience railway travel for the first time? Turn, we are told, to *Dombey and Son*; and so on. The accuracy and sheer inexhaustible scope of Dickens' observations of contemporary urban life alone would make him the most important Victorian writer for such a study as this. One need only compare the London of Dickens' novels to that of many of his contemporaries to appreciate the difference in the quality of the reportage. The city as it appears in the earliest of London novels, Pierce

Egan's *Life in London* (1822–4), is curiously flat and insubstantial. That of Bulwer Lytton's *Paul Clifford* (1830), one of the few city novels of the early 1830s, is a cardboard backdrop lacking in authenticity.

It is also true that Dickens is virtually the only English writer of any great stature to engage in a sustained effort to write about the city during the first two-thirds of the nineteenth century. With the later exception of Mrs Gaskell, who wrote about Manchester, no other important writer of fiction dealt extensively with the city. To find writers other than Dickens who wrote about London in any detail and over a substantial period of time, one must turn to people of much lesser talent, like Augustus Mayhew (brother of Henry Mayhew, author of *London Labour and the London Poor*) and Douglas Jerrold, or the prolific hack, G. W. M. Reynolds, chief author of the immense serial, *Mysteries of London* (1846–50). Even later in the century, many major literary figures avoided London material, as for many years did George Eliot, who detested the metropolis, and Tennyson, who rarely could come closer in his verse to London than Camelot. Several concentrated upon contemporary London in single works—Thackeray in *Vanity Fair* (1847–8), Trollope in *The Way We Live Now* (1874–5), George Eliot in *Daniel Deronda* (1876) and Henry James in *The Princess Casamassima* (1886). But they cannot rightly be called city writers, for they rarely wrote about the city elsewhere. Dickens alone offers an *oeuvre* which is 'about' the city, and is of great literary merit.[5]

In addition, there is another facet of Dickens' genius that makes such a study of his work vitally important. Trollope mockingly referred to Dickens as 'Mr Popular Sentiment' in *The Warden* (1854), but he understood that Dickens did have a special gift for comprehending, representing and even guiding the popular mind. Dickens' own thoughts, opinions and pronouncements on every matter from penal reform to the suppression of the Indian mutiny often may be contradictory and inconsistent, but almost always reflect the broad consensus of enlightened public opinion. Even in his life-long campaigns for Poor Law and sanitary reform, both of which were initially unpopular, minority Radical causes, one senses that Dickens was acting as spokesman for the 'Good Angel' of contemporary conscience, and eventually Parliament and the governing classes were brought round to accept his point of view.[6]

Dickens' special gifts went further than enabling him to act as the voice of contemporary opinion: he had the ability, as has perhaps no other English writer since Shakespeare, to enter into the heart and mind of a character so completely, that the character can virtually walk off the page, and be treated as a personage with an identity distinct from that of its creator. Dickens' characters seem to have been created with ideas, beliefs and views of their world which appear uncannily real. They appear to speak and think autonomously, as other people actually did, and to hold thoughts in their minds that Dickens himself often did not. And so, for all these reasons, to read Dickens is to read the imprint of the consciousness of an age. Dickens is *the* representative Victorian.

By calling Dickens representative, I do not mean to say he was in any way typical, for he was certainly a most atypical man. Rather, I believe that he is representative by virtue of his unique creative imagination. It was this gift which allowed him to evoke in his writing a world as close to that in which he lived as one ever could in words. By understanding him and the development of his work, we can understand a great deal about his entire culture and society. Therefore, while this volume studies the interrelations of the city and the life and work of Charles Dickens, and so is primarily the story of an individual, I trust that if it does this adequately, it will also illumine a larger and now obscure area of Victorian culture.

At the same time, I intend that the implications of this work should be much wider. Although primarily a study of literature, of necessity it has entailed the study of the development of the city itself during Dickens' lifetime. For this reason, I have found it necessary to move beyond those areas of study to which literary criticism recently has confined itself, and to bring to bear upon the central problem insights derived from the disciplines of history, social history, sociology and psychology, as well as from the close study of the texts themselves. Though I am well aware of my limited competence in these fields, I hope that my utilisation of them, however inadequate, may yet indicate what of value they can add to literary studies. And, in so far as I have been successful, I also hope I shall have demonstrated that literary studies shed light on the history and culture of a period as well.

II

Charles Dickens was born in 1812 in the small naval town of Portsea, the first son of John Dickens, a clerk in the Navy Pay Office. From time to time, John Dickens was transferred to different offices, and the family moved several times during Charles' childhood, first of all to London toward the end of 1814. Apparently the family remained there until the summer of 1817, when they moved to Chatham, a large shipbuilding town close to Rochester in Kent, where they were to stay some four years. Young Charles retained almost no memory of his first years in London, and little at all of anything before the move to Kent. But throughout his life, those years he would spend at Chatham constituted the stuff of his happiest and most treasured memories —centred around long walks in the surrounding rural areas, to Strood, Cobham and Gad's Hill, where there stood a large house that Dickens' father told him he might one day own if he worked very hard.

John Dickens worked very hard, and by 1820 was earning over £350 per year, a very substantial salary. But he was impecunious by nature, and as his family and income grew, so did his debts. In March 1821 the Dickenses economised by moving to a smaller house; then, probably in November, John Dickens was recalled to Somerset House in London. Charles, at school under a kindly master named William Giles, stayed on until Christmas. Then, travelling alone by coach, he came to London to join the family, now living in a small house in Bayham Street, Camden Town, then a lower middle class suburb where less affluent clerks and tradesmen were their neighbours.

But even by stringent economies, the family finances could not be rescued, and though Charles remained idle for some time, eventually it was decided that he should go to work. On 9 February 1824—just two days after his twelfth birthday— Charles was sent (through the influence of a near relation) to work at Warren's Blacking Warehouse off the Strand, pasting labels on blacking pots.[7] Two weeks afterwards, the final collapse came, and John Dickens was imprisoned in the Marshalsea for debt. The family, all except Charles, moved inside the prison shortly after that, while the boy lived in a succession of lodging houses, first in Camden Town, and then in Lant Street near the Marshalsea. Meanwhile, John Dickens had initiated proceedings to be freed under the Insolvent Debtors Act, and to be pensioned off by the Navy Pay Office. Late in May he was released from prison. But Charles, to his horror and despair, was allowed to remain at the Blacking Warehouse. One day shortly afterward, it seems his father saw him at work, exposed to public view in a large window as a kind of working advertisement. His father was humiliated on his account, and either at once or a few days later he was taken home. He had been there about four or five months. In June, he resumed his education, as a day pupil at a nearby school, Wellington House Academy.

Dickens remained there until 1827, when he was found a place as a clerk in a legal office. While there, he taught himself short-hand, and eighteen months later became a freelance reporter (or stenographer) at Doctor's Commons, an obscure and antiquated London court, situated between St Paul's and the Thames. Then, with the aid of a journalist uncle, he began a career as a parlia-mentary reporter, a job for which shorthand was essential, as most of the work consisted of transcribing debates *verbatim*. At this work he was extremely successful, and was said to have been the finest reporter in the House when he left it. While still a reporter, he began writing short stories, and achieved a modest success with them in the literary world—but that is to anticipate another story.

This outline of Dickens' childhood and youth contains only the barest facts. It is the history of a young boy who grows up in a small seaport with pleasant rural surroundings; is taken to London at the age of eleven, and about a year later is sent to work, if not actually in a factory at least in a manual trade; and then with a little bit of luck and a great deal of personal exertion, raises himself to a financially secure social rank in a respectable journalistic, and later literary, career. It is one version of the typical Victorian success story. Samuel Smiles' *Self-Help* (1859) contains capsule biographies of dozens of Dickens' successful contemporaries, self-made men whose lives follow the same rough outline. The story, in this respect, is not unique, but is highly typical.

Indeed, so far is it from being unique, this story of the move from country to city is typical not only of many of Dickens' more eminent contemporaries, but is the story of millions of English men and women during his lifetime. Even an amateur can sense this from a glance at some of the statistics of population growth and change at this time. (See accompanying table.)[8]

Population of England and Wales

1801	8,893,000	1811	10,164,000
1851	17,928,000 [102%]	1821	12,000,000 [18%]

[Figures in brackets are percentage increases]

Population of Towns of 100,000 or greater in England and Wales (inc. London)

1801	1 (i.e. London)
1811	2
1821	4
1851	8

Number of Towns of 50,000 or greater in England and Wales (inc. London)

1801	6
1811	8
1821	9
1851	22

Ratio of Rural/Urban Population

1801	70%/30%
1851	49%/51%

Percentage of Population by Age Group, 1821

0–4	13.5
5–19	34.0
20–44	32.0
45+	19.0

From 1801 to 1851, a period spanning the ten years prior to Dickens' birth to about his fortieth birthday, England's population doubled. The magnitude of this increase was unprecedented, and historians still do not agree on an explanation of how and why it happened; yet even more unprecedented was the shift of that burgeoning population towards cities. In 1801, 70 per cent of the population had lived in rural areas; by the census of 1851, the balance between town and country had shifted, albeit by one percentage point, in the opposite direction. London's population alone grew from 1,088,000 in 1801 to 2,491,000 in 1851, and by almost a quarter of a million in just the first decade of Dickens' life. The rate of increase, averaging 20 per cent per decade, was always in excess of the national growth rate. And even London was growing slowly in comparison with provincial cities like Manchester, Bolton and Birmingham, which were experiencing decennial growth rates of over 40 per cent at various times early in the century.

Throughout the first half of the century, migration was the major component of this increase in the numbers of city dwellers.[9] It is not difficult to understand why this must have been so. In the first place, it appears that fertility rates were considerably lower in the city than in the country. Perhaps more importantly, cities were places which tended to devour their inhabitants even as they were born. The infant mortality rate for all of England remained level at roughly 155 per 1000 over the entire period, 1800–50. (By contrast, the rates in modern industrial nations at the present time are generally lower than 20 per 1000.) But this average, however high it is by current standards, masks the even more appalling rates that prevailed inside large cities. Figures of about 250 per 1000 were typical urban averages, and in certain districts of Manchester, for example, it is estimated to have exceeded 500 per 1000. A child born there had less than a one in two chance of living to a first birthday. It was only as late as the 1850s and 1860s that English towns were beginning to produce their own population growth, rather than continuing to import it.

The conclusion to be drawn from these figures is that if there were in 1851 approximately six million more city dwellers in England and Wales than there had been in 1801, most of them must have been born in the country and moved to the city at some point in their lives.[10] This, too, was likely to have happened to most of them when they were fairly young, for as the figures quoted here indicate, in 1821 virtually half the population, 47.5 per cent, were nineteen years old or younger. Quite naturally, it was the young who were most able and most likely to attempt a dramatic move: children and young unmarried persons made up the bulk of the internal immigrants.

Clearly then, keeping these statistics in mind, to say that Dickens' story is representative is if anything a gross understatement. Dickens' childhood experiences were a small part of a truly national experience. But his experiences are representative not only in so far as the events were experienced by many millions of his contemporaries. They are representative as well because of the way in which they affected him, and the way in which he responded to them.

To come from the country to the city was to move from a familiar and known world to an unfamiliar and unknown one. Not only was this new environment strange, but it was horrific, terrifying and dangerous, for during the first half of the century there occurred a rapid and great deterioration of living conditions in cities. During the previous century, the population of London had been relatively stable, rising from some 650,000 in 1700 to just over 1,000,000 in 1800. The services and institutions designed to serve the people of eighteenth-century London had been able to cope, in a fairly adequate manner by the standards of the time, with their needs. But they could not adapt quickly enough to maintain their balance under the pressure of rapid population growth. Transport, education, sanitation, food distribution, religious institutions, government, housing—all these collapsed under the pressure of numbers. (The situation was even far worse in those once small provincial cities where growth was yet more rapid than in London.)

In the slums of any large town whole families would inhabit single rooms; have access to an indifferent water supply, which meant perhaps as little as two hours of filthy river water from a public standpipe one or two days a week; be forced to use a public privy, which might have drainage through the inhabited cellars of adjoining houses, sharing it with dozens, or even hundreds, of other families; and be exposed, especially after 1830, to the scourge of several recurrent epidemic and endemic diseases, including cholera, typhus, typhoid, influenza and tuberculosis.

Even the traditional consolations of religion were denied them: there were, it was estimated early in the nineteenth century, sittings in Anglican Churches for less than half the Christians then living in towns.[11]

But even more than this, the experience of the city was one of profound dislocation, of being cut off, physically and psychologically, from one's roots and one's community. Whatever its faults or virtues, the country had had its accepted values, codes of behaviour, and rules and rewards; it had given its people a way of life successfully adapted to its conditions and contingencies. The modern city had no way of life, at least as yet: as E. J. Hobsbawm writes unequivocally, 'the city destroyed society.'[12] The new dwellers in cities were completely unequipped by anything in their previous experience not only to survive the town, but even to understand it. It was becoming an environment seemingly devoid of meaning, and actually devoid of any cultural traditions or institutions which could assist them in making an adjustment to it. And whatever way of life had been successful in the past for city dwellers was itself made obsolete by changing conditions. Whatever positive institutions the city would contain—the public houses, penny theatres, workmen's institutes and chapels—they themselves would create.

The immediate consequences of such an extreme dislocation, as one can well imagine, are profound and profoundly crippling. It is, I believe, by no means inappropriate to compare the experience of entering a life in the early nineteenth-century city in England to that of inmates of concentration camps in Germany or communist prisoner-of-war camps in Korea in the early 1950s. The effects on the personality of such extreme circumstances are similar.[13] The events surrounding the experience are perceived as arbitrary and meaningless. In addition, one's own sense of identity is shattered, and the sense of self becomes uncertain.

Keeping this in mind, Dickens' reactions can be taken as typical: he saw the events surrounding his move to London as inexplicable and unjust, and he felt his sense of self collapsing under the pressures of poverty and work. He could, as a child or an adult, find no explanation whatsoever for his parents' decision to deny him the education he felt he deserved, to put him to work in a low and mean trade, and to allow him to remain there for so long after their financial crisis had ended. In addition, young Dickens felt that he was losing his rightful social station. His greatest fear was that rather than be a young gentleman, as he had been at Chatham, he would become a poor working class drudge, or even a common thief. All in all, he could take no solace from the knowledge that others had gone through similar ordeals: his sufferings were perceived by him as unique, both in nature and degree.

It is unlikely, however, that anyone could long endure such an experience of dislocation. However great the shock to the self, eventually one begins to domesticate and accommodate it, by ascribing to it some form of meaning. What happens, in essence, is that one creates a myth, a word which the *Concise Oxford English Dictionary* usefully defines as, a 'fictitious narrative ... embodying popular ideas on natural phenomena, etc.' By using the word 'myth' in this context, I mean to suggest the manner in which we adumbrate explanatory models, fictitious only in varying degrees, which account for happenings in the actual world for which there are no readily available (or acceptable) explanations. A myth in this sense need not refer to history or natural phenomena; it can deal with man-made occurrences as well. Such a myth is a variety of experiential fiction—a model which rearranges and transmutes past events and present circumstances into a consecutive narrative with order and meaning. In other words, it is a way of making sense of a world that does not itself, at least on the surface, make sense. It allows us to understand and even accept that which may yet be experienced as unpleasant and dangerous.

This is precisely what Dickens did: he created a personal myth to account for the events of his childhood which had seemed at once arbitrary and terrifying. Perhaps more important than this was that the creation of such a myth also helped to reestablish the sense of identity he had felt so threatened; for if the world did have an identifiable structure after all, he could once again apprehend his own place in it. Furthermore, from that time on, the possession of such a myth allowed him to deal more satisfactorily with the debilitating emotions of fear, anxiety, anger and frustration, that were the natural result of undergoing such an experience.

And equally as Dickens was not alone in having undergone such an experience, he was not alone in creating a mythic explanation for it. His myth was but one version of the one created and shared by millions, one which governed the Victorian apprehension of the city. It is this myth that I hope to explore below, beginning first by examining in detail Dickens' own account of his experience of the city.

III

The most complete exposition of Dickens' mythic version of his past is to be found in the unfinished autobiography he began writing at some time between 1845 and 1847, most probably late in 1846. It dealt with the first twelve or thirteen years of his life and contained information that in his lifetime he had confided to no one but his wife and his close friend and literary advisor, John Forster. It was published in fragmentary form for the first time in 1872 in Forster's biography of Dickens. But, though none of Dickens' readers knew this story nor any of the details of his early life, and while it surprised them to learn of it, it must have seemed oddly familiar when they did. Dickens' novels contain many versions of this same story, the clearest analogues of which are those of Oliver Twist, David Copperfield and Pip Pirrip. In one form or another, he had told the story many, many times over.

As a middle-aged man, looking back at his early experiences, Dickens recast them into something other than they had been, as he had already been doing unconsciously in his fiction for many years. He made of them the sort of explanatory myth about which I have been writing. The portions of Dickens' autobiographical fragment extracted below present a condensed version of this personal myth of the past. I hope that those who are familiar with it will excuse the length of the narrative below, for no understanding of Dickens' special imaginative relationship with London can be achieved without a careful consideration of this account, and of the ways in which Dickens saw the key events of his childhood.[14]

He was not much over nine years old when his father was recalled from Chatham to Somerset House, and he had to leave this good master [William Giles] and the old place endeared to him by recollections that clung to him afterwards all his life long. . . . It was the birthplace of his fancy; and he hardly knew what store he had set by its busy varieties of change and scene, until he saw the falling cloud that was to hide its pictures from him for ever. The gay, bright regiments always going and coming, the continual paradings and firings, the successions of sham-sieges and sham-defences, the plays got up with his cousin in the hospital, the navy pay-yacht in which he had sailed to Sheerness with his father, and the ships floating out in the Medway, with their far visions of sea—he was to lose them all. He was never to watch the boys at their games any more, or see them sham over again the sham-sieges and defences. He was to be taken away to London inside the stage-coach Commodore; and Kentish woods and fields, Cobham park and hall, Rochester cathedral and castle, and all the wonderful romance together, including a red-cheeked baby he had been wildly in love with, were to vanish like a dream. A longer time afterwards he recollected the stage-coach journey, and in one of his published papers ['Dullborough Town', UT, 116] said that never had he forgotten, through all the intervening years, the smell of the damp straw in which he was packed and forwarded, like game, carriage paid. 'There was no other inside passenger, and I consumed my sandwiches in solitude and dreariness, it rained hard all the way, and I thought life sloppier than I expected to find it.'

. . . Bayham Street was about the poorest part of the London suburbs then, and the house was a mean small tenement, with a wretched little back-garden abutting on a squalid court. Here was no place for new acquaintances to him: not a boy was near with whom he might hope to become in any way familiar. A washerwoman lived next door, and a Bow Street officer lived over the way. Many, many times has he spoken to me of this, and how he seemed at once to fall into a solitary condition apart from all other boys of his own age, and to sink into a neglected state at home which had always been quite unaccountable to him. 'As I thought', he said on one occasion very bitterly, 'in the little back garret in Bayham Street, of all I had lost in losing Chatham, what would I have given, if I had had anything to give, to have been sent back to any other school, to have been taught something anywhere!

... '—In an evil hour for me, as I often bitterly thought: [Warren's Blacking's] chief manager James Lamert, the relative who had lived with us in Bayham Street, seeing how I was employed from day to day, and knowing what our domestic circumstances then were, proposed that I should go into the blacking warehouse, to be as useful as I could, at a salary, I think, of six shillings a week. . . . At any rate, the offer was accepted very willingly by my father and mother, and on a Monday morning I went down to the blacking warehouse to begin my business life.

'It is wonderful to me how I could have been so easily cast away at such an age. It is wonderful to me that, even after my descent into the poor little drudge I had been since we came to London, no one had compassion enough on me—a child of singular abilities: quick, eager, delicate, and soon hurt, bodily or mentally—to suggest that something might have been spared, as certainly it might have been, to place me at any common school. Our friends, I take it, were tired out. No one made any sign. My father and mother were quite satisfied. They could hardly have been more so, if I had been twenty years of age, distinguished at a grammar-school and going to Cambridge.

'The blacking warehouse was the last house on the left-hand side of the way, at old Hungerford Stairs. It was a crazy, tumble-down old house, abutting of course on the river, and literally overrun with rats. Its wainscotted rooms and its rotten floors and staircase, and the old grey rats swarming down in the cellars, and the sound of their squeaking and scuffling coming up the stairs at all times, and the dirt and decay of the place, rise up visibly before me, as if I were there again. The counting-house was on the first floor, looking over the coal-barges and the river. There was a recess in it, in which I was to sit and work.

... 'I know I do not exaggerate, unconsciously and unintentionally, the scantiness of my resources and the difficulties of my life. I know that if a shilling or so were given me by anyone, I spent it in a dinner or a tea. I know that I worked, from morning to night, with common men and boys, a shabby child. I know that I tried, but ineffectually, not to anticipate my money, and to make it last the week through by putting it away in a drawer I had in the counting-house, wrapped into six little parcels, each parcel containing the same amount, and labelled with a different day. I know that I have lounged about the streets, insufficiently and unsatisfactorily fed. I know that, but for the mercy of God, I might easily have been, for any care that was taken of me, a little robber or a little vagabond.

. . . . 'Until old Hungerford Market was pulled down, until old Hungerford Stairs were destroyed, and the very nature of the ground changed, I never had the courage to go back to the place where my servitude began. I never saw it. I could not endure to go near it. For many years, when I came near to Robert Warren's in the Strand, I crossed over to the opposite side of the way, to avoid a certain smell of the cement they put upon the blacking-corks, which reminded me of what I was once. It was a very long time before I liked to go up Chandos Street. My old way home by the Borough made me cry . . . after my eldest child could speak.'

Dickens' account of this period of his childhood speaks powerfully for itself. It retells vividly the formative incidents of his life, and reveals how he felt—and how very strongly he felt—about them. Modern critics and biographers (and indeed Dickens himself) have stressed it as a key to understanding the man and his fiction. Edmund Wilson provided the classic formulation of their importance: 'These experiences produced a trauma in Charles Dickens from which he suffered all his life.'[15] Yet the account does present certain problems and cannot always be taken at face value, persuasive as it is. A closer analysis of it reveals what these problems are.

Looking at the overall structure of the account, we can see that Dickens divided it into three distinct sections: his childhood in Chatham, his move to London and the time he spent there before being put to work, and his short spell at the Blacking Warehouse, which last part makes up the bulk of the narrative. But these events are not simply described. They are given—by tone and texture—a mythic shape and significance. The mythic interpretation Dickens cast over them is really a very simple one. Basically it divides the world and life in it into two parts. The first, set in the country, corresponds to the years of earliest childhood, and is seen as paradise; while the second, set in the city, corresponds to adult life and work and its responsibilities, and is seen as a literal hell. To move from one to the other was to experience a secular equivalent of the Fall, with the emphasis on permanent loss ('As I thought ... of all I had lost in losing Chatham ...'). The horrible physical city is the objective correlative of Hell, with its prime locus the Blacking Warehouse at Hungerford Stairs.

Key words in the descriptions of Chatham reinforce its paradisical nature—'picturesqueness', 'sunshine', 'gay', 'bright', and 'wonderful romance'. Those associated with London stress its infernal qualities—'mean', 'wretched', 'squalid', 'dirt', 'decay', and 'common'. And like those of Hell, the sufferings of London seemed eternal: 'My rescue from this kind of existence I considered quite hopeless, and abandoned as such altogether' (*Life*, I, 26). The profound shock of dislocation, the overwhelming sense of loss, the sudden and grave threats to the sense of self, and the genuine physical horrors and dangers that the boy felt, are all absorbed into the country–city opposition.

Several relevant observations about Dickens' account of his childhood ordeal should be made at once.[16] To begin with, there are a number of discrepencies of fact in the account. Dickens thought (or so at least he told Forster) that he had left Chatham at about age nine; actually he was nearly eleven. In a letter to Forster in November 1846, he alluded to some experiences that were contemporaneous with Warren's Blacking, and wrote, 'I don't suppose I was eight years old' (*Life*, II, 28), misdating it even further. He also gave the impression that the period at Warren's Blacking began soon after his arrival; actually thirteen months had intervened. He was uncertain, too, how long he had been at Warren's, but guessed it was a year; it was probably four months, and certainly no more than five.

How are we to explain this? Admittedly, it may be a simple matter of a lapse of memory. Dickens did write this some twenty-five years after the events took place, and may well have forgotten a great deal. But such an explanation is not entirely convincing to me. After all we know that even at nine or ten, and certainly twelve, Dickens' powers of observation were remarkably acute; his detailed recollections of certain experiences and incidents from that time are so accurate and complete that it seems oddly inconsistent for him merely to have forgotten the rest. It is at least possible that these errors were the result of Dickens not correctly remembering the past, but rewriting it.

It is important to remember that this autobiography was written not by the child but the man, the successful author ('famous and caressed and happy' in his own words) looking back at the helpless and impoverished child. It is not, as so many commentators have assumed, a literal account but is in certain respects a fabrication, or, if that sounds too extreme, an imaginative reconstruction, of his childhood. After all, what autobiography is not? And as such, certain elements of fact were made subservient to the myth, or fiction, that Dickens had made out of his past. Indeed many (if not all) of the factual inaccuracies of the account can be accounted for if we endorse this explanation.

The power of the myth was great indeed. As an adult, he relocated *all* of his happy childhood memories in Kent, and so nothing could be allowed to precede them: therefore those early years had to evaporate completely. And so, though Dickens was perhaps over six years old when he left London for Chatham, he remembered virtually nothing of that first stay in the metropolis. In the same way, the experiences of coming to London—at first being left to take care of himself (employed chiefly in blacking his father's boots) for a year, and only later being put to work tying blacking pots, all distinct and separate events—tended to become one event for Dickens. The time separating them collapsed, but the time they elapsed stretched out. And by relocating them further back in the past, when he was younger and more vulnerable, their effect was further magnified.[17]

The initial shock, and no doubt the most important and damaging shock, was leaving Chatham, placed inside a coach like a parcel, and coming to the new and disappointing family home in Bayham Street. 'That he took, from the very beginning of this Bayham Street life,' wrote Forster, 'his first impression of . . . struggling poverty . . . there cannot be a doubt' (*Life*, I, 12). This again was a distortion, for in the 1820s Bayham Street was a lower middle class suburb, but hardly the slum this description implies. Looking back, Dickens made the move seem a far greater descent than it had been. (Forster did not doubt the description because by the time he was writing, in the early 1870s, Bayham Street was a shabby slum.) The way Dickens recast these events in *Oliver Twist* suggests that this class decline was a key part of Dickens' sufferings: he was not only poor, but in danger of becoming common as well. Dickens' paternal grand-parents had been domestic servants, and a maternal uncle had been an embezzler. Perhaps half understood remarks about these skeletons in the family closet haunted the boy too, and gave even greater force to his fears of becoming *déclassé*, or a criminal.

The move and the social decline it heralded, and the removal from school, were all damaging enough to the boy, long before entering Warren's Blacking. Clearly, coming to London was the substance of Dickens' initial shock. The Blacking Warehouse was only the confirmation and final decree of what he already had begun to see as a sentence to a life of shame, poverty, toil, isolation and misery.

The way in which Dickens restructured these events in *David Copperfield* makes this mythic reordering of the past more obvious. This novel was begun after the autobiographical frag-ment had been put away, but the relation between the two is clear, for as Forster reports, Dickens abandoned any ideas of completing it once he was at work on *David Copperfield* (*Life*, I, 455n). The process of recording the past was to be completed so successfully in the novel, that there was no need to continue the earlier effort. David, for the first two hundred pages of his 'Personal History' (as the novel calls itself in the full title), is an almost direct cipher for his author. (The signicant fact of the transposition of Dickens' own initials and those of David, C.D. and D.C., was noted by Forster even before the novel was written.)

Unlike his creator, however, David is placed in a rural home from the start of his life, Blunderstone in Suffolk, which is a metaphorical if not literal equivalent of Chatham. There is in the novel an added complication, the fulfilment of an Oedipal dream;

David is a posthumous child who enjoys the affection and attention of not just one but two mothers, Clara Copperfield and Clara Peggotty, his nurse. What happens next can be summarised as follows: the Oedipal dream turns nightmare when a tyrannical stepfather marries his mother, replaces David with a son of his own, and then when his mother dies, replaces him in earnest by throwing him out of the house, exiling him to London and putting him to work at Murdstone and Grinby, a wine merchant's warehouse which is nothing other than the Blacking Warehouse with a new name. (David has just turned ten at this time.) In the passages describing this time of his character's life, Dickens preserved the tone, and often the exact wording, of his autobiographical essay. What is important to note about these events is that the expulsion from the country Eden, the arrival in London, the start of the job at Warren's Blacking (i.e. Murdstone and Grinby), and David's sufferings throughout are all seen as nearly simultaneous events. This was the view of his own past Dickens had come to hold.

IV

But Dickens' imaginative view of the opposition of town and country in his own life, though derived largely from personal experience, was not only a personal view. In England, during the first half of the nineteenth century, a new attitude toward city life was taking hold of human consciousness. The nature of that attitude will be more clearly seen if it is contrasted to earlier attitudes toward the city.

Traditionally, from Roman times to the early eighteenth century, town life and country life have been seen as an opposition between good and evil, conventionally expressed in the language of disease—the moral and physical health of the country was opposed to the moral and bodily corruption of the town. This myth, then, is nothing new: but something about its use was changing. In English literature after the Restoration it had developed into a stock convention; that is, an attitude which was not so much based on real experience as on a purely literary device which need not have any serious relation to life as it was actually lived. By the latter half of the eighteenth century, it had been relegated to the status of a cliché. No one took the contrast seriously. That is to say, the fact that the literature of the time often debunked town life as wicked and unhealthy did not reflect the way most people felt about London. Dr Johnson's famous remark—that a man tired of London was tired of life— more closely captures the spirit of the age. The metropolis in his lifetime was more than ever before the cultural, political and economic centre of the nation, and attracted its finest minds. Perhaps an accurate gauge of the sensibility of the age is the growing usage during the eighteenth century of the adjective 'urbane' to mean not merely 'of the city', but 'knowledgeable, sophisticated and cultured'.

During the first half of the nineteenth century all this was to change, as the equilibrium of eighteenth-century urban society was shattered under the weight of massive immigration. Country people were to experience the city in ever larger numbers, and those very numbers would materially change the nature of city life, and for the worse. The reputed (and often illusory) economic advantages of the town attracted many. But other factors forced people to leave the land: renewed waves of enclosures, increasing agricultural productivity, growing population, and after about 1810, as steam replaced water as the major source of industrial power, the growth in urban industrialisation, all made it virtually unavoidable that they should migrate. With 40 per cent of all agricultural workers on parish relief in the 1840s, according to one estimate, country people needed little to entice them to desert the village for the town.

Perhaps those who knew how difficult village life had been should have known better. But the miseries of country life notwithstanding, once the even more hellish nature of town life had been experienced, that rural past almost of necessity became transformed into a pastoral myth. In response to the pressures of urban experience, it became seen as a lost golden age of community and economic well being. There was no turning back to it in reality, but there was no bar to such a return in fantasy and fiction.

What we can see happening during the first decades of the century is a hackneyed literary device, whose significance long had been totally absorbed into its conventionality, being made into a living myth, to which millions firmly held as an accurate version of their individual and collective past; one which offered some alleviation, at least on the level of fantasy, of the unendurable horrors of life in overcrowded towns and cities. Against the stark reality of their present lives was set this pastoral dream, the myth of a lost rural Eden. That even those who had good reason to know better still could become convinced that this was the way it had been back in the country, gives us an idea of its power.

The popular fictions of the period reveal this change in process. It is not accidental that one of the most popular songs of the entire century was 'Home, Sweet Home', from John Howard Payne's *Clari, the Maid of Milan* (1823)—the home referred to was of course a village home. Similar material dominated the popular stage from the 1820s well into the 1860s. As Michael Booth, historian of the nineteenth-century stage, has commented:

> Praise of country life at the expense of the city has been a theme common in Western literature...but...there is nothing like it in previous English drama and it can hardly be found before the 1820s. What is praised specifically is the village, not rural life in general, a village that is no longer a real place but a dream, a lost Eden in the sharpest contrast to the dirty streets and the wretched dwellings which the rural poor now inhabited. ... It appears again and again in plays seen and enjoyed by metropolitan audiences in their tens of thousands, and the great London in which these audiences lived, in these same plays, vanished before the Ideal Village from which thousands of them came (or thought they came), many of them long ago. This is what countless Londoners saw as the stage version of their own past—illusion, it is true, but with all the complex significance of illusion.[18]

(Dickens later wrote such a drama himself, *The Village Coquettes* (1836), which achieved some popularity; it will be discussed below in Chapter Two.)

Not only the popular stage, the most influential of early Victorian cultural institutions, but popular fiction and poetry stressed the same theme. Louis James quotes this example of popular verse written in 1854:

> Leave the town, leave the town, come,
>> To the quiet, green woods we will be bound,
>> Like true friends, like true friends roam
> Where there's health, if not wealth to be found!
>> In happy fancy we can raise
>>> An altar there,
>>> Or sylvan temple....[19]

Street ballads, too, constantly return to rural settings, often not for any obvious reason connected with their subjects, but because their audiences would be more appreciative if some mention of a village home were made. 'Twas down in a snug country town', many begin, and proceed to tell a domestic or humorous story that could easily have been set in London. And the traditional ancient ballads that warned of the perils of the city—as in, 'Be cautious in great London town,/Or, in trying to do, you'll be done'—were as popular in the cities as out of them, no doubt because so many could remember when they had come up to town 'green' from the country and been done themselves.

While I have examined them so far only on a personal level, Dickens' childhood experiences, and what he made out of them, also offer perfect illustration of this process of convention becoming myth. That Dickens as a child of seven or eight in Chatham did not think he was enjoying pastoral bliss in sylvan glades, we can be reasonably certain. First of all, Chatham was hardly a village, but a bustling town. It was only much later— and in Chapter Three I shall attempt to say precisely when and why—he recast Chatham in that mould. Yet in a certain sense, he was ideally prepared to do so, for his childhood had been a bookish one, apparently because of chronic ill health, and the books he read and reread contain numerous references to the conventional town–country opposition. His favourites included *Roderick Random*, *Peregrine Pickle*, *Humphrey Clinker*, *Tom Jones* (an especial favourite), and the *Vicar of Wakefield*; and the *Tatler* and *Spectator*, *Idler*, *Citizen of the World*, and later Goldsmith's *Bee*, a gift from his schoolmaster when he was leaving Chatham. Dickens absorbed the conventional wisdom about the horrors of town life as he read, unwittingly preparing himself to deal with the experience of it which was to come.

Later as a young man, from about 1827 to 1832 or 1833, Dickens attended various London theatres of all types, from the patent theatres to penny music halls, nearly every single night of the week. The stage convention of city evil and country virtue was one with which he must have been quite familiar. In fact it is hardly surprising to learn that in April 1833 Dickens arranged with his friends and family an evening of amateur theatricals in which two scenes of *Clari* figured prominently, in one of which his elder sister Fanny sang 'Home, Sweet Home' to great effect.

As we can see from the autobiographical fragment, Dickens, like Tom Jones in fiction and millions of English men and women in life, did 'fall' into city life. In the face of the incomprehensible experience of the city, a pattern, or structure, which could help order and explain what had happened was available to him ready made, in the popular and pervasive convention of the town–country opposition. But for Dickens, unlike his childhood hero Tom, the fall was irreversible—there was no rural haven to which later he could retreat. The convention was changed by ineluctable experience into myth, and as such, allowed the child and the man after him to make that experience a little more understandable, and as a result, perhaps a little more bearable.

V

In writing his autobiography, Dickens remoulded certain elements of his own experience into a fiction, a process which I have tried to show involved certain distortions of fact. My account of it has also involved distortions, for it has stressed only the dark aspect of Dickens' childhood in London. But his view of London was not entirely negative, as every reader of his writing knows: in some ways it was as very positive as it was negative in others. Indeed, it was in some sense the negative aspects of the city which were a great advantage to him. Dickens had a phrase of his own to describe this—'the attraction of repulsion'. The phrase occurs several times in the autobiographical fragment, and a number of times in his fiction and reportage. Its use almost always is connected in some way to the emotionally highly charged material of his childhood experiences in London.

For even from the very start, London did have its genuine attractions for the boy. The first time he was in the city, as a small child, he may have paid visits to his godfather, Christopher Huffam, and his shop near the docks in the East End, which were the germ of Sol Gills' marvellous shop in *Dombey and Son*. Later, once arrived from Chatham, Forster notes that, 'neglected and miserable as he was, he managed gradually to transfer to London all the dreaminess and all the romance with which he had invested Chatham' (*Life*, 1, 14). Forster lets this theme lapse, following Dickens' persuasive lead in the fragment, but at other times in his career Dickens was more favourably disposed toward remembering that period as being at least occasionally less than terrifying. In the essay 'Gone Astray' (HW, 13 August 1853; MP, 395–405), Dickens recalled an incident from the first months of that time, the Spring of 1823, when he was taken into the City (perhaps by James Lamert, the cousin who later found him the job at Warren's) and became lost. He spent the day wandering on his own, quickly forgetting his initial terror, and growing enthralled by what he saw, 'like a child in a dream' (400). His thoughts are of endless bounty and the fortune awaiting him, punctuated by treats of food the shilling or so he has with him can purchase. That evening he goes to a cheap theatre, and only afterwards decides to find home. He locates an old watchman who takes charge of him, and shortly after that he is called for by his father.[20]

From this time, too, dates his lifelong fascination with Covent Garden:

> To be taken out for a walk into the real town [Forster writes], especially if it were anywhere about Covent Garden or the Strand, perfectly entranced him with pleasure. But, most of all, he had a profound attraction of repulsion to St. Giles's. If only he could induce whomsoever took him out to take him through Seven Dials, he was supremely happy. 'Good Heaven!' he would exclaim, 'what wild visions of prodigies of wickedness, what and beggary, arose in my mind out of that place!' (*Life*, 1, 14)

Covent Garden, he wrote later, was one of those places of child-hood he had never outgrown ('Where We Stopped Growing',

HW, 1 January 1853; *MP*, 358–64). He returned to the market countless times in his literal wanderings, later in his fiction, and eventually even lived there, when in the 1860s he often stayed while in town at the *All the Year Round* offices on Wellington Street. It was a place of endless motion and excitement, variety and mystery, promising wealth as well as revealing squalor. And though the squalor and the misery of the poor neighbourhoods around the market were horrifying they were yet somehow immensely appealing as well. Perhaps they were similar in their appeal to the frightening stories of murder and depravity that his Chatham nurse, Mary Weller, had delighted in telling him, about which he wrote in 'Nurse's Stories' (*AYR*, 8 September 1860; *UT*, 148–58). He remembered being too frightened to listen to them, yet derived great pleasure from hearing them all the same. Dickens sensed a deeper connection himself, writing, 'If we all knew our minds (in a more enlarged sense than the popular acceptation of the phrase), I suspect we should find our nurses responsible for most of the dark corners we are forced to go back to, against our wills' (*UT*, 150).

Whatever the reason for his initial fascination with it, it grew more important to him soon afterwards. Proximity to Covent Garden was one of the few compensations of working at Warren's, for the Warehouse was so close to it that even during his lunch break he could wander through it, and we can assume he did so often. Later, when the firm moved a few streets away to Chandos Street, he was even closer to it. In fact, all of the places he could reach on foot in a few minutes from Warren's figure importantly in his writing throughout his life: Covent Garden, the Temple, St Giles, Waterloo Bridge, The Strand, Temple Bar, and so on. As important, and as frequently used in the novels, are the places in and near the Borough he passed walking from Warren's home to Lant Street and the Marshalsea.

The 'attraction of repulsion': the phrase applies to the places and to the entire experience. For by returning to this period in his fiction, Dickens was not only being attracted by the suffering he had endured, but by elements of the experience of it that were genuinely attractive. This time at Warren's was not only the greatest shock of his young life, but his first great accomplishment. Despite his abandonment, he had managed to survive the

ordeal and even to flourish as he did so. For a previously sheltered
and sickly child of twelve, he exhibited astounding courage and
self-reliance, existing very much on his own for several months,
and earning his own keep. (Indeed, he was then the only active
wage earning member of the family.) Also, whatever shame he
felt tying blacking pots among common men and boys, he felt
equal pride in his skill at it. Being placed in a window as a
working advertisement and having his salary raised from six to
seven shillings testify to that skill.

Dickens did hint at this other side of the time at Warren's, for
Forster adds 'that he used to describe Saturday night as his great
treat. It was a grand thing to walk home with six shillings in
his pocket, and to look in at the shop windows, and think what
it would buy' (*Life*, I, 23). One can sense more of his pride in
this passage of the fragment, referring to the decision to relocate
him nearer the family:

> 'A back-attic was found for me at the house of an insolvent
> court agent, who lived in Lant Street in the Borough, where
> Bob Sawyer lodged many years afterwards. A bed and bedding
> were sent over for me, and made up on the floor. The little
> window had a pleasant prospect of a timber-yard; and when
> I took possession of my new abode, I thought it was a
> paradise.' (*Life*, I, 26)

Much later in life, Dickens became accustomed to wandering
these same parts of London at the times when he was either
planning a writing project, or actually writing. Over the course
of his writing career, he began to sense the connection between
his inspiration and walking the city streets. He grew fully
conscious of this need to return physically to the scene of his
childhood experiences, when in the mid-1840s he was spending
the better part of three years on the Continent. In 1844, working
on a Christmas book, he wrote from Genoa: 'Put me down on
Waterloo Bridge at eight o'clock in the evening [the time he
finished work at Warren's], with leave to roam about as long as
I like, and I would come home, as you know, panting to go on
[writing]' (*Life*, I, 333). Writing fiction away from England for
the first time, Dickens experienced difficulty writing for the
first time. And once that particular book, *The Chimes*, was done,

he raced back to London in December, to read it to a group of close friends.

The problem intensified when he began a more serious project, his next novel, *Dombey and Son*. He travelled from place to place, seeking a substitute for London. In June 1846 he settled on Lausanne: 'On consideration . . . I thought it best to come on here, in case I should find, when I begin to write, that I want streets sometimes. In which case, Geneva (which I hope would answer the purpose) is only four and twenty hours away' (*Life*, I, 384). Geneva did not answer, for later that month (Forster observed), he was 'feeling sometimes the want of streets in an "extraordinary nervousness it would be hardly possible to describe," that would come upon him after he had been writing all day' (*Life*, I, 399). In August he complained, 'the difficulty of going on at what I call a rapid pace, is prodigious: it is almost an impossibility. I suppose this is partly the effect of two years' ease [i.e. not writing novels], and partly the absence of streets and numbers of people' (*Life*, I, 419). In Geneva that October he was physically ill, he wrote, 'attributable, I have not the least doubt, to the absence of streets' (*Life*, I, 427).

Dickens had long been in the habit of taking nocturnal walks. He did so first while at Warren's, for they offered the only relief and amusement available to him. They continued to furnish relief and amusement for the rest of his life. Part of the relief was emotional: for example, during the late 1850s, at the time of the breakup of his marriage, he often worked off his frustration by walking thirty miles a night. But the greater part of the relief was, as we have seen, linked specifically to the tensions and emotional effort of writing. As his daughter Kate later recalled, 'he would walk through the busy, noisy streets, which would act on him like a tonic and enable him to take up with new vigour the flagging interest of his story and breathe new life into its pages'.[21]

As Duane DeVries has demonstrated, Dickens was using story telling as a source of amusement and gratification even as a young child of five or six.[22] Even at that age, fantasy was a vital part of his life. He would sing or recite for company, to his father's great delight. His first written piece, based on an Arabian tale, apparently dates from Chatham. In London, however, especially after the books he had read at first in Chatham and then in Bayham Street had been pawned, and once he was at work at Warren's and was unable to read at all, he had an increased need to create his own fictions as a substitute for written fiction. Not only as a substitute, but also as a means of asserting the special social status he felt he deserved: to set himself apart from and above his workmates, he told them stories based on his former reading while they worked. He told them other kinds of stories, too, lying about his family to keep the secret that they were in the Marshalsea from his fellows' knowledge. Later, when he waited each morning at the Marshalsea gate with the Dickens' servant girl (a necessary luxury even in prison) to be let in for breakfast, 'he would occupy the time before the gates opened by telling her quite astonishing fictions about the wharves and the tower' (*Life*, 1, 27). The very next phrase Dickens wrote, as a qualifier, is itself astonishing: 'But I hoped I believed them myself'.

That Dickens should feel it necessary to apologise for his telling tales by saying he believed them true himself, indicates also that he must have been using those tales as a substitute for the truth, a personal truth too horrible to believe—that he was a pauper and a drudge. The same use applied more and more to those fictions that were closer to the painful truth, as when one evening he had been accompanied 'home' from Warren's by Bob Fagin, and in desperation stalked up to a big house and pretended to live there so the older boy would walk away, and not follow him to the prison. The supreme touch, when the door was answered, was to ask if Bob Fagin were at home. Another time, the debtors of the Marshalsea, John Dickens chief among them, petitioned the King on a small matter, and Charles observed the ceremony of reading and signing the document carefully. 'I made out my own little character and story for every man who put his name to the sheet of paper. . . . I thought about it afterwards, over the pots of paste-blacking, often and often' (*Life*, 1, 30–1). Tale telling had changed from amusement and palliative device to a deeply felt need: a way of transfiguring reality.

What was happening was that the boy was already growing into the novelist. Steven Marcus writes, 'Dickens enlisted those powers which are quintessentially novelistic—the powers of observation and responsiveness to the world about him, the delight in associating himself with it—in order to remain alive.'[23] Those powers were exercised from the very first on the parts of London in which he spent that trying time. His art, his personality, and the city were thus inextricably bound together. That he returned to them in prison and in fiction for many years afterwards should not be taken as a sign of weakness or defeat, though those two attitudes characterise his autobiographical account of that period. What they signified most of all was severe trial *and triumph over it*; and on the deepest level, Dickens did know 'how all these things [had] worked together to make me what I am' (*Life*, 1, 32). What he was above all was a great novelist, and a great novelist of the city.

VI

One of the important components of Dickens' greatness is the way in which his fiction makes free and creative use of every detail of his outer and inner life. The seventy some odd volumes of the journal of the Dickens Fellowship, *The Dickensian*, contain hundreds and hundreds of accounts of the 'originals' of characters, places and incidents in Dickens' life which appear in one form or another in his writing. This alone, of course, is not necessarily an important, nor even an interesting, quality of his work. What made his use of all this material so transcendent, was that he could in touching the important experiences of his own life characterise and analyse the important experience of his age. His interest in and focus on children and childhood is a fine example of this. As I have tried to show, another of those key, formative experiences, for the man and his society, was the experience of the modern city. In his response to the city, Dickens was moulded by and in turn helped to mould the sensibility of his culture, and of ours, as its inheritors.

It is not only fitting, but perhaps inevitable, that Dickens' first imaginative writings should have taken their substance and setting from the metropolis. In his early sketches, written from 1833–6 and later collected as *Sketches by Boz*, Dickens appears as the genuinely and completely urban man, with a truly urban sensibility. Those first essays and articles and stories are the record of the young author discovering his ideal subject, the city, one which would remain at the centre of his creative imagination and his fiction for the rest of his writing career.

CHAPTER ONE

Sketches by Boz: Fiction for the Metropolis[1]

Until quite recently, *Sketches by Boz* was one of the few of Dickens' books that few people read, and even fewer wrote about. Fortunately, judging by the current renaissance of critical interest in *Sketches*, that situation has begun to change.[2] Despite this, readers of the book still seem to approach it with a tinge of condescension, no doubt inspired by Dickens' own negative comments about the pieces, written for the preface to the Cheap Edition of 1850, and reprinted with *Sketches* ever since: 'extremely crude and ill-considered, and bearing obvious marks of haste and inexperience' (xiii).

Forster, though, thought quite highly of the book, and felt that Dickens, by 1850, had 'decidedly underrated it' perhaps because 'he did not care to credit himself with the marvel of having yet so early anticipated so much' (*Life*, I, 60). Yet, before *Pickwick Papers* had even begun to be published, *Sketches* had been a great success. Indeed, it was upon its reputation alone that Chapman and Hall commissioned Dickens to write *Pickwick Papers*.

Sketches contains Dickens' first writings, essays and short stories published in various magazines and newspapers from December 1833 to October 1836, and collected in two series during 1836. Even a glance at contemporary reviews of the first editions of *Sketches* suggests how great its initial success was. We can excuse George Hogarth, soon to be Dickens' father-in-law, for remarking that the author was 'evidently . . . a person of various and extraordinary intellectual gifts' (*Morning Chronicle*, 11 February 1836). But other reviewers were equally laudatory: 'We have seldom read two more agreeable volumes' (*Satirist*, 14 February 1836); 'Two more amusing volumes in their way have not appeared this season' (*Sun*, 15 February 1836); 'These volumes are the merriest of the season' (*Court Journal*, 20 February 1836). It seems to have been virtually

impossible for contemporary critics to refer to *Sketches* in anything but superlatives. Phrases like 'infinite skill' and 'perfect
picture' stud the reviews.[3]

In addition, what we know of the sales of *Sketches* tells us that
the book was a popular as well as a critical success. Published in
February 1836, the First Series (as they came to be known) had
reached a second edition by August; a Second Series of new
material was added in December. In June the following year,
Chapman and Hall were paying Macrone the astounding sum
of £2000 for the copyright; almost immediately they began a
reissue in monthly parts that extended over the next two years,
and they published a collected edition in 1839.[4]

There can be no doubt, then, that at the time *Sketches* was
published, the book was seen as a remarkable literary work.
What remains puzzling is to account for the reasons behind its
success, especially in the light of later readers' (and Dickens'
own) apparent indifference to it. Kathleen Tillotson has suggested
that its reception was largely a result of the subject matter, that
the sketches were *metropolitan* sketches, introducing new physical and social areas—London and the middle classes—into the
realm of respectable popular fiction. She notes in particular 'the
sharpness of the difference between the world of Boz and the
worlds of "silver-fork" novels, of the Annuals, of romantic-
historical thrillers and "political-economy" tales, or . . . the less
sharp but still distinctive difference from the comic worlds of
Hood and Hook and the lower grade imitations of Egan's *Life in
London*.'[5] Dickens, it would appear, was merely breaking new
literary ground. And to be sure critics unanimously did note the
metropolitan nature of the work.

This analysis is certainly true, as far as it goes, but it does not
go quite far enough; for one thing, as I will demonstrate below,
Dickens was not entirely alone in his use of metropolitan
material. *Sketches* was indeed metropolitan in choice of subject
and location, but even more so in its entire spirit and outlook. In
it, for perhaps the first time in English literature, Dickens
apprehended something of the essential nature of modern urban
life, the sensibility of the city. And it is not only because we tend
to see *Sketches* in the long shadow of *Pickwick* that it now seems
so unexceptional to us, but also because we have become too

accustomed to the way of looking at and writing about the city that it embodies to appreciate its originality. It is difficult, almost 150 years after the sketches were written, to understand how truly revolutionary the outlook of *Sketches by Boz* was.

II

Turning again to reviews of *Sketches*, one can see that it was seen at the time not only as a work of great talent but as an entirely new literary phenomenon. Almost all the notices stress the accuracy of the reportage and great fidelity to 'life' of *Sketches*; yet one senses reviewers were attempting to say more than this, but lacked a vocabulary to do so. These comments are representative:

> The graphic descriptions of 'Boz' invest all he describes with amazing reality. (*Morning Post*, 12 March 1836)
>
> He ... perceives traits which are not consciously noted by ordinary observers, and yet, when mentioned, remind everybody of the thing described. (*Chambers's Edinburgh Journal*, 9 April 1836)
>
> He shows his strength in bringing out the meaning and interests of objects which would altogether escape the observation of ordinary mortals. (*Examiner*, 28 February 1836; by John Forster)

These remarks indicate that it was important not only that Dickens' short pieces were about the metropolis, but that they were accurately metropolitan in a distinctly unique and novel manner.

Boz himself, in fact, rarely misses an opportunity to point out the special metropolitan nature of his pieces. He usually makes his proclamations of metropolitan uniqueness for comic effect, with tongue securely in cheek, as in the opening of the sketch 'Hackney-Coach Stands', where London cabs are defended against the pretensions of provincial cabs in respect of their superior dirtiness and slowness (81). But often they indicate a deeper insight, too, as when he notes in 'Shabby-Genteel People' that whole social classes seem native to the metropolis and can be found nowhere else: 'they seem to be indigenous to the soil, and to belong as exclusively to London as its own smoke, or the dingy bricks and mortar' (262).

He is, in effect, observing how urban existence has become a new way of life, one in which traditional kinds of knowledge and customs no longer apply. City life for Boz has become self-referential. By this somewhat opaque term, I mean to describe the underlying assumption of the pieces that only by experiencing the city can one ever know it. (The very fact that the occasional slang words or idioms in the book are never glossed, as they had been in Egan's *Life in London*, itself indicates that a certain degree of metropolitan knowledgeability in his readers was taken for granted by Boz.) The city is seen as a new mode of social organisation where outside norms do not apply, and whose very nature is one of continuous, institutionalised change.

And of course, London at that time was changing its aspect with unprecedented rapidity, and becoming a place which even lifelong residents could find strange and altered from one day to the next.

The magnitude of London's population growth early in the century is astounding. It had risen from approximately 1,000,000 in 1811, the year before Dickens' birth, to 1,650,000 in 1837, the year after the publication of *Sketches*—an increase of 65 per cent altogether, and better than 20 per cent per decade.[6] The physical appearance of London was changing even faster. The built-up area of the city in the 1830s had more than doubled since 1800. The post-Waterloo speculative building boom had produced ever lengthening tentacles of terrace houses that led to outraged complaints as early as the 1820s. William Cobbett was exclaiming in 1822 that between Southwark and Croydon, 'There are, erected within these four years, two entire miles of stock-jobber's houses on this one road, and the work goes on with accelerated force!'[7] And the speed with which this was happening was in many senses quite literally beyond comprehension: new tools for its comprehension, like the fledgling science of statistics, now had to be invented merely to quantify the immense changes.[8]

Sketches is full of examples of this rapid 'change, and restlessness and innovation' ('Scotland Yard', 67). 'Shops and Their Tenants' presents Boz watching the numerous tenants who follow each other in setting up various business establishments in one house over a short period; each time he passes it, another has moved in. The house itself, once grand and elegant, was abandoned and fell into disrepair when the owner had become involved in a Chancery suit; the first new tenant refits it elegantly and ostentatiously, but goes bankrupt; and as each succeeding tenant is poorer than the last, it is soon a ruin again. But, despite the surface of constant change, almost nothing has changed—the house starts as a ruin and reverts to one, in a never ending cycle of transformations.

It is precisely this awareness of the paradoxical continuity of ceaseless change in the city that marks Boz's urban observations. His city is not only outside traditional social modes of behaviour, but it is outside reference to traditional concepts of time and history as well. The past of a place doesn't seem to matter very much; it is only what it is at the moment he sees it that is important to him. This is an attitude many have found striking and original in the much celebrated 'Staggs's Gardens' episode of *Dombey and Son* (Chapter vi), but it is equally present here. Perhaps we can see this more clearly by a comparison with similarly conceived sketches of city life that were being written at about the same time.

III

Leigh Hunt's sketches of metropolitan life are among the earliest and the best of those few others roughly contemporaneous with Dickens' own earliest work. Hunt had begun writing his sketches late in the summer of 1833, first for the London *Weekly True Sun*, and then in his own *Leigh Hunt's London Journal*, which ran from April 1834 to May 1835. The subjects included were as various as the Sunday amusements of different classes, the habits of London waiters, and, in a long series, 'The Streets of the Metropolis'. It is impossible now to say whether Dickens was influenced in any clear way by Hunt's work when he began his own series of 'Street Sketches' in the *Morning Chronicle* in September 1834, or whether Hunt was in turn influenced by Dickens' sketches in his own later pieces, and it probably does not much matter. There is, to be sure, a certain similarity between their pieces, and not only in subject matter. (Since they were writing metropolitan pieces, that at least was inevitable.) They share also the conceit of the loitering observer, traversing the metropolis on foot, and recording along the way the peculiarities of various neighbourhoods and social groups. The same narrative tone, supercilious, superior and suave, is common to both as well.

Yet the results are quite different. In one of Hunt's earliest of what he called his 'most metropolitan papers', 'A Ramble in Mary-le-bone', he unequivocally states this general principle: 'The five things that make a place interesting are—personal feelings connected with it, its beauty, its antiquities, its eminent men, and its future destiny.'[9] In practice, each building or street Hunt sees immediately leads him to recall something else, usually its history—how it first came to exist, how it came to be what it is now, what famous individuals of the past were associated with it, and so on. But to Dickens, all that matters is the 'now' of a thing—what it looks like *now*, what it does *now*, what people do in or around it *now*. Its history or its future are immaterial. For him the city exists only in the present tense. At the close of one sketch, he imagines a 'future antiquary of another generation looking into the mouldy record of the strife and passions that agitated the world in these times', completely unable to understand anything about what Boz has written, despite all 'his knowledge of the history of the past' ('Scotland Yard', 68): London is a place entirely of the here and now.

Comparisons with others of the many metropolitan works that began appearing more and more frequently in the 1830s yield similar results. In a work issued in parts over the years 1837–9 entitled *Select Illustrated Topography of . . . London*, William Edward Trotter advised his readers that he would concentrate on the subjects of 'Antiquity, History, and Topography' to help them understand their 'crowded metropolis'; Charles Knight, prefacing his massive work *London*, also issued in parts, 1841–4, stressed that the 'chief' importance of the sights of the metropolis 'consists in the associations which they suggest' in the past, and even ancient, history.[10]

If one does perceive any common ground among the metropolitan writers of the period, from Egan's *Life in London* onward, it is that the works of Dickens and others were independently conceived and written in a climate of growing interest in and demand for naturalistic and detailed 'sketches' of metropolitan life by an increasingly selfconscious and vocal metropolitan middle class reading public. One must be wary of making facile generalisations linking politics and literature, but it seems clear that it is not accidental that this demand rose dramatically in the years immediately surrounding the passage of the Reform Bill in 1832. Whatever Reform may or may not be credited with, in the final analysis, at that time the middle classes most certainly felt that it had been a great class victory, the signal for their entry into a proper role of responsibility and power in the nation. What they lacked was a literature of their own, and it was not slow to materialise.[11]

Even so, Dickens' metropolitan pieces stand out from the others, and his contemporaries seem to have sensed the uniqueness of his approach. When William Harrison Ainsworth was planning a new periodical early in 1838, 'to be entitled "Ancient and Modern London"', he intended that, 'Mr Dickens will illustrate the metropolis of the present day: I shall endeavour to revive its departed glories.'[12] (Edgar Allan Poe, reviewing an American pirate edition of *Sketches* in 1836, also noted their unusual quality; he praised especially their overall 'unity of effect'.[13])

This 'now-ness' of *Sketches* is to be found almost on any page of it. A sketch that illustrates this strange everchanging changelessness particularly well is 'Meditations in Monmouth Street', which seems at first to be presenting only a lively, ordered succession of events. In it, Boz wanders among secondhand clothing shops, and in one of them notices several suits of clothes that all seem to have belonged to the same man at different times of his life. He animates each suit in turn, imagining from it the man himself, and in a series of tableaux recounts the conventional old story of a boy who gets in with the wrong crowd and embarks on a life of crime, while his patient all-suffering mother silently endures. This piece is notable first for the way in which the author's imagination is engaged by, interprets and eventually overwhelms the dumb, inanimate artifacts it encounters; but also because it demonstrates this other curious perception. The events

in the imaginary life of this imaginary man are presented as a
progressive chronological sequence: but the clothes themselves,
in fact the only remaining signs of that imaginary life, are all
hanging in the same place and are all present at the same time,
as are the fictitious events themselves in the mind of Boz. The
surface, while seeming to embody change, only masks a kind of
timelessness, for the succession of changes, visible to Boz all at
once, is itself permanent. '... [It] is the times that have
changed', he writes, 'not Monmouth-street' (74).

'The Pawnbroker's Shop' presents a similar situation. At the
close of the sketch three women are shown to us: one very young,
reduced by want; another, scarcely older, but clearly a prostitute,
although ashamed of her fallen state; and a third, a few years
older still, already coarsened by her life into open vulgarity and
lewdness, and entirely without shame. They are three definite
stages in the inevitable downward progress of women impelled
by poverty to sell themselves. But by placing all three women in
one place at one time, rather than telling the story of the
downfall of one single girl, Dickens confounds the notion of
sequential time with considerable moral effect: 'Who shall say',
he asks, 'how soon these women may change places?' (195). This
story, he is stressing, does not only happen once, nor does it
have an end—it is present in every stage of its terrible development in a thousand instances at any given moment anywhere
in the city.

This sketch also hints at another way in which Dickens' vision
of metropolitan life is surprisingly modern: the way in which
change, whenever it does occur, is inevitably felt to be decay.
Perhaps it was Dickens' very personal and very poignant awareness of the fragility of middle class respectability, demonstrated
by the speed with which John Dickens had declined into bankruptcy in London, that accounts for this uneasy feeling. Quite
often, his lamentations of decline are masked by comic intention,
as in the protest against cleaning those traditionally filthy
hackney-coaches as evidence of 'the little respect paid to our
time-honoured institutions' ('Hackney-Coach Stands', 81). Less
frivolous, however, are the changes presented in one of the last
sketches he wrote, 'Scotland Yard' (published 4 October 1836 in
the *Morning Chronicle*, well after the successes of both the First

Series of *Sketches* and *Pickwick Papers*). It describes the society of the Thames rivermen who once lived in the Yard (incidentally, near Hungerford Stairs) as a veritable golden age, even breaking into the present tense better to evoke the feeling of their timeless community. But the construction of Waterloo Bridge breaks up their trade and livelihood, and Scotland Yard becomes a sterile, soulless collection of gaudily pretentious shops. 'We marked the advance of civilization,' he concludes, 'and beheld it with a sigh' (66). The loss, one feels, is genuine and irreparable.

IV

This last, brief consideration of what we can take to be an autobiographical irruption into the detached vision of *Sketches* raises a more important question. The unique and modern approach to urban experience Dickens takes in his earliest writings is evident, but what remains unaccounted for is why he should have been able to take such an approach.

What we know of Dickens' childhood experiences of and in London, and his mature reconstruction of them, would prepare us rather to expect that Dickens would characterise the metropolis as a nightmarish hell to be reviled, if he could bring himself to discuss it at all. The sense of impending decline mentioned above, or the attacks on middle class smugness and mercenary morality that also appear in many of the pieces (especially the short tales), are more in keeping with the expectations we might base on biographical knowledge.

Yet these are only minor preoccupations of *Sketches*. The lighthearted, bantering narrative persona of Boz is far more characteristic than this other sardonic one. If we can reconstruct an image of Dickens from *Sketches* at all, it is of a young man full of excitement and life, far closer to his pose as Boz than to his misanthropic characters like Dumps and Minns.

That Dickens knew the metropolis fully as well as his omniscient persona is beyond doubt, from the testimony of those who knew him at the time, and even long before he began writing, while he was still a clerk at the law firm of Ellis and Blackmore.[14] The 'attraction of repulsion' of which Dickens later spoke of his relationship with London was at this time simply far more attraction than repulsion. Dickens' long walks through London —even now often twenty miles in a single evening—were already part of his routine in the early 1830s, as we can see from his casual references to them in letters to friends. And there was infinite variety to be found on such a walk: 'What inexhaustible food for speculation, do the streets of London afford!' he opens one sketch. '[We] have not the slightest commiseration for the man who can take up his hat and stick, and walk from Covent Garden to St. Paul's Churchyard, and back into the bargain, without deriving some amusement—we had almost said instruction—from his perambulation' ('Shops and Their Tenants', 59). This city was a world in which everything a young writer might need to observe was present.

However, more than his intimate knowledge of London, it was Dickens' willingness to build a career upon it that makes his street sketches so surprising. Flushed with the success of having risen as far as he had, from law clerk to the premier Parliamentary reporter of his day in but five years, he was willing to accept and use his past to build a future. The reluctance even to mention his childhood in the city that characterises his manhood is hardly evident at all in his youth. As he began writing, the thrill of being able to use his dismal experiences to raise himself to even greater fame and fortune communicates itself in the vibrant prose with which he wrote about London. Remarkably enough, it appears that at this time Dickens was even writing advertising verses for Warren's Blacking, and had no objection to his uncle, John Barrow, mentioning the fact while introducing him to John Payne Collier.[15] As much as being a literary discovery, *Sketches* are a personal discovery too—of a subject which had great importance to him that was also eminently suitable for his literary efforts.

This sense of exuberant joy, born in his ability to transcend the burden and stigma of the past, is evident too in the many sketches which describe London's amusements and recreations: 'The River', 'Astley's', 'Greenwich Fair', 'Vauxhall Gardens by Day' and 'Making a Night of It', among others. In *Sketches*, despite a persistent tone of snobbery toward 'the humbler classes' ('London Recreations', 92), Dickens approached the genuine satisfactions of metropolitan life far more directly than ever again in his long writing career after it.

V

Dickens, as we have seen, was not alone in his literary interest in the metropolis. His early tales, written from late 1833 to mid-1834,[16] are metropolitan solely by virtue of being set in London and the near suburbs, but little else distinguishes them from the stage farces and comic tales of those of his contemporaries to whom Dickens was at first typically compared, Hood and Hook. Nothing, that is, distinguishes them but Dickens' skill as a literary craftsman, already evident in his more subtle plotting and lively prose. But on 26 September 1834 the first of his series of 'Street Sketches' for the *Morning Chronicle* appeared, and the 'Boz' we have discussed above truly came into being. (The name Boz had first been used in print by Dickens only the previous month.) The sketches that immediately followed over the next three months show how quickly and completely Dickens had taken to his material: 'Shops and Their Tenants' (10 October); 'The Old Bailey' (23 October): 'Shabby-Genteel People' (5 November); and 'Broker's and Marine Store Shops' (15 December).

Of course here too Dickens was not entirely novel, in subject or in style. The major stylistic influence on *Sketches* was not, as has been suggested, the eighteenth-century essayists and their Romantic successors—Goldsmith, Addison and Steele, Lamb and Hunt—but contemporary journalism. After all Dickens was a reporter, not only a shorthand recorder of Parliamentary debate, but out of session covering more general assignments as well. If one reads the criminal and court trial reports of newspapers like those for which Dickens worked while he was writing *Sketches*, the affinity is clear: the direct, matter-of-fact treatment of ordinary people and events, the relatively unadorned and unrhetorical prose style, and the use of reported dialect dialogue that mark *Sketches* are all there.[17]

Still, as these comparisons invariably do reveal, what is more striking than the similarity is the difference between Dickens' work and its literary context. Even if the material and style are to a certain extent derivative, what is Dickens' unique contribution to writing about the city is the unifying vision of urban experience which lies behind it: a vision of the urban milieu as an eternal here and now, 'whose content was transcience, but whose transcience was permanent'.[18]

We have tended for some time now to see this view of the quality of life in the city as beginning much later than this: perhaps first in Dickens' late novels, or more usually, with Baudelaire, the French Impressionists, and the English Decadents. For example, meditating on the nature of life in London, Thomas Hardy made this entry in his journal for 28 March 1888: 'There is no consciousness of where anything comes from or goes to— only that is present.'[19] *Sketches by Boz* embody this same perception: a new, and unmistakably urban, sensibility.

Seen in this perspective, *Sketches* represents far more than merely the first ephemeral writings of the man who later became the great novelist, Charles Dickens. It was a manifestation of the birth of what, for lack of a better term, must be called the essentially modern consciousness, an outgrowth of the revolutionary experience of the modern city. It is this that makes the author of *Sketches* as much our contemporary as the contemporary of Hook, Hood or Hunt. And this alone is not an insignificant achievement for the twenty-four year old author then still known only as Boz.

CHAPTER TWO

Pickwick Papers, *Oliver Twist*, and *Nicholas Nickleby*: Labyrinthine London

On 10 February 1836, a day or two after the publication of the First Series of *Sketches*, a man named William Hall called on Dickens. Hall was partner in the publishers, Chapman and Hall, who were planning to issue a humorous monthly periodical chronicling the adventures of a Cockney sporting club, to be centred around plates drawn by Robert Seymour. Hall proposed that Dickens write the accompanying letterpress. The work was hack work, but would pay well—£14 a month—and Dickens quickly agreed. How it was that this venture became *Pickwick Papers* no one really can say—and least of all could Dickens himself once it had happened. But somehow it did happen, achieving in time a success which dwarfed even that of *Sketches*, and beginning a five year period of unparalleled literary creativity, during which Dickens would write (often concurrently) five full novels, and numerous minor works, ranging from political pamphlets to operettas.

Even from the beginning of *Pickwick*, though he was taken on as a junior collaborator, it seems Dickens was manouvering to gain more control over the project, with the object of better exploiting what he felt were his own particular talents. Then, in April, Seymour committed suicide; Chapman and Hall hesitated, but decided to continue *Pickwick*, and Dickens was now in a position to take command. What he appears to have been aiming for initially was to turn *Pickwick* into a vehicle which would allow him to do more of the kind of writing he was already doing in *Sketches*: with incidents, like the hunt, which were similar to the comic tales; with stories, like the more serious and melo-dramatic tales, directly interpolated into the text; and with much general journalistic observation, like that of the remainder of *Sketches*, but set in new locations, *outside* London and its suburbs (which handily made use of Dickens' travels as a political reporter).[1] It was only after a half dozen or so of the monthly numbers had appeared that Dickens gained some instinctive insight into the material he was creating, and began to organise it into a connected, organic work of fiction, transforming it from a continuation of *Sketches* into something more like a great novel.[2]

This had begun with the fourth number, in which Sam Weller made his first appearance, and shortly afterwards, as everyone knows, *Pickwick Papers'* sales took off like a rocket. It is usually said that Sam Weller, a lively Cockney servant whose not entirely original style of comic aphorism is now called after him, was the cause of this tremendous popularity. This is probably at least partly the case, but in the fourth number along with Sam's introduction something else occurred: Mr Pickwick returned to London. From this point on, he was really never to leave it, for wherever he travelled he took with him Sam, the living embodiment of London life. Dickens' imagination was engaged and excited by London in a way it was not by any other place—as soon as Mr Pickwick set foot again on the paving stones of a London street, *Pickwick Papers* sprang to life almost as if by magic.

It was a magic that Dickens' contemporaries understood. They recognised the special character of his relationship with London: one reviewer in 1837 dubbed him 'the literary Teniers of the metropolis', while a few years later Ruskin was writing in a letter that, 'in London, and to his present fields of knowledge, he [Dickens] ought strictly to keep for some time.'[3] Dickens must have understood this in some way, too, for the novels that immediately followed *Pickwick Papers*, that is, *Oliver Twist* and *Nicholas Nickleby*, though they wander from it at times, are set mainly in and around London.

Indeed, one can treat London as it appears in all three as virtually one fictional entity.[4] Yet, as soon as this statement is made, it must be qualified. The endless excitement and variety of the broad metropolitan canvas of *Sketches* and the early numbers of *Pickwick* is not the same as the setting of the remainder of *Pickwick*, after Mr Pickwick enters the Fleet, nor of *Oliver Twist*, nor of a large part of *Nicholas Nickleby*. Here by contrast it is a dark, foul and revolting city in which characters are trapped like rats in a maze. The contrast could not be starker.

II

This dark London is most intensely imaged in *Oliver Twist*, though the novel actually begins in a small provincial town.[5] The opening chapters are a vitriolic satiric attack on the horrific cruelties of the New Poor Law, its inhumane administration, and the misguided zeal of the political economists who had drawn up the legislation for it. Young Oliver Twist is an innocent victim of the Poor Laws, and his experiences under them make up the first part of the novel. But either by Dickens' original design, or because the potential material in such a satire was quickly exhausted, in Chapter vii Dickens has him run away from the town of his birth to seek his fortune elsewhere. On the road, Oliver pauses to rest at a milestone, on which he sees the name 'London', which conjures up for him a vision of boundless opportunity:

> The name awakened a new train of ideas in the boy's mind. London!—that great large place!—nobody—not even Mr. Bumble—could ever find him there! He had often heard the old man in the workhouse, too, say that no lad of spirit need want in London; . . . It was the very place for a homeless boy, who must die in the streets unless some one helped him. (*OT*, 50)

London is presented as a place of endless bounty, a collective dream vision of fulfilment where Oliver's instinctive need for 'more'—more food, more love, more everything—can be filled. By virtue of its size, it has the additional advantage of granting him anonymity, and thus is the perfect place in which to hide from his pursuers. But once he arrives in the metropolis, Oliver's expectations are met only with a heavy twist of irony. What he expects to find, in effect, is the London of *Sketches*, but the London he does find is in every way the opposite of that city of hope and opportunity.

He is led into London by Mr John Dawkins, the Artful Dodger himself, who meets and befriends Oliver in the nearby village of

Barnet. They agree to go into town together. Significantly, however, the Dodger waits until dark to begin their journey inward:

> They crossed from the Angel into St. John's Road; struck down the small street which terminates at Sadler's Wells Theatre; through Exmouth Street and Coppice Row; down the little court by the side of the workhouse; across the classic ground which once bore the name of Hockley-in-the-Hole; thence into Little Saffron Hill; and so into Saffron Hill the Great: along which the Dodger scudded at a rapid pace, directing Oliver to follow close at his heels. (55)

The details of their route are scrupulously accurate—every street and turning is carefully and exactly named. And yet, the effect is not, as one might expect, an enhanced sense of realism. The seeming precision is only on the surface: by naming the streets, and giving us no other detail about or description of them, the passage shatters their particularity and renders them virtually interchangeable. Reading the paragraph is like entering a maze, which is precisely what Oliver has done. This is the labyrinth of London.[6]

When Oliver finally looks around him, the description of what he sees explodes with all the power of a nightmare:

> A dirtier or more wretched place he had never seen. The street was very narrow and muddy, and the air was impregnated with filthy odours. There were a good many small shops; but the only stock in trade appeared to be heaps of children, who even at that time of night, were crawling in and out at the doors, one screaming from the inside. . . . Covered ways and yards, which here and there diverged from the main street, disclosed little knots of houses, where drunken men and women were positively wallowing in filth; and from several of the door-ways, great ill-looking fellows were cautiously emerging, bound, to all appearance, in no very well-disposed or harmless errands. (55)

Here the frightening things which Oliver sees, though they are evoked with dramatic intensity, reinforce the surreal quality of the scene. As in a surrealist painting, there are present recognisable bits of reality, but reassembled in a new and frightening set of relations. These details have even less of a fixed relation to actuality than the list of featureless names; they float ominously around Oliver, threatening and claustral.[7]

This evocation of horror has at its core one startling observation—that the people who inhabit this place, whose salient characteristics are filth, stench, darkness and a terrifying closeness, are animals. They are not *like* animals; they simply *are*. Their children are the 'stock and trade' of the shops, chattel to be bought and sold as mere merchandise. No human activity occurs, but instead they crawl, scream, and wallow in filth like swine. It is an environment in which the only mode of existence possible is bestial.

This same analogy informs the description of the Smithfield Market which occurs later in the novel, as Oliver is dragged past it by Bill Sikes on the way to the robbery at Chertsey:

> The ground was covered, nearly ankle-deep with filth and mire; ... All the pens in the centre of the large area, ... were filled with sheep; tied up to posts by the gutter side were long lines of beasts and oxen, three or four deep. Countrymen, butchers, drovers, hawkers, boys, thieves, idlers, and vagabonds ... were mingled together in a mass; the whistling of drovers, the barking of dogs, the bellowing and plunging of oxen, the bleating of sheep, the grunting and squeaking of pigs, the cries of hawkers, ... and the unwashed, unshaven, squalid, and dirty figures constantly running to and fro, and bursting in and out of the throng; rendered it a stunning and bewildering scene, which quite confounded the senses.[8] (153)

The carefully interwoven mixing of the human and animal sights and sounds successfully confuses the two. Our confusion, aided by the syntactic complexity, is so complete that when the 'squalid, and dirty figures' appear at the end of the passage we hardly know whether to take them for man, or beast, or both. The difference between them has collapsed.

This process, in which carefully defined and described details of actual things, places and people, in the city of London are used in *Oliver Twist* to evoke a nightmare vision of a bestial city of death, is the essence of Dickens' technique in the novel—what one critic has called 'the genius of abstraction', an 'extraordinary impulse to compel the typical from the particular'.[9] Though every detail can be placed on a map, nevertheless we are certain that the labyrinth we are in is Hell itself. And at the same time that we know Fagin is, as the Dodger describes him to Oliver, the ''spectable old genelman ... wot'll give you lodgings for no-think' (54) he is also the Devil himself, an incarnation of the pure evil of the world he inhabits.

This dark world, the labyrinth of London, appears to exist in a state of complete separation from the rest of the world. To enter it, as we have seen, one must pass through the maze. It is a necessary ritual. After Oliver is recaptured by Nancy and Sikes he must be dragged through it yet another time:

> Darkness had set in; ... resistance was useless. In another moment he was dragged into a labyrinth of dark narrow courts, and was forced along them at a pace which rendered the few cries he dared to give utterance to, unintelligible. (108)

The passage into the dark world is signalled and sealed by the fall of night.[10]

All of the neighbourhoods which make up this dark world are, but for their names, mutually indistinguishable. Saffron Hill, Bethnal Green, or Smithfield, are all localised manifestations of the same place. The final term in the series is Jacob's Island, a piece of land both morally and physically cut off from the rest of London. Yet, Dickens insists, it is in some special sense typical, only one 'of the many localities that are hidden in London, wholly unknown, even by name, to the great mass of its inhabitants.' A landscape more fantastic than the set of an expressionist film, it is a tangled 'maze of close, narrow, and muddy streets', thronged with people who are 'the raff and refuse of the river', the stench, din and houses sinking into the mud over which they totter, 'every conceivable sign of desolation and neglect' (381). This is the London of *Oliver Twist*.

While this version of the dark labyrinth of London is most powerfully actualised in *Oliver Twist*, it is not confined to that novel alone. In *Pickwick Papers* this dark world emerges once Pickwick is incarcerated in the Fleet Prison, described as a 'place which was never light' (PP, 575). The prison itself is another maze, made up of dark passages and infernal galleries filled with idle, often terrifying inmates. It is a scene of human suffering and degradation almost beyond belief, and which in the end, 'Mr. Pickwick's heart was really too full to bear' (580). This is most poignantly symbolised by a haggard woman watering the stump of a plant, which clearly like her will die inside the prison walls (596).

In *Nicholas Nickleby* the first metropolian scene Dickens presents to us, in Chapter iv, seems full of vitality and movement. But this is only an illusion. The 'giant currents of life' from all parts of the city that 'flow ceaselessly' toward its heart converge at Newgate prison 'and meet beneath its walls'. Here surrounded by a jeering, callous crowd, as many as eight men may be hanged on a single day. (*NN*, 29) Despite appearances, the heart of the city is not only a source of life, but a source of death.

The crowd, which appears in this description in *Nicholas Nickleby*, is in fact central to Dickens' conception of the city in these three novels. It is virtually the only social institution that the city can be seen to have in it. The crowd watching the military exercise at Rochester in *Pickwick Papers* is typical; it forms spontaneously, and it is ready to inflict upon any object casual and meaningless violence—on Pickwick, in this case, merely because he happens to be there. Or, later, Pickwick sitting locked in the pound has done nothing obviously wrong, yet he is treated to a barrage of vegetables solely because 'of the playful disposition of the many-headed' (*PP*, 46, 260).The crowd in *Oliver Twist* is yet more ominous. Each of the three times a crowd forms it is equally ready to 'whoop and scream with joy' chasing either Oliver, Sikes or Fagin, or one assumes anyone else, because, as Dickens observes, 'There is a passion *for hunting something* deeply implanted in the human breast' (*OT*, 67; Dickens' italics). This passion, and indeed all that is worst in man, is magnified in the crowd.

But crowds do have one advantage: they offer the opportunity of losing oneself. That, after all, is Oliver's thought as he decides to come to London. Noah Claypole makes the same observation when he runs away from Mr Sowerberry. Likewise in *Nicholas Nickleby*, Newman Noggs' most noticeable characteristic is his habit of making an exit by melting 'among the crowd' and disappearing 'in an instant' (NN, 15). Nicholas too escapes from a moment of powerful emotional agitation by 'plunging into the crowds which thronged the street' and similarly disappearing (682). And Bill Sikes, fleeing from the terrible consciousness of the murder he has just committed, can only escape it at the scene of a fire as he plunges 'into the thickest of the throng' (OT, 369).

Unfortunately, being lost in the crowd is not always this pleasant. One can lose one's pursuers, but one runs the risk of losing one's selfhood as well. Inside the dark world, Oliver is likewise hidden from the knowledge of his heritage, which would make him rich and establish him as a gentleman. All that he is conscious of is his own isolation. The society of thieves led by Fagin offers him the only physical sustenance and human companionship he has ever known, but in it he is still 'desolate and deserted, . . . alone in the midst of wickedness and guilt' (146). Pickwick in the Fleet is similarly cut off from the society of the debtors, and experiences a profound 'depression of spirit and sinking of heart' while he sits 'alone in the coarse vulgar crowd' (PP, 579). For both, it is at once a blessing and a curse that their inherent goodness isolates them within the labyrinth.[11]

In all three novels there is but one mode of response to this terrifying urban world—escape. No attempt can be made to reach an accommodation with or within it. To put it simply, it cannot sustain life and he who would live must flee. As J. Hillis Miller writes, 'There is only one way to protect oneself: permanent withdrawal.'[12]

After Pickwick loses his case in Bardell v. Pickwick, he leaves London entirely, until he must return to enter prison. And at the end of his travels, he retires from London again to Dulwich, taking Sam Weller with him; note that even Sam, whose 'knowledge of London was extensive and peculiar' (269), abandons city life with no remorse. In *Oliver Twist*, escape is even more patently the only conceivable response to urban life (except for death itself). Oliver's first impulse upon entering London is to run away from it, and that impulse is sustained until it is permanently effected. Even in *Nicholas Nickleby*, where Dickens, I shall argue, is making a conscious attempt to delineate the possibility of a healthy existence in the city, Nicholas and his entourage in the end settle at his father's old home in Devon, going to London solely when obliged to by 'the cares of business' (831).

This attitude stands in sharp contrast to the treatment of urban life we saw in *Sketches by Boz*, and the metropolitan sensibility that lay behind it. Yet only a brief period of time separates the writing of the one from the other. What must be explained is how and why this dramatic change came about; but before doing so, it will be helpful to examine briefly the world in which the characters of these novels seek refuge.

III

This other world must be entered as definitively as the dark world. When Mr Brownlow rescues Oliver from the courtroom of Mr Fang, they travel 'over nearly the same ground as that which Oliver had traversed when he first entered London in company with the Dodger; ... turning a different way ... [at] the Angel at Islington' (OT, 76), the precise point at which Oliver's initial descent into the labyrinth had begun. This ritualistic backward retracing of his steps symbolises Oliver's departure from the dark world and his entry into the light. The 'quiet shady street near Pentonville' (76) where Mr Brownlow lives is clearly in a different world, and not at all like the London we have been seeing. Before Oliver can complete his entrance into it, he must experience a long, cleansing period of unconsciousness, as he does again at the Maylie home in Chertsey. The separation of these worlds seems absolute, and the one time Fagin crosses from his to the other it is apparently accomplished only by supernatural means.[18]

In every respect, this world of light is the opposite of the dark labyrinth. For one thing, as here at the Maylie cottage, it has remarkable restorative powers:

> Oliver, whose days had been spent among squalid crowds, and in the midst of noise and brawling, seemed to enter on a new existence there.
> ... It was a happy time. The days were peaceful and serene; the nights brought with them neither fear nor care; no languishing in a wretched prison, or associating with wretched men; nothing but pleasant and happy thoughts. (238)

Here he is free to wander where he pleases in the 'pure air' and to enjoy 'all the pleasures and beauties of spring' (232). The openness of the country fields is reassuring, no longer terrifying as it was when he trudged across the barren wastes between the town of his birth and London. He no longer has to steal, let alone work, to earn his keep; he has little to do at all but gather flowers and run trivial errands for Rose Maylie, who immediately responds with 'a thousand commendations . . . on all he had done' (239). (Indeed, withdrawing from all active commerce with the world is an essential condition for entry into this community.)

This world is sunny where the other was dark; open where it was threateningly close; and even 'sweet-smelling' and 'neat and clean' (239) where it was foul and filthy. Each day is the same as the next, or the one before it: time almost ceases to have meaning. It is 'a little society, whose condition approached as nearly as one of perfect happiness as can ever be known in this changing world' (413). It is, in short, 'Heaven itself' (94). Here, in a temple made up of a snug country cottage, whose hearth is the altar, and in which Rose Maylie is the object of worship, the true Christian virtues of kindness and generosity can be established as the hallmark of all human relations, and existence in a modern urban world again becomes possible.[14]

Like the various localities of the dark world, those of the light—Pentonville, Chertsey and the Maylie country cottage—are all really manifestations of the same place. But this world of light has its fullest and most convincing actualisation in *Pickwick Papers*, in Dingley Dell at Christmas. For many generations of readers, this part of the novel has been the centre of their enjoyment of and reverence for all of Dickens. Truly there would be no way even to do summary justice to this triumphant celebration of a human community based on mutual affection, trust and boundless generosity, merely by selecting quotations from the novel, unless one were to present several chapters intact. The achievement of Dingley Dell is most remarkable in that Dickens never once falls to the level of hackneyed sentimentality while describing it. However, what we can say about it is that Dingley Dell is in the *countryside*, where Mr Pickwick characteristically rises with the sun and looks out upon the placid and reassuring landscape from his bedroom window. By contrast, the Fleet (and

the city) is a place trapped in time, where 'life' is not a precious
gift but a harsh criminal sentence. But at Dingley Dell, and even
more so at Mr Pickwick's Dulwich cottage at the close of the
novel, where Dickens shifts his narrative into the eternal present
to take leave of his character, immortality is attained in the here
and now.

IV

From these sketches of what I have called the dark world and
the light world of these three novels, it will be obvious that
Dickens has elaborated in them a very traditional view of the
city and country. As was discussed in the Introduction above,
this conventional wisdom, which Dickens absorbed in large part
from his favourite childhood authors and from the popular stage,
characteristically praised largely imaginary country virtues, and
denigrated city vices. Yet we know that after the time at
Warren's Blacking, the city had been a place of genuine opportunity to Dickens, in which his rise to social eminence and
financial success had been rapid and secure. At twelve he was a
little drudge; at twenty-four, the premier author of the English
speaking world. Moreover city life was really the only life he
knew. Though he clearly fancied himself, as he wrote to a
correspondent in 1840, 'a Kentish man bred and born',[15] it was
many years before he considered revisiting Chatham, let alone
taking up residence there. And as we have seen, this conventional
view is hardly at all evident in *Sketches*, which elaborates a
revolutionary and quite modern approach to urban life.

Nevertheless, this view does appear occasionally in *Sketches*,
but it does so, as we might expect, in formulations that are
extremely conventional, even hackneyed and trite. In a digression
in the piece, 'Our Next Door Neighbour', a country boy dying
in London asks as his last wish to be buried 'in the open fields—
anywhere but in these dreadful . . . close crowded streets; they
have killed me' (*SB*, 46). The deadness of the language betrays its
wholly conventional and derivative nature. And we know that
those 'close crowded streets', at the time these words were
written, far from being deadly, were more than anything else
exciting to Boz.

Early on in *Pickwick Papers*, one also finds Dickens invoking similarly hackneyed pieties about country and city. 'Who could continue to exist' in the city, soliloquises Mr Pickwick early in the novel while surveying a pastoral scene,

> where there are no cows but the cows on the chimney-pots;
> nothing redolent of Pan but pan-tiles; no crop but a stone crop?
> Who could bear to drag out a life in such a spot? Who I ask
> could endure it? (82)

The staleness of this sentiment is transparent, and it was, Dickens unashamedly assures us, made 'after the most approved precedents' (PP, 82). In *The Village Coquettes*, written at about the same time, the entire plot (such as it is) revolves around this tired cliché. In it, the Hon. Sparkins Flam, 'the pet of the court and the city' (CP, 119), corrupts the weak country Squire Norton, and together they attempt to seduce two honest but flirtatious village maidens. Of course, virtue triumphs in the end; Squire Norton mends his ways, and decides the country is really the place for him, singing out that,

> A country life without the strife
>   And noisy din of town,
> Is all I need, I take no heed
>   Of splendour or renown.
>
> And when I die, oh, let me die
>   Where trees above me wave;
> Let wild plants bloom, around my tomb,
>   My quiet country grave!   (CP, 138)

This song is simply so bad it is comical, though hardly in the way Dickens intended it to be. It stands in sharp contrast not only to the intense and powerful urban descriptions of *Oliver Twist*, but even to that novel's sincere and earnest (if equally turgid) passages which endorse country life and condemn the city, and certainly to those about Dingley Dell in the latter part of *Pickwick Papers*. A dramatic difference in imaginative force, emotional intensity and the sheer energy Dickens poured into the writing itself, separates these passages.

After completing *Sketches*, and while he was writing *Pickwick Papers* and the early chapters of *Oliver Twist*, it is evident that a substantial and pronounced change took place in the nature of Dickens' writing about the city and the country. The fictional events which coincide with this change are Mr Pickwick's entry into the Fleet prison (PP, Chapter xl) and Oliver's arrival at Fagin's den (OT, Chapter viii). Because of the circumstances of their simultaneous publication, they occurred in print at about the same time, respectively in July and May of 1837. Both fictional events correspond roughly to an important event in Dickens' life—the sudden death, early in May 1837, of his young sister-in-law, Mary Hogarth. In working on *Oliver Twist*, and in bringing Oliver to London, Dickens had begun to delve into the buried memories and emotions relating to his own childhood in the city. Mary's death and the grave shock it caused him accelerated his autobiographical impulse, and reawakened in him the original fear and agonies of London and Warren's Blacking. This fear and pain coloured his fictional treatment of the city in those novels, and helped make it into the dark world which we have already found in them.

Before proceeding any further, it will be as well to note that this explanation differs greatly from the view of Dickens' attitudes toward the city presented persuasively by Alexander Welsh in *The City of Dickens* (Oxford: Clarendon, 1971). Welsh takes a synchronic approach to the Dickens *oeuvre*, perceiving in all his writing a pattern of imagery and a structure of feeling not unlike that expounded immediately above in relation to the dark and light worlds of *Pickwick Papers*, *Oliver Twist* and *Nicholas Nickleby*. In Welsh's analysis the city is always seen by Dickens as a place of danger and death; the country as unreal pastoral refuge; and the good woman, wife or sister, presiding over the domestic circle, as a latter day Angel of Mercy. Welsh's thesis, far more subtle and convincing than this oversimplification of it, is a valuable contribution toward our understanding of Victorian attitudes toward death and the home, and the role of women, and sheds insight on more than Dickens' novels alone. What it does obscure, however, is the development—often dramatic—of Dickens' attitudes and their fictional correlatives over his long and varied writing career. The most important of them is that brought about by Mary Hogarth's death.

The serious nature of Dickens' relationship with her can only be surmised from his reaction to her death, for the evidence we have of it during her brief life is far from exceptional.[16] Mary was lively and pretty, but only fifteen at the time of Dickens' marriage. She seems to have stayed with the Dickenses for several months during the winter of 1836–7, and when they vacated Furnival's Inn and took a larger house in Doughty Street in April 1837, she probably moved in with the family to help with the housekeeping as her sister was again pregnant. It has been speculated that Dickens was already quarrelling with his wife and becoming discouraged by her moodiness, and that the impressionable and flirtatious Mary offered him a convenient means of escape from her company. Certainly, with Catherine restricted to her bed and the house, he spent time with Mary doing many things he otherwise would have done with his wife, for example, choosing new furniture. Whether this was an open flirtation or not, it is likely that Dickens was at least tempted by Mary, and imagined one.

Then, on 7 May, after an evening at the theatre at which he and Mary saw performed Dickens' own farce *Is She His Wife?* (which features the bickerings of a newly wedded couple), Mary collapsed. She died that night, in Dickens' arms. (It has even been suggested that the shock of seeing the Dickens family situation on stage may have caused her to suffer a heart attack, and thus caused her death.) The guilt Dickens must have felt can be imagined. Reeling from such a blow, he might well have wondered if his desire had in some way provoked her death as an extreme form of retribution; at the death of someone close, guilty thoughts of this kind are unavoidable. Even worse, because of the provisions of the law then in force relating to a deceased wife's sister, such a relationship would have been virtually incestuous.

Dickens reacted extremely, with a show of grief which must have shocked Catherine and the Hogarths: even as Mary died, he took a ring from her finger and, placing it on his own, vowing never to remove it. He said that when he died, he would be buried in the grave next to hers. He took his family off to a secluded farm in North London to mourn her. The most telling sign of his distress was that he was unable to write the next month's instalments of *Pickwick Papers* and *Oliver Twist*, the only time in his career he was to miss such a deadline.[17] The later deaths of his parents, siblings or even his children, caused no such outward show of grief. For several years afterward, Dickens dreamed of Mary every night, and the dreams ceased only once he had managed to bring himself to tell his wife of them.

As Dickens himself admitted, Mary Hogarth's death was the greatest emotional shock of his life. At the time it occurred, Dickens had already begun to explore (albeit in an indirect manner, with Oliver and Fagin's den) the circumstances of his early life in London. Sending Oliver to the city and into the den of thieves was in a way a reenactment of his own journey to London and Warren's Blacking Warehouse. Rummaging among these buried experiences was bound to revive some of the feelings of isolation and fear associated with them. And as one of the most common reactions to great emotional shock is regression, it is hardly strange that Mary's death weakened his psychic defences against those debilitating emotions, and brought yet closer to the surface of his psyche the conflict and pain of the earlier time.[18]

The memories of his ordeal at Warren's Blacking had, after all, never really been very far from his consciousness, and now, in his unstable condition, they returned with renewed intensity. But Mary's death did not only revive them, it changed them. For at the same time, as it were retrospectively to defuse any guilt he felt about his relationship with her, Dickens began to idealise Mary Hogarth. She had not been a young woman at all, but a sweet and innocent child, with whom nothing even remotely illicit could have happened; therefore nothing had. And somehow, as Dickens thought this, by association Mary became for him an image of himself as a child, 'of that conception of himself which he saw as still existing in the past'.[19] (It may be that at this time he also had a recurrence of the painful kidney ailment he had suffered from quite often at Warren's.) Her death and his childhood alone in London came to be regarded by him on a deep level as simultaneous events; and he linked both to an even more distant past, his memories of his earliest years in the Kent countryside.

Dickens, as we have seen, looked back on his boyhood in Chatham as the happiest years of his life, though when he later tried to write about them, he remembered but little and that vaguely. 'Kentish woods and fields, Cobham park and hall, Rochester Cathedral and castle, and all the wonderful romance together . . . were to vanish like a dream' (*Life*, I, 11), Forster wrote, probably using Dickens' own words. The specific incidents Dickens recalled from those years do not make them seem particularly happy ones to us, but the whole experience later was transformed into an impression of an idyllic interlude spent among 'beautiful hawthorne trees', 'buttercups and daisies' and other typical rural delights (*Life*, I, 11). He came to regard it in exactly the way he had Nicholas Nickleby look back on his childhood, as a bright and happy time spent wandering in 'green fields' and gathering 'wild flowers' (*NN*, 759). Nicholas here is a very transparent vehicle for Dickens' own musings; in fact, the Nickleby's ancestral home is in Devon, where Dickens had just resettled his parents before writing this.

What was happening in Dickens' imagination was something like this (though to formulate it so baldly is to make it sound far too mechanical and crude): Dickens had been attracted strongly to Mary Hogarth; she died suddenly; he felt unsupportable grief and guilt after her death, and that he was in some way responsible for it; and under the impact of these powerful emotions, was laid open to a resurgence of the childhood sufferings at Warren's Blacking he had already begun to explore in *Oliver Twist*. At the same time he combated this double shock by trying to reshape Mary into an ideal, innocent child, and also by again holding on to the memories of his happy years in Kent before London, memories which once before had sustained him in a period of great emotional turmoil and stress. London then had nearly been the ruin of him, a poor, innocent child who could not protect himself. Mary, also poor and innocent, had been killed in London. And so on some profound inner level, London again became for Dickens a place of danger and distress. So, during the months and years that followed, Dickens' fictional image of London was less and less the city it actually was, and more and more the city he had seen a dozen years before as a lonely and terrified little boy. It became the nightmare labyrinth of *Oliver Twist*.

The isolated and abandoned workhouse boy, wandering the

dark and winding streets of London at the mercy of unknown
and unseen forces of evil, is as much the way Dickens now saw
himself as he had been as a child, as the way he imagined Oliver
Twist.[20] The nightmarish labyrinth of the novel is described in
terms which uncannily suggest the language and imagery of his
description of his childhood bondage in London in the autobiographical fragment written some ten years later. That he could
sustain them so long in the same form itself suggests the power
this personal myth held. The Blacking Warehouse itself, for
example, described in the fragment as 'a crazy, tumbledown old
house, abutting of the course of the river, and literally overrun
with rats' (*Life*, I, 25), reappears as the decayed house over a
river where Monks meets the Bumbles to destroy all proof of
Oliver's birth (and also in *Nicholas Nickleby* as the house in the
City that Kate and Mrs Nickleby are given by Uncle Ralph,
which does not itself serve any clear purpose in the narrative).[21]
The London of the dark labyrinth was similarly a precise reflection of the London of the Blacking Warehouse.

This argument about the significance of Mary Hogarth's
death for Dickens has rested until now mainly upon biographical
assertions not readily proven at this great remove in time. But in
his writing there are further evidences that her death was the
key element behind the change in his attitude toward city and
country. All three novels, though most of all *Oliver Twist*, are
marked by long, expository passages which offer theoretical
justifications, and conscious rationalisations, of the movement
away from the city back to the country, which refer clearly to
Mary's demise.

One of the most complex of these passages occurs midway
through *Oliver Twist*. In an 'inland village', Dickens writes,

> ... scenes of peace and quietude sink into the minds of pain-
> worn dwellers in close and noisy places. ... Men who have
> lived in crowded, pent-up streets, through lives of toil, ... to
> whom custom has indeed become second nature, and who
> have come almost to love each brick and stone that formed the
> narrow boundaries of their daily walks; even they, with the
> hand of death upon them, have been known to yearn at last
> for one short glimpse of Nature's face; and ... have seemed

to pass at once into a new state of being. . . . The memories
which peaceful country scenes call up, are not of this world,
nor of its thoughts and hopes. . . . [There] lingers, in the least
reflective mind, a vague and half-formed consciousness of
having held such feelings long before, in some remote and
distant time, which calls up solemn thoughts of distant times
to come, and bends down pride and worldliness beneath it.
(OT, 237)

This passage was written in April 1838, on the eve of the first
anniversary of Mary Hogarth's death, and for some years afterward at this time of year Dickens penned similar commemora-
tions of the event.[22] What it constitutes is an attempt to erase
the sting of that death.

To begin with, it moves in two directions, forward to the
afterlife, and back to distant memories. The countryside links
both, for it is here where the childhood paradise once was, in
that 'distant time' which is in fact 'a foretaste of heaven'.
Children are allowed to begin life in pastoral paradise; death only
restores this actual past. The peril of the city is seen as separation
from this past, but above all as the most final form of separation,
death; Dickens had himself risked it alone as a child, and it had
come now suddenly to Mary Hogarth. The country, then, serves
not only as a refuge from this special danger (which after all
must eventually come to all), but removes its pain in a round-
about way: it allows us to experience, or more precisely to
re-experience, paradise itself. Dying is then something not to
fear but eagerly to await. In a way this was to say that the time
in the Blacking Warehouse and Mary's death had never been,
for both his image of himself as a child and Mary herself could
be placed in a future life which was only a reflection of that past
one spent in the green fields of Kent, in that time 'before we
knew what death was' (NN, 759). The process by which death
can be accommodated is illustrated by Smike's last days: removed
to Devon by Nicholas, he vicariously lives Nicholas' (and Kate's)
childhood through Nicholas' memories of it, and so having
experienced paradise in this and his 'pleasant dreams' (762) of it,
he knows he has nothing to fear from death and can face it
cheerfully.

We can see here too how the very special role in life which Dickens came to give to memory was developing. The subject of memory was increasingly displaced from the novels to the Christmas books, and has its fullest treatment in *The Haunted Man*. Note also how in these novels the word 'old-fashioned', applied to Pickwick, Brownlow and the Cheerybles, among others, is given a particularly positive connotative value, equivalent to virtuous, cheerful, generous and sincere rolled into one. Since the past was paradise, anything old must be good.

Still, this process is problematical, for the flight from the city to the country does not lead to freedom from death, the city's great terror, but only embraces it in another form. *Pickwick Papers* neatly sidesteps the issue, for by the end of the novel the audience and the author both have come to believe in the immortality of its leading characters. In the less transcendent worlds of *Oliver Twist* and *Nicholas Nickleby* this situation is more squarely faced, and both close with the living (or more accurately, perhaps, those who have survived) quietly gathered in worship at a country grave, that of Agnes in the former, Smike in the latter. The dead are what link the living to a vision of their childhood memories which prefigure the joys of paradise.

V

It is this insistence upon the essential oneness of the peace and quiet of the country with the somewhat more permanent peace and quiet of the tomb which is one of the reasons why we tend instinctively to reject the affirmation of idyllic life in the later two of these novels. For one thing, we cannot accept that Dickens—in his mid-twenties already a popular and widely praised novelist, fathering books and children with equal rapidity, engaged in editing a magazine and writing numerous lesser works at the same time, dazzling his friends with the relentless energy he invested in what to most people would be merely leisure activities—should think of himself as a world-weary philosopher identifying so closely with the 'pain-worn' city dwellers 'with the hand of death upon them' about to sink passively into the tomb. Yet we cannot but appreciate how earnestly he wished to believe that passivity and a calm, serene acceptance of death (in suitably rural surroundings) was the way of life he should be following.

There is no doubt about how strongly he did at times wish to consider himself in such a way. For example, he could write this to Forster, on 5 March 1839, while looking for a cottage in Devon in which to settle his parents: 'I am sure they may be happy there; for if I were older, and my course of activity were run, I am sure I could, with God's blessing, for many and many a year' (*Life*, I, 109). In a way he did put this philosophy into practice, by spending increasingly long summer vacations in country resorts like Petersham and Twickenham, or later in Broadstairs,[23] and by establishing his own personal cult of remembrance at the altar of Mary Hogarth's country grave.[24] But the hectic and almost feverishly intense activity he was involved in at the same time demonstrates that he never came too close to accepting his own philosophy, however passionately he could espouse it in the novels he was writing, or, for that matter, in his letters and conversations with friends.

This tension between the life of repose, represented by the country, and the life of activity, by the city, surfaces everywhere in these novels, most obviously in the character of the writing about them. Dickens, as was noted above, was from the start of his career constantly forced to borrow conventional language and imagery to describe the country, resulting in writing as boring as it is unimaginative. But now his writing about it was marked also by an emotional intensity which added nothing so much as bathos, as here: 'The earth had donned her mantle of brightest green; and shed her richest perfumes abroad. It was the prime and vigour of the year, all things were glad and flourishing' (OT, 240). The vacuousness of such a description stands in sharp contrast to the stark poetry of even this brief phrase from the same novel, part of a much longer passage about Jacob's Island: '. . . rooms so small, so filthy, so confined, that the air would seem too tainted even for the dirt and squalor which they shelter' (OT, 382).

The country scenes or provincial towns in these novels are rarely differentiated or invested with any memorable qualities whatsoever. Having read about them in the novels and never seen them, would one ever guess Kent and Devon to be in any way different? Or could one describe in detail the landscape of Dingley Dell? In *Pickwick Papers*, Bristol, then in fact a large city, is described in a mere half sentence, while Lant Street in the Borough has two long paragraphs lavished upon it. It is not only the amount of detail that distinguishes Dickens' writing about London and its main imaginative extensions in these novels, the workhouse and Dotheboys Hall, but the precise and powerfully evocative prose with which he describes them. Forster noted this quality in Dickens' metropolitan scenes in *Nicholas Nickleby*: 'Its [London's] hidden life becomes familiar as its commonest outward forms, and we discover that we hardly knew anything of the places we supposed that we knew the best' (*Life*, I, 99). London was to Dickens a real place, in his life and imagination; this other was only an idea, and no matter how desperately he willed it to life, it remained to him literally and figuratively dead.

The tension is reflected not only in the prose of the novels, but in the fact that so often all of their imaginative power allies itself with the dark city world and tends to subvert the position of the light. This is especially true of *Oliver Twist*. I do not refer here to Dickens' sympathy for Fagin, or the shallowness of good characters, like Rose or Harry Maylie. The former convincingly can be accounted for by the complex, and here more or less extraneous, autobiographical impulses in the novel, and the latter by difficulties Dickens shares with any writer creating a believable virtuous character. What I do refer to is a wide range of structural elements which undermine the neat separation of country and life from city and death.

To begin with, every societal institution that does appear in these novels is implicated with the dark world and not the light. The courts, the magistrates and the workhouse in *Oliver Twist* are all as corrupt and evil as Fagin's den, and considerably more hypocritical. The Artful Dodger's remark that a court is not 'the shop for justice' (OT, 335) is, if one considers his sentence of transportation for stealing a snuffbox, rather an understatement.[25] In this society, in both the light world and the dark world, poverty is treated in exactly the same manner—as a crime whose punishment is death, either in the workhouse or on the scaffold. Oliver at birth is simply another 'item of mortality' (1). For the vast majority of the poor, who are not lucky enough to be saved like Oliver, by their father's name and fortune, no escape from this harsh sentence is possible.

The principles which govern both the light and dark world are the laws of political economy (synonymous for Dickens with 'philosophy'), the theoretical dogma of the most politically advanced segments of the early Victorian middle class, and one which seemed to be moulding the nation in its image with the enactment by Parliament of such bills as the New Poor Law. However, in *Oliver Twist* it is not the 'overworld' of the middle class but the criminal underworld that is the one in which the concept of enlightened self-interest, 'the beautiful axiom' (66) of philosophy which Oliver never manages to learn, has already been adopted as the guideline for all human intercourse. But far from its resulting in the universal betterment philosophic radicals promised, we see instead a society whose relations are governed by universal deceit and mutual treachery.

Fagin eloquently explains the principle of the 'magic number', one:

> '. . . [You] depend on me. To keep my little business snug, I depend on you. The first is your number one, the second is my number one. The more you value your number one, the more careful you must be of mine; so we come at last to what I told you at first—that a regard for number one holds us all together, and must do so, unless we would all go to pieces in company.' (328)

Only the possibility of betrayal and the gallows makes cooperation possible. The significance of this similarity between the two worlds is outlined even more strongly in *Nicholas Nickleby*; for here the school, the one societal institution whose avowed purpose is to spread civilisation and promote humanity, becomes by application of this same rule of enlightened self-interest, an instrument of de-educating children, turning boys into savages. Dotheboys Hall is a Hobbesian inferno, where the students and teachers exist in a state of open warfare. Mr Squeers is another moralist for whom 'the only number in all arithmetic that I know of . . . is number one' (NN, 782). Philosophy is reduced by Squeers to anything which will serve him financially by killing off his charges: ' "Measles, rheumatics, hooping-cough, fevers, agers, and lumbagers," said Mr. Squeers, "is all philosophy together; that's what it is. . . . Philosophy's the chap for me" ' (751).

The separation of the light and dark worlds collapses in practice as well as in theory. The ease with which Nancy can, both at the police station and later when she recaptures Oliver in the street, impersonate a virtuous woman, and make Oliver seem the guilty and unnatural transgressor, undermines the appearance of all virtue. Commenting on the deflation of Bumble after he is stripped of his beadle's hat, Dickens comments that, 'Dignity, and even holiness too, sometimes, are more questions of coat and waistcoat than some people imagine' (OT, 267). By changing one's clothing one changes one's identity. And if one recalls the way in which Oliver's old clothes are sold to a second-hand dealer, are there found by Fagin, and so lead Fagin to discover Oliver's whereabouts, one concludes Dickens may well be implying a circular relationship that joins the two disparate halves of society.

In addition to all this, it is not possible to accept, at least on the basis of the evidence Dickens presents to us, that the light world of passive virtue can ever sustain itself against the aggressiveness of the world of evil invoked against it. The dice seem loaded against it from the start: not only are its members often pathetically unreal but they are usually ineffective as well. Mr Pickwick would, we are sure, have perished inside the Fleet were it not for the knowing Sam Weller. In *Oliver Twist* it requires the ceaseless efforts of an entire community of rich and powerful grown men to save one small boy.

More than this, the system founders on financial grounds. Dickens never successfully solves the problem of how one is to come by the cash necessary to enter the suburban world where the community of the good must live. Sam Weller, himself a *de facto* orphan who grew up on the streets of London, must be taken up by Mr Pickwick and rewarded with sums far greater than his station deserves to escape the city. Furthermore, where Mr Pickwick acquired his money is never revealed; we know only that he is 'retired from business, and . . . a gentleman of considerable independent property' (486). As far as we know in the novel, the only way to get money is by 'doing' someone else, as Dodgson and Fogg do Pickwick. Does this mean the young Pickwick was really a Scrooge?

Oliver is rescued by his inheritance without himself ever doing a thing to gain it, conveniently absolving him of the taint or guilt incurred by earning it. In *Nicholas Nickleby*, however, Dickens attempted a more honest and realistic approach to this problem, though an equally unsuccessful one in the end.

VI

In *Nicholas Nickleby*, his answer to the problem is embodied in the portrayal of the Cheerybles. They are businessmen, but ones whose stock in trade is mainly generosity and geniality, large quantities of which they dole out as regularly as physics in Dotheboys Hall, and in a manner almost as unpleasant. They are meant to represent, in the way they run their business, a vaguely old-fashioned kind of merchant who treated his workers as his family, and who gladly shouldered his social responsibilities. Yet they are, we know, German-merchants—in other words, in the cotton trade, at that time the most mechanised and brutally modern of all industries.[26] Dickens is just fudging the facts. In this highly competitive part of the business world, dominated by the factory system, no firm that carried on as the Cheerybles do could ever have survived. The villain of the novel, Ralph Nickleby, is truly an old-fashioned businessman, a miser: but it would have been entirely more realistic to have made the Cheerybles the villains rather than him.[27]

Conspiring in the same way against the relentless pressure of social reality, whenever Dickens puts Nicholas in the position of actually having to earn his own living in the world, he resorts to a *deus ex machina* to extract him. As a teacher working in Dotheboys Hall Nicholas has a very dull future, so Dickens quickly pulls him out of that profession; as an actor in a provincial company, he can support himself adequately, but not gain respectability, so he is made to leave again; only as a clerk for the Cheerybles, who pay him £120 per annum, roughly twice his market value, can Nicholas be allowed to settle down.

And in the end, his fortune is not earned but pulled out of a hat, given to him along with his lovely bride.

However, despite the failure of the Cheerybles to demonstrate a way of doing business in the city without succumbing to its inhumanity and resisting contamination from its evils, it is notable that the London of *Nicholas Nickleby* is conceived as a city in which life is still possible. To be sure, the dark world exists in this London, personified by Ralph Nickleby—a cruel and aggressive userer. The garden of his house is a symbol of the social and personal evils he represents: it is a desolate place containing only shrunken and deformed living things, 'a crippled tree', a 'rheumatic sparrow', and 'stunted everbrowns' (NN, 8). This garden has nothing in common with nature, having been created from the debris of the city, 'pieces of unreclaimed land, with the withered vegetation of the original brick-field' (NN, 8). It is as much as saying that the city has created a second nature for man, in which nothing whole or healthy can grow.

But, Dickens insists, this is not the only kind of urban environment possible. Opposed to it is the City square in which the Cheeryble warehouse is located, where a happy and good life *is* available, though it is in London. In fact, the square's first function is to shut out the din and bustle of the city, creating a 'desirable nook' (468) where, though it be devoid of vegetation, one can experience something akin to the serene tranquility of the country. A city dweller here can be happy, though perhaps only after the fashion of Tim Linkinwater's blackbird, which being blind cannot see the bars of its cage. This life may be only second best, for a man like Tim who has lived all his life in the city knows nothing else, but at least it is still life.

Tim, and not his employers the Cheerybles, is the character who does demonstrate the possibility of survival in the city. He has never slept a night out of their warehouse, and positively loathes the country. To him the country has no attractions 'but new-laid eggs and flowers' (514), both of which he can get more easily in London. He even goes so far as to aver the superiority of city graveyards, and remarks that Smike should have been buried in one, which in the context of the novel is surely the highest praise conceivable. Most significant of all of Tim's defences of London is his description of the sickly crippled boy across the yard from his back window who has managed to grow a remarkable 'double-wall flower'. Nicholas scoffs incredulously:

> 'Yes, is there!' replied Tim, 'and planted in a cracked jug, without a spout. There were hyacinths there, this last spring, blossoming in—but you'll laugh at that.'
> 'At what?'
> 'At their blooming in old blacking-bottles,' said Tim. (514)

The mention of blacking bottles, knowing their secret meaning for Dickens, together with the fact that the crippled boy watching other children at play is described in the same way Dickens once described himself as a sickly child (in *David Copperfield*, Chapter iv), indicate that Dickens was trying here to come to grips with his own past suffering. The secret pain and suffering that the city contains, Dickens seems to be saying, cannot be erased, and in fact the little crippled boy eventually dies. But out of that pain and suffering can come life and growth itself. Life can flourish in the city, Tim triumphantly asserts—and flowers can grow even in blacking bottles.

CHAPTER THREE

The Old Curiosity Shop and Barnaby Rudge: Breakdown and Breakthrough

Though editing *Bentley's Miscellany* had proved to be a disastrous experience, during the summer of 1839 Dickens decided he would again edit a magazine of his own, and arranged for Chapman and Hall to publish it. It was to begin appearing on 31 March 1840, some time after *Nicholas Nickleby* was completed, and though at first would be written entirely by Dickens, need not contain a long narrative, nor even continue to be his work alone once it had become established. Dickens hoped, vainly as it turned out, this would be less taxing work than writing monthly novel parts.

The conception of this weekly, *Master Humphrey's Clock*, was from the start obsessively involved with the past—historical, mythical and personal. The format would be that of the eighteenth-century periodicals Dickens had read as a child. The stories it contained were to be set in 'the old simple times' (*MHC*, 20), and would perhaps use the legendary ancient London giants Gog and Magog as narrators. The original formula of Dickens' success with *Pickwick Papers* would be recapitulated as well, with the figures of Master Humphrey and his club and their adventures. (Eventually, Mr Pickwick himself and both the Wellers were trotted out, too.) But already, something had gone wrong in this attempt to recapture the past: Master Humphrey and his associates are all mental and physical cripples, and their ways solitary and doleful. Nothing further from the jovial and animated Pickwick Club could be imagined.

The movement into his own past that Dickens had undertaken as a way of coping with Mary Hogarth's death was being crystallised in his conception of *Master Humphrey's Clock*.[1] But whereas in the novels before it, Dickens had dealt with this wish to return implicitly and indirectly, in *Master Humphrey's Clock* and in the novel he soon began in it, *The Old Curiosity Shop*, he did so quite openly. This work, and that which followed it, *Barnaby Rudge*, continue to explore responses to the question, how is it—indeed, is it at all—possible to live in the city, the repository of suffering, guilt and death. The conclusions in each are quite different: in *The Old Curiosity Shop* Dickens breaks down and surrenders completely to his most neurotic fears and impulses in a manic flight from the city. But somehow, through this breakdown, he was able to free himself of those fears and break through them, and go on, in *Barnaby Rudge*, to confront the problem of life in the city with vitality and dynamism.

II

The Old Curiosity Shop began as a short tale in the third number of *Master Humphrey's Clock*, centring about the image of a young girl and her old grandfather (suggested by Dickens seeing such a couple in Bath). Two circumstances made him decide to expand it to a novel. Firstly, when readers found the new magazine contained no new novel by Boz they stopped buying it, and circulation fell ominously. Secondly, Dickens found the subject so congenial once begun that it seemed to write itself. So, Forster wrote, the story of Little Nell took form 'with less *direct consciousness* of design on his part than I can remember at any other instance throughout his career' (*Life*, I, 117; my italics). As this comment suggests, Dickens was yielding to unconscious promptings in taking hold of, or being taken hold of by, this narrative.[2]

Little Nell is a magnificently naïve, pure and innocent young girl who quickly became for Dickens, as he wrote on, an idealised image of Mary Hogarth. Through Nell, Dickens made explicit all he had thought in response to her death: she is placed in a city which is quite literally a city of death, then is made to flee London for the unspoiled countryside, where she seeks a total and absolute peace and stillness which is none other than death itself. That she approaches death joyfully as the true fulfilment of her young life reflected back reassuringly on Mary; she too must have desired her own death.

Nell is set at first in the Curiosity Shop, which is really a microcosm of the city around her, a collection of dead objects, the detritus of urban life.[3] Trapped in this 'black, cold, and lifeless' shop (OCS, 12), she still remembers how 'happy and . . . cheerful and contented' (48) she and her grandfather were at some vague time in the past. She also remembers her dead mother, who 'was not lying in her grave, but had flown to a beautiful country . . . where nothing died or ever grew old', not unlike the place where she and her grandfather once had 'walked in the fields and among the green trees' (49). The connections between death, the city, memories of childhood, pastoral bliss and heavenly paradise are perfectly clear. Her memories of happiness and the country and her intuitions about death are all visions of one place and one experience.

The city is wholly a place of terror. Its associations are exclusively 'mournful fancies' (69), like her nightmare vision of her grandfather's blood creeping under her door at night. In the surreal landscape of London at night, the streets are deserted, except for the sudden appearance of death itself figured in the apparition of 'a man passing with a coffin on his back' (69). Here in the city of death, Nell will either starve, or what is worse, be sexually violated by Quilp.[4]

Without even a moment's hesitation, Little Nell flees the city. The strategy of retiring to the suburbs after acquiring a fortune, successfully realised by the protagonists of *Oliver Twist* and *Nicholas Nickleby*, is not even considered. It is rejected here, in fact, with a good deal more truthfulness, for Nell's grandfather's attempts to make them rich only entangle him with Quilp and so if allowed to continue would prove her undoing. The activity of seeking a fortune is reduced in the novel to the old man's obsession with gambling, and even further to blatant sexual aggression. To lust after money is thus to be fatally compromised. This connection is made clear in Chapter xxx, when the grandfather enters Nell's room at night to steal a piece of gold she has sewn into the lining of her dress: the act is described as if it were a sexual violation, and Nell (unaware at first it is he) fears it is an act of violence, an attempt by some villain to murder herself or the old man.

Their only hope appears to be in a complete rejection of

money. '"... Oh hear me pray that we may beg ... to earn a scanty living, rather than live as we do now"', Little Nell pleads with her grandfather:

> 'Let us be beggars. . . . Let us walk through country places, and sleep in fields and under trees, and never think of money again, . . . but rest at nights, and have the sun and wind upon our faces in the day. . . . Let us never set foot in dark rooms or melancholy houses, any more, . . . and I will go and beg for both.' (71)

Begging in the countryside, or working in a non-cash economy by bartering work for food and shelter, is the only way of life which will allow Nell to remain uncontaminated.

There is never any doubt that this flight from London is also a return to the actual historical past: 'an *escape* from the heartless people by whom she had been surrounded . . . the *restoration* of . . . peace, and a life of tranquil happiness' (94; my italics). This can only be interpreted as a conscious rejection of modern urban England, and a search for an older, even mythical, way of life. Thus immediately upon leaving 'the labyrinth of men's abodes' (114), they duly experience the 'deep joys' that country life gives 'to those whose life is in a crowd or who live solitarily in great cities as in the bucket of a human well' (116).[5]

At this point, we are close to one of the novel's central paradoxes. It would seem to be, from what I have said about it, no more than a thinly disguised personal allegory and fantasy; but at the same time we know that *The Old Curiosity Shop* was immensely popular (selling over 100,000 copies per weekly instalment) and Little Nell herself something like a mass hysterical obsession: when she 'died', it is said, people went into mourning. The pathetic figure of Nell herself is central to this popularity (a Victorian Lolita, Steven Marcus has called her), but I think in addition to this, another great part of the novel's appeal derived from its general tone of nostalgia and its overall retrogressive movement.

For one thing, we must consider the fact that Dickens felt he was writing in this novel a rather sharp social protest on behalf of the poor and exploited. He seems to have meant this to be true of the entire novel, and not merely of the ineffective, hallucinatory episode set in an industrial town (apparently a conflation of Wolverhampton and Birmingham), which bears as little relation to the actual experience of factory life as Nell herself does to flesh and blood. Yet the confused response of rejection in the novel, the rejection of industry, the city and the town, the cash nexus and the capitalist economy altogether, and the search for a better way of life in a dimly remembered but already mythic rural folk past, was one which struck a deep and sympathetic note in Dickens' readers.

The time when this was being written was a period of extreme industrial depression—the beginning of what would be remembered as 'the Hungry Forties'. It was the most severe economic distress yet experienced in England, and perhaps the worst ever experienced: certainly it was bad enough to convince many observers that industrial capitalism was now in its death throes. It is crucial to remember about this period that industrial development was yet a recent thing, a phenomenon which had grown to its present state from almost nothing wholly within the memory of men little older than Dickens. A man hardly more than thirty living in Bolton, for example, could have remembered a time when there was not a single cotton mill in the town. By 1840, it was a booming industrial city of 50,000 people, and a centre of the cotton trade.

The move from village to city had destroyed a traditional way of life for millions, but had replaced it so far with little more than bestial living conditions, depersonalisation on a factory floor, and much physical suffering. Now, in what to many seemed to be the final collapse of this new economic system, it was only natural that they should look backward to a real or imagined far better way of life in the historical past. Even the Chartist movement was, in a limited sense, reactionary, for it began by demanding ancient rights and usages, believing (at least for a time) that a direct appeal to the Sovereign over the heads of Parliament could yet set things right. Even in the late 1840s, some Chartists persisted in believing that a return to peasant proprietorship of the land could end poverty.[6]

This was an illusion, but not one confined to the working classes. Many Tories, like Disraeli and his followers in the loose Young England movement, also envisioned a solution to the nation's problems by a return to an earlier, organic state of society, with the aristocracy once again shouldering its burden of responsibility and setting things straight. Carlyle, too, in *Past and Present* (1843) was looking backwards, leaning toward the former of his two terms of reference as a model for the latter. Dickens had little patience for tomfoolery about the magnificence of medievalism, but there was nevertheless something about the lost pastoral myth that he, like so many others, found irresistibly alluring. Nell's flight to a rural idyll somewhere off in the English heartland is his fullest expression of it.

But Nell's flight is a failure. The more he wrote, the more inevitably Nell moved towards death. Her country odyssey at times is more like a Cook's tour of English graveyards than an actual journey. Dickens was at last coming to face the implications of his endorsement of the pastoral myth, and one of the ways in which this surfaces in the novel are frequent attempts to imagine what it would feel like to be dead. When he did so, the result was not always as comforting as it should have been.

The novel opens with Master Humphrey imagining a man 'condemned to lie, dead but conscious, in a noisy churchyard, [with] no hope of rest for centuries to come!'(1) This death is hardly restful peace; it is but a 'poor hollow mockery . . . of sleep' far different from true sleep (92). Still Dickens piles up endorsements for the other view, as when an old widow assures Nell that, ' "Death doesn't change us more than life, my dear" ' (129). Country graveyards still are seen as desirable locations, 'beneath which slept poor humble men' (122). The final term in this series of glimpses beyond the tomb is Nell's vision of the stars at night, 'eternal in their numbers as in their changeless and incorruptible existence', which is exactly the same when reflected before her in the river, the symbol of 'dead mankind, a million fathoms deep' (311). The experience had first been Dickens' own, 'the fruit', he wrote to Forster, 'of a solitary walk by starlight on the cliffs' (*Life*, I, 120). The meaning of the passage is not difficult to grasp: the order of creation will not change after death. Death is but a mirror image of all that is unchanging in life. Once this is stated, Nell's days truly are numbered, and all who meet her know it. Even the wretched creature who tends the furnace in the industrial town cannot see Nell without recognising this, and in a symbolic gesture he gives her two coppers, no doubt to aid her passage into the next world.

The village where this will take place is sketched by Dickens as a semi-primitive paradise, a physical representation of the mythical past in which he had located his hopes for societal and personal regeneration. As soon as Nell sees it, she knows it— 'visions of such scenes . . . had always been present to her mind' (347). Whatever or wherever this place really is, Dickens leaves its identity vague and unspecified, because it too is already dead, 'for even change was old in that old place' (385). It is overrun with graves, and the people in it have but two visible occupations, digging new ones, and tending the old. Dickens still attempts to invent a new metaphoric means of redeeming death, by calling graves gardens, and the sexton a gardener. Nevertheless, when he has Nell gaze down the churchyard well, a sort of direct passage to the other world, even she cannot repress saying that it is 'a black and dreadful place!' (413) Dreadful or not, it is where she desires to be. When Nell finally does die, the peace and tranquility the novel has so assiduously sought are finally achieved: 'Time itself seemed to have grown dull and old, as if no day were ever to displace the melancholy night' (529). It is almost as if her entire world had died along with her—and in a sense it had.

III

For all its cloying necrophiliac sentimentality, *The Old Curiosity Shop* does reveal that Dickens was beginning to reject his fantasy of peace and death even as he was surrendering his fiction to it. For one thing, the quality of his writing was deteriorating. Dickens' tendency to lapse into execrable blank verse, especially when dealing with Nell and related material, was noticed as he wrote it and has been commented upon many times since. As Nell progresses—or more precisely, regresses—to her inevitable rest, the novel begins to wind down as well. The ending chapters of the novel, as Ruskin opined, 'seem to indicate a sense of failing power in the writer's own mind.'[7] The passages about pastoral bliss and the grave, which are more and more one and the same, are so badly written that they carry no authority. Ruskin sensed this too, and went on to say that, 'It is evident the man is a thorough cockney, from his way of talking about hedgerows, and honeysuckles, and village spires'.[8] Again, as has often been said, Quilp's evil vivaciousness dominates the novel—simply because there is no living opposition.

Even more subversive of the conscious thrust of the novel is the running satire of its endorsed values provided by Quilp. For example, what makes Nell's sexual innocence so difficult to admire in the way Dickens intended is Quilp's openness about his wishes to deflower her. Quilp also parodies the pastoral theme, by naming his wretched summer house the Wilderness, and by using it only in the foulest weather. And if he is prevented from laughing at Nell's demise, with characteristic largeness of spirit he laughs at his own. His subsequent 'resurrection' is a parody of Dick Swiveller's transformation from wastrel to country squire, under the benign influence of another child prodigy, the Marchioness.

These indications suggest that the process of writing the novel and so explicitly dramatising his innermost wishes was acting as a kind of ritual exorcism of them. We might today prefer to call it a variety of auto-therapy, but whatever the term, it was a means by which Dickens could escape from a psychological, and certainly a fictional, cul-de-sac. To believe in the philosophy of *The Old Curiosity Shop*, in both his life and his art, was his most earnest desire. But the marriage of philosophy and art remained a consummation devoutly to be wished, and never fully effected: the novel's insistence on the virtues of death resulted only in a dead novel. This could be no more evident than from the novel which immediately followed, *Barnaby Rudge*, which even from its opening pages is full of a vitality its predecessor attains only fitfully, if ever.

Indeed, the description of the Maypole Inn which opens Chapter i is virtually a conscious refutation of the view of nature presented in *The Old Curiosity Shop*. The Inn is very old, and much rebuilt, yet its alterations are 'naturally fantastic' (1), that is, lively and natural all at once. Over the centuries it has not become decrepit, but has increased in soundness and usefulness, acquiring as it grew many apparent 'resemblances to humanity' (2). There is a suggestion that here man and nature have grown into an organic relationship, a second nature in which each has accommodated the other. What is significant is that the tranquillity is not that of stillness and death, but rather of vigour, a sign that building and occupant are 'hale and hearty . . . still' (2). Even more striking about *Barnaby Rudge* is that it is set almost entirely in London. True, it may well seem odd that a novel set in the past and whose subject was the near destruction of the city should yet be seen as an affirmative view of London and life in it. Yet, it is an affirmation of city life, all the more striking because of the thoroughness with which it attacks the pastoral.

To begin with, the peace that Nell finds in nature is in this novel allowed only for Barnaby, and only then because he is an idiot, and simple enough to take delight in it, and view the natural world as 'full of happiness' (355). But the healing influence of nature is no longer to be taken for granted in *Barnaby Rudge*. It may well be that nature has the power to reinforce in man only what is already there, regardless of its moral value: 'There are times,' Dickens writes, 'when the elements being in unusual commotion, those who are bent on daring enterprises, or agitated by great thoughts, whether of good or evil, feel a mysterious sympathy with the tumult of nature, and are roused into corresponding violence' (17). The import of this statement is already preparing us for the 'naturalness' of the violent outrages of the Gordon Riots to follow.

For also there is in *Barnaby Rudge* an entirely different attitude toward the historical past. Dickens' flirtation with the idea of a pastoral utopia located somewhere in the actual English past was over—the days of the Gordon Riots in the novel are seen unequivocally as the baddest of the bad old days. The past does persist in the present, but as something with a paralytic stranglehold over it. The Warren, an ancient country house—whose name cannot have been accidental— is one symbol of this oppressive past 'the very ghost of a house, haunting the old spot in its old outward form, and that was all' (102). The entire impulse of the novel is toward a confrontation with the past (mirrored in the many subplots of rebellious sons fighting tyrannical fathers), violent conflict with it, and triumph of a sort over it. This clearly is also the contemporary political message Dickens intended to be read into it: the latent violence in Chartist protests would erupt in revolution unless antiquated and paralysing political and social institutions were modernised immediately.

The violence, when it does come, is extreme. It has been noted of this novel, and of many other Victorian novels of social protest, that having precipitated an inevitable crisis, the author cannot bring himself to endorse the violence and pulls back in horror.[9] Dickens, at least, was consistent here, and violence tends always in his novels to the self-destructive. The most striking instance here is in Chapter lxviii, the unforgettable self-immolation of the mob outside a looted vintner's warehouse, with men, women and children alike dying as they gorge themselves on the flaming wine flowing in the street. What is equally certain about this violence is that, horrible though it is, it accomplishes much that must be done.

The major accomplishments of the mob are burning the Warren and destroying Newgate prison. On the political level of the novel, this is symbolic of the necessity of ending an archaic and brutally severe legal system, before they cause a revolution. They indicate also a personal purgation. There is no need to elaborate upon the very personal significance of the name 'Warren' for Dickens: its fictional destruction signals the novelist's sense of growing power over his past suffering, and his mastery of the pastoral myth of death that came to be associated with it in his mind. Newgate, as in *Nicholas Nickleby*, is an objective correlative of the guilt and misery physically embedded in the entire city, in its very buildings and streets. To destroy it along with the Warren in *Barnaby Rudge* is another announcement of Dickens' power over himself, and over a paralysing view of the city controlled by the hated past; and with it came the consequent freedom to see London again as it was *now*.

The two major acts of destruction are neatly balanced in another way, in that one is rural and one urban. This, and other incidents, such as Stagg's intrusion at the Rudges' pastoral retreat and the pillaging of the Maypole, stress that evil, personal and social, is not confined to the city and miraculously excluded from the country. If the good life were possible, it would be so in London as much as anywhere else. Significantly, *Barnaby Rudge* does not end with death but with life—in the appearance of a cheerful crowd of lively 'small Joes and small Dollys' (631).

Dickens' earnest and impassioned espousal of the pastoral myth—and the deathly escape from the city it represented—had ended. From this time, his fiction was committed to the city: to exploring and explaining it, and to delineating the possibilities for human existence and development within it. For, though set in the past and about destruction, *Barnaby Rudge* is a novel which looks forward to life in a constructive—and urban—future.

CHAPTER FOUR

Martin Chuzzlewit:
Architecture and Accommodation

Martin Chuzzlewit marks a dramatic change in the quality of Dickens' urban observation, and his use of it in his fiction. In this novel, and in those that follow, the role of the city can no longer sufficiently be described simply as setting, a topographical entity in which characters and events are placed in a totally independent manner as they might be anywhere else, nor even as a motif with certain tonal or emotional qualities, which colours the action of the novel and regulates the response of the reader. In *Martin Chuzzlewit* Dickens uses London quite consciously as a model of the social organisation of England. What is more, for the first time, we can say that Dickens is beginning to be interested in the idea of the city as a modern social community in general, quite divorced from the specific city, London. Furthermore, in the city, beneath its teeming, anarchic surface, Dickens discovers a mysterious organising social principle. Paradoxically, that hidden structure becomes evident in the seemingly accidental relations and random interactions of the novel's characters—a process that will figure more importantly in Dickens' next novel *Dombey and Son*. In some sense, *Martin Chuzzlewit* is about this principle and about the city itself—London has become setting, symbol and subject all in one.

The novel is also the first of Dickens' works to show in any important way the influence of Carlyle.[1] The major problem of the novel is still the great Dickensian question, how the individual can survive and flourish in a hostile world. But now, in part because of Dickens' reading of Carlyle, it is a world dominated by selfishness and the cash nexus. Dickens is amazingly ambitious in his attempt to answer this question, exploring two very different solutions: one utopian, i.e. the possibility of advancing to a simpler, freer, and more 'natural' way of life as apparently had been done in America; and the other pastoral, i.e. a continuing flirtation with the possibility of escaping modern, commercial England by retreating into the countryside. But Dickens considers them both only to reject them both. The solution Dickens eventually does affirm is the acceptance of society as it is presently constituted, and proceeding to seek an accommodation with and within it.

The word 'accommodation' is especially appropriate to *Martin Chuzzlewit*, in both the wide and narrow senses of its meaning. The novel deals not only with the individual's accommodation *to* society, and *vice versa*, but with the physical accommodation *of* society—houses, streets and cities. In a novel about society—one of the very first in English literature—Dickens with characteristic acuity focussed on housing as a key parameter of social well-being. For housing, in so far as it is crude minimal shelter from the physical elements, is one of the basic human needs, and to provide adequate shelter must be the first responsibility of any society. *Martin Chuzzlewit*, then, considers at length and in great detail the buildings and communities which represent the various kinds of living accommodation provided by America and England.

Keeping this social dimension in mind it is clear that architecture, which features prominently in *Martin Chuzzlewit*, is quite properly a concern of the novel. It is a means of expressing Dickens' preoccupation with the physical aspects of accommodation, but it also allows him to comment upon the broader social implications of architecture, representing as it does one of the primary modes of social action which man uses to reinterpret the past in creating the future. To rebuild a society requires bricks and mortar as well as ideas. And so the movement of the novel away from utopia and pastoral back toward an acceptance of society in its given historical context, symbolised first by the movement of the action away to America and then back to England, is appropriately seconded by Dickens' emphasis on England's architectural heritage.

There are a great many casual and not so casual references to architecture in the novel.[2] Its main character, Pecksniff, is himself an architect, and several of the other major figures, Tom Pinch, John Westlock, and young Martin Chuzzlewit, are apprentice

architects under his tuition. Martin even sets himself up as an
architect when he travels to America, expecting to earn his
fortune designing homes and public buildings on the frontier.
Martin's major occupation throughout the early part of the book
is erecting castles in the air, and Tom Pinch indulges in the like
activity of building statues of Pecksniff in the air. The major act
of villainy perpetuated by Pecksniff is the theft of a design for a
school executed some time before by Martin, a design which
wins a competition and much public admiration for Pecksniff.
References to the Monument and the Great Fire, and to the
community of Eden in America, add to this a level of reference
to city planning as well.

As was so often the case with his secondary material, Dickens'
use of architecture in the novel was extremely topical. Architecture was much in the news in the early 1840s, and Dickens
created in Pecksniff a figure who was in many ways representative of the changing condition and problems of the profession. In
the 1830s the architectural profession had reached a low point in
public reputation, no doubt because so many of its practitioners,
like Pecksniff, were qualified only by their greed and a brass plate
on the door. The Institute of British Architects was founded in
1834 to counteract this adverse image and to raise the standards
of architectural practice. By the early 1840s, it had achieved a
large measure of success, though no doubt there were many
Pecksniffs left. A number of factors contributed to the resurgence
of the profession. One was the impetus provided by the work
of and controversy over the new Gothic school, sparked by the
publication of the Pugin's *Contrasts* in 1836. Perhaps even more
important was the sudden upsurge in the planning and construction of public buildings in London, and in provincial cities, the
latter just beginning to sense their new position of national
importance and develop commensurate civic pride. In London,
the public competitions for the designs of the buildings and
interior decorations of the new Palaces of Westminster, necessitated by the fire of 1834, brought architecture very much before
the public eye. The arrival of the railways in or near central
London created an entirely new form of public architecture, the
railway terminus, which in the cases of Euston and King's Cross
Stations (opened in 1838 and 1842, respectively) was a grand

style indeed. And the new limited liability assurance companies, created after the change in company law in 1844, began competing for attention by erecting large City offices, often in the imposing style of the remodelled Bank of England, which itself had opened in 1843.

This architectural material was no doubt also helpful in assisting Dickens to focus his thoughts on larger social questions, by providing him with an apt metaphor for depicting society. The analogy between a building and society was a quite common one in the literature of the previous century, furnishing a convenient device for describing the social edifice.[3] The separate parts of a building are distinct and individual, and when examined too closely may well appear to be unrelated and insignificant. Yet when viewed as a whole, the separate parts work in unison, contributing to and deriving meaning from the building's organising principles and relations. Whether the eighteenth-century model was in his mind or not, in *Martin Chuzzlewit* Dickens clearly sees the apparently hidden organising principles of the structure of society operating in a similar manner.

There is yet another way in which the architectural influence in *Martin Chuzzlewit* can be perceived, and that is its effect on tightening the organisation of the novel as a whole. As Steven Marcus notes, it is the first of Dickens' novels in which 'scarcely a page goes by which does not in some way further the central course of development; no detail is too small or by-the-way for it not to be discovered as elaborating some larger theme—even as it stands by itself, as a locally justified detail.'[4] Here too the construction of the novel is analogous to the construction of a building, with detail laid upon detail as brick is upon brick, and chapter upon chapter as storey upon storey. And likewise, all derive strength from the firm foundation and planning that lie beneath.

These many dimensions of reference and allusion can be seen in operation in this passage, quoted from a speech of Montague Tigg early in the novel. Tigg is explaining that his associate Chevy Slyme is being held at the Dragon Inn for failing to pay his bill:

'If it had been for anything but a bill, I could have borne it, and could still have looked upon mankind with some feeling of respect: but when such a man as my friend Slyme is detained for a score . . . I do feel there is a screw of such magnitude loose somewhere, that the whole framework of society is shaken, and the very first principles of things can no longer be trusted.' (102–3)

Even in this apparently comic passage, which in no way advances the story, Dickens almost effortlessly brings in the central concerns of the novel, referring to the 'framework of society' being shaken by some key organising part having gone wrong, and this being the causal agent of his friend's troubles. Dickens was in agreement: there was a screw loose somewhere in English society, but to discover it, he had to visit America first.

II

The appositeness of the American episodes of *Martin Chuzzlewit* to the rest of the novel is so striking that, as K. J. Fielding comments, it would be difficult to believe they were not part of Dickens' plan from the start, had we not Forster's express statement that this was so.[5] Forster tells us that the decision to send Martin to America was made in the hope of raising disappointingly poor sales (*Life*, I, 285). Yet, despite the fact that the American material was improvised, what Dickens had experienced in America and what he had come to believe about American society informs and shapes every page of the novel. Paradoxically, it is in the American episodes that Dickens makes his clearest statements about English society.

The novel, we know, was to have as an overarching theme and organising principle the vice of Self. Pecksniff is the supreme embodiment of this modern social evil, perhaps meant by Dickens to represent the English middle classes as a whole. (The motto of the novel was to have been 'Your homes the scene, yourselves the actors, here', but Forster wisely vetoed it [*Life*, I, 296].) Pecksniff is a consummate hypocrite, who nurtures and propagates an image of himself as virtuous and benevolent which all (or most of) the world accepts as genuine. His constant effusions of verbiage and self-puffery are an attempt to fill the universe with his own ego, and extend even to equating his will with the Divine will; as when Mrs Todgers resists his sexual advances and he rebukes her with the reproach, ' "This is irreligious! my dear creature!" '(150) But beneath Pecksniff's surface is only inflated greed and impotent self-aggrandisement, with the implication that such is the moral nature of the worst elements of the commercial and professional middle classes. But having created this character, it almost seems as if Dickens had asked himself, what an entire nation of Pecksniffs would look like— only to find that such a fictional country tallied perfectly with his view of American society.

Dickens had had the idea of going to America in the back of his mind perhaps as early as 1837, but as *Master Humphrey's Clock* wound down he revived the idea with characteristic fervour. Early in the autumn of 1841 the plan was arranged, domestically to Catherine's satisfaction and professionally to Chapman and Hall's, and he and Catherine sailed after Christmas.

After a tumultuous and dangerous passage, they arrived in Canada, and then went to Boston, where Dickens was welcomed as if he were visiting royalty. That analogy was his, and especially pleased him, for he had brought with him to America firm radical principles: he saw (or expected to see) in the young republic an embodiment of freedom and equality, a living example to and confutation of the repressions of the authoritarian monarchies of Europe. This belief was grounded far more in the vague political sentiments he had picked up as a young man at the *Morning Chronicle* and in the Parliamentary galleries than in any real knowledge of America; perhaps it was because of this that his disillusionment with the real America came so rapidly. His hopes had outdistanced actuality: as he later wrote to a friend, 'This is not the republic I came to see; this is not the republic of my imagination' (To W. C. Macready, 22 March 1842; PL, III, 156). This disappointment was the principal cause of his disenchantment, though there were many specific grievances to focus on. Among them were Dickens' increasing irritation over the problems and responsibilities of being lionised as a public personality, his mistrust of and clashes with the press, his vocal anti-slavery beliefs, his inability to tolerate American manners and the universal habit of spitting, and the famous international copyright controversy.[6]

Dickens' general disappointment quickly led him to take a more analytic critical stance, almost as if he now had to find objective reasons for his dislike of the country. But if the motives were suspect, the fruits of the search were not. The problems he had as a public man—even his dress was now a matter of journalistic scrutiny—led him to understand that in certain respects private life in America had actually ceased to exist. A new form of social authority, not reactionary or monarchical but progressive and democratic, had taken over in America. This was public opinion, a joint creation of the press and the politicians, which dictated the nation's beliefs, mores, manners and even emotions, and did so with dictatorial imperiousness. There was no possibility for individual assertion in face of the general will: Dickens knew this from the campaign of vilification and character assassination that had followed his statement in support of an international copyright agreement.

On an individual level, the American character had become curiously externalised. Americans seemed to have no inner lives, and existed only in their (mainly verbal) expressions of public opinions and dogma. Here the links with Pecksniff are clear; but the essential difference is that while Pecksniff is a hypocrite, Americans believed their own cant. For there is no inner life for Americans to mask, and though this is in one sense more honest, as they are hiding nothing, in another it is far more frightening, in that there is nothing to hide. The linguistic implications are most frightening of all: it is impossible to tell the difference between a lie and the truth, since all statements have only surface meaning. When Mrs Hominy asks Martin where he 'hails' from, he doesn't understand her; she shakes her head as if to say, 'They corrupt even the language in that old country' (369). The reversal is complete: when a word means what it really means, it is false, and only the false meaning is true. This is the effect of a completely public life upon language.

Yet another of the results of the public nature of American life is the curious abstract uniformity that pervades the American character and American culture. In a country where ladies attend lectures on 'The Philosophy of Vegetables' it is no suprise that the people seem to have the same opinions, the same ideas, or for that matter are perfectly interchangeable in almost every respect. Individuality was simply gone, and this prospect terrified Dickens.

Even in the *American Notes*, where Dickens exercised great restraint in his remarks, something of the nature of his social analysis comes through, but only in isolated instances. And already we can find in his remarks on American architecture and cities evidenced most clearly the germs of his developing critique of American society. (But not wholly successfully: *American Notes* was an attempt to write a direct social critique as well as a travel book, but it does not really work as either. Dickens was far more successful at social analysis in his fiction, where his imagination was engaged by his material and his deepest creative powers stirred in a way that they never were in his ordinary, nonfiction prose.)

For example, in Boston, the first American city he saw, though he found it a beautiful place, his unfamiliarity with and surprise at the exclusive use of wood rather than brick or stone as building material made the suburbs seem to him curiously 'unsubstantial' (AN, 26).[7] Still, the provisions for social welfare and the generally clean and pleasing layout of the city impressed him. Only a week later, in New York, less of a model metropolis, he was having second thoughts about the quality of urban life in America. He found slums there equally vile 'in respect of filth and wretchedness' as any of the worst in London (AN, 80). Visiting the then already infamous Tombs prison, he was shocked by barbaric practices within its walls as repulsive as the 'bastard Egyptian' architectural style of the building itself (AN, 83).

Moving South and then West, what Dickens gradually came most to detest about American cities was their sameness and tediously monotonous appearance. Every house was indistinguishable from the next, the streets were laid out with geometrical precision, and each city seemed no different from any other. Philadelphia he felt was 'distractingly regular', and he exclaimed, 'I felt I would have given the world for a crooked street' (AN, 98). In Washington, the public buildings were as precise, uniform and empty as the rest of the city. To Dickens, American architecture and the quality of American city life was a reflection of and a contributing factor to the dehumanising effects of American society. However, it is in *Martin Chuzzlewit* rather than *American Notes* that this is made fully explicit.

Here again it is the architectural dimension which serves to elucidate the more general social concerns of the novel. This, for example, is the description of an American hotel, at which Martin and Mark Tapley briefly stay:

> Close to the railway was an immense white edifice, like an ugly hospital, on which was painted 'NATIONAL HOTEL.' There was a wooden gallery or verandah in front, in which it was rather startling . . . to behold a great many pairs of boots and shoes, and the smoke of a great many cigars, but no other evidences of human habitation. By slow degrees, however, some heads and shoulders appeared, and connecting themselves with the boots and shoes, led to the discovery that certain gentlemen boarders, who had a fancy for putting their heels where the gentlemen boarders in other countries usually put their heads, were enjoying themselves after their own manner in the cool of the evening. (350)

This vast 'edifice' is not even visually attractive. Its very lack of colour, its whiteness, signifies its lack of content. Somehow, this building, like American cities, and by implication American society, has lost its social meaning. Intended as a place of human accommodation, it is manifestly uncomfortable. Quite literally, it dehumanises its occupants by chopping them up into boots and cigars, heads and shoulders—they are no longer whole human beings. Even in the position in which they sit, upside down, the gentlemen boarders reveal the reversal of the natural order of things in American society.

Indeed, America is a society almost entirely without proper homes, as Martin learns in conversation with Mr Bevan. After watching the social life of Major Pawkins' Boarding House for an evening, Martin asks Mr Bevan, ' "When you say 'home', do you mean a house like this?" ' His honest friend answers: ' "Very often." '(294) When the people are so undifferentiated as to be interchangeable, why should not their homes—or houses

—be similarly interchangeable? And how convenient for a totally public society that all its members should live in each other's close company, where secrets would be impossible. Dickens had discovered an intimate relation between the physical accommodation of a society and the quality of its life: 'Observing how they [the Americans] lived, and how they were always in the enchanting company of each other, Martin even began to comprehend their being the social, cheerful, winning, airy men they were' (350).

Opposed to this stark dehumanising American hotel is the comfortable old inn at which Martin and Mark stop after their return to England. Martin and Mark realise they are home again at last when they see not the land itself, but its buildings, 'the old churches, roofs, and darkened chimney stacks of Home' (548). Indeed, all their experiences that same day are in one sense or another architectural, including (coincidentally) seeing Pecksniff laying the cornerstone of a grammar school, the design of which he has stolen from Martin. Inside the old inn, they eat heartily in an old little front room that they find refreshingly comfortable. A heavy mist on the window makes the street into a 'fairy street'; then the magical atmosphere begins to embrace the room itself:

> It was one of those unaccountable little rooms which are never seen anywhere but in a tavern, and are supposed to have got into taverns by reason of the facilities afforded to the architect for getting drunk while engaged in their construction. It had more corners in it than the brain of an obstinate man; was full of mad closets, into which nothing could be put that was not specially invented and made for that purpose; had mysterious shelvings and bulkheads, and indications of staircases in the ceiling; and was elaborately provided with a bell that rung in the room itself, about two feet from the handle, and had no connexion whatever with any other part of the establishment. It was a little below the pavement, and abutted close upon it; so that passengers grated against the window-panes . . . and fearful boys suddenly coming between a thoughtful guest and the light, derided him, or put out their tongues as if he were a physician; or made white knobs on the

ends of their noses by flattening the same against the glass, and vanished awfully, like spectres. (549)

The prose explodes into rapturous and affectionate detail in describing this impossible room. What it is meant to represent is really English society itself, the society to which Martin and Mark have returned.

To understand this, it is necessary to look back to America. There is yet another dimension of American society that deeply disturbed Dickens which can be sensed from the passage about the National Hotel, but more directly elsewhere in the novel. The Hotel, white and new, has no discernible relation to the past. Like so much in America, it was intended to be a dramatic departure, a fresh start in the development of human society. In effect, America was going to create human nature anew, by casting off the accumulated burden of the past. This would be, then, a return to man's original nature, the human character before civilisation had corrupted it. Coincidentally, the virgin nature of wilderness of the continent mirrored the hopes it embodied for mankind. It was, in a way, a hopeful example, for it was untouched by the corrupting influences of civilisation.

But here, for Dickens, the equation had already gone wrong. When Dickens travelled West to the frontier and was confronted by the raw, untamed power of nature, he was quite simply terrified. The place in which this perception emerges in the novel is in Chapter xxiii, at the ironically named settlement of Eden. As if the name were not transparent enough in indicating its prehistoric nature, Dickens adds that, 'The waters of the Deluge might have left it but a week before' (377). Here is what this paradise is like:

> As they proceeded further on their track, and came more and more towards their journey's end, the monotonous desolation of the scene increased to that degree, that for any redeeming feature it presented to their eyes, they might have entered, in the body, on the grim domains of Giant Despair. A flat morass, bestrewn with fallen timber; a marsh on which the good growth of the earth seemed to have been wrecked and cast away, that from its decomposing ashes vile and ugly

things might rise; where the very trees took the aspect of huge weeds, begotten of the slime from which they sprung, by the hot sun that burnt them up; where fatal maladies, seeking whom they might infect, came forth at night in misty shapes, and creeping out upon the water, hunted them like spectres until day; where even the blessed sun, shining down on festering elements of corruption and disease, became a horror; this was the realm of Hope through which they moved. (377)

Nature is anything but benevolent here—it is the very source of all that is vile and corrupting. This was nothing at all like the peaceful green fields of Kent. And similarly, the American national character, a return to man's original nature, had revealed only evil.[8]

By contrast, in England, human society has gone so far toward creating a second nature for man that he can no longer repudiate it and attempt to exist outside it, as the failed American experiment has decisively proved. Its rules and relations have become, like the odd room in the inn, in which nothing can be introduced that is not designed for the purpose, entirely self-referential. Taken outside their context, they have no meaning. Their accepted usage is their social meaning. Inside the room, as do the rules in English society, they make up a positive and supportive structure.

In addition, this passage describing the room symbolises Dickens' acceptance and affirmation of his personal stake in English society. For Dickens' voyage of discovery around America had been one of self-discovery as well. Having had every aspect of his appearance and beliefs and conduct taken up by the American press and analysed in depth, it was only natural that he would begin to examine his image of himself, too. The longer he stayed on, the more he began to realise that if America was not the nation he imagined it to be, nor was he the man he had thought himself. What he came to understand was his own Englishness—that there was deeply rooted in him an irrational, complex component of his personality over which he had no control, in other words, his nationality. As he told Albany Fanblanque, 'he had discovered he was an Englishman.'[9]

Similarly, the very irrationality of the room in the inn—or of

English society itself—is beside the point: they are both there, and must be accepted before one can change them. That Martin and Mark return to England and this room signal that Dickens had indeed come to terms with this.

III

The implications of the description of this snug, little room carry yet further. The room suggests a model of society as benevolent protectress. In it are supplied food, drink, warmth and well-being. The room, so close to the pavement that it is almost on top of it, is in the midst of the stream of life, and yet its shielding influence is such that the gravest of its terrors are small boys making faces on the windowpanes.

This view of society, in a more complex and extended form, lies behind Chapter ix, 'Town and Todgers's'. Todgers Commercial Boarding House, a microcosm of the city in which it is nestled, is quite intentionally presented as an example of the possibility of a positive human community in the very midst of a modern urban environment. It is a form of physical accommodation which allows its boarders peaceful accommodation in and with their society. Not that it embodies a simple affirmative view of society: the tone of the chapter is delicately balanced, characterised by a full awareness of the advantages and disadvantages of the urban milieu in which it must exist.

An example of this balanced and sensitive tone is the first paragraph of the chapter, which proclaims Todgers' uniqueness. Dickens immediately places it within the metropolis:

> And surely London, to judge from that part of it which hemmed Todgers's round, and hustled it, and crushed it, and stuck its brick-and-mortar elbows between it and the light, was worthy of Todgers's, and qualified to be on terms of close relationship and alliance with hundreds and thousands of the odd family to which Todgers's belonged. (127)

The threat of the city is substantial, and the celebrated passage describing the view from the roof of the boarding house as a 'wilderness upon wilderness' of 'housetops, garret windows . . .

smoke and noise' (130), which almost overwhelms and destroys the viewer, indicates it cannot be taken lightly.

Yet another startling reversal of Dickens' earlier attitudes takes place in the creation of Todgers'. Its physical location is inside a maze of 'lanes and bye-ways, and court-yards, and passages', so lost that, 'Nobody had ever found Todgers's on a verbal direction, though given within a minute's walk of it.' In fact, 'Todgers's was in a labyrinth, whereof the mystery was known but to a chosen few' (127). In vivid contrast to the hostile and dangerous labyrinth of *Oliver Twist*, this labyrinth is one of Todgers' principal advantages. To be lost in it is no terror, but rather to approach the secret of entry into a community of, if not the good, at least the moderately happy. Even to approach it without entering it confers a pleasant tranquility. Those who search for it but fail to find it, rather than becoming angry, go 'home again with a gentle melancholy on their spirits, tranquil and uncomplaining' (127).

Within Todgers', a new, synthetic kind of family has been created to replace the natural family which, epitomised by the Chuzzlewits, has been corrupted and perverted in modern England into a community of hatred and duplicity. Here, the dehumanising and fragmenting tendencies of the modern world are countered on their own terms; in a sort of social application of the division of labour, each lodger supplies for the group one part of the whole man none of them is any longer capable of being. One gentleman of the house is of a sporting 'turn', another of a theatrical turn, another of a literary turn, or a vocal turn, a convivial turn, a witty turn. Mrs Todgers, who supplies the roof over their heads, bountiful food, and consoling advice, is almost a surrogate mother. Mr Jenkins, the leading gentleman of the House (himself of a fashionable turn), is more or less the father of the group. Todgers' does have its conflicts, but even they are mild and comic, centring on the pratfalls of that pitifully hilarious misfit, Augustus Moddle. Todgers' is furnished even with a household genius, Young Bailey, the 'remarkable boy' whose powers extend to changing his identity, becoming his own father and son simultaneously, and returning from death itself.

Nor is Todgers' insulated from any less glorious parts of social existence. Its neighbourhood contains fruit and vegetable sellers, pumps and fire companies, drowsy old taverns, and 'churches by the dozens, with many a ghostly little churchyard, all over-grown with such straggling vegetation as springs up spontan-eously from damp, and graves, and rubbish' (128). In these graveyards, significantly described as the urban equivalent of country gardens, 'paralysed old watchmen' guard the dead until they join them, and 'their condition can hardly be said to have undergone any material change when they in turn were watched themselves' (128). There is something strangely reassuring in this urban variety of death, in which the final change comes so gradually that there is no pain or suffering.

Todgers' has a mystery, too:

> The grand mystery of Todgers's was the cellerage, approach-able only by a little back door and a rusty grating: which cellerage within the memory of man had had no connexion with the house, but had always been the property of someone else, and was reported to be full of wealth: though in what shape . . . was a matter of profound uncertainty and supreme indifference to Todgers's, and all its inmates. (129–30)

The process of death, seen earlier as so gradual that it seems not to involve any change from life at all, which produces the spontaneous growth in the graveyard, suggests a connection by. association with the underground treasure buried in Todgers' cellar. The implication is, then, not only that time has subdued death, or domesticated it, but perhaps even transformed it into wealth and a source of life. Through centuries of contact with human society, Todgers' neighbourhood and the society it repre-sents have almost begun to be human themselves.[10]

This gradual mutual accommodation of the human and the inanimate is seen as an exclusively urban process. This is most sharply shown through Pecksniff's pastoral associations, which are worked into the novel as an integral part of his character. While he is in Salisbury, Pecksniff is almost always framed in pastoral terms. As he remarks, spade in hand, to old Martin Chuzzlewit, ' "I do a little bit of Adam still" ' (384); while his daughters are described as 'worthy of the pastoral age' (15). One could list many such details, but their import is already clear: in linking the odious Pecksniff, the novel's chief villain, with his own former pastoral yearnings, Dickens was declaring his independence from such a dream.

Pecksniff, through his architectural connections, also offered Dickens an opportunity to better understand exactly what had gone wrong with the pastoral ideal. When Pecksniff sets his pupils to work, he has them make elevations of a medieval monument, Salisbury Cathedral, or construct models of other old structures, St Peter's in Rome, or the St Sophia mosque in Constantinople. As he tells Jonas (while standing in his garden), ' "It is here we contemplate the work of bygone ages." '(679) Pecksniff's false art is the uncritical worship of the past, and is therefore sterile and dead. Similarly, he tends to prefer art to reality. For this reason, he is unable to see any notable difference between a wooden leg and the real thing—'the difference between the anatomy of nature and the anatomy of art' (152).

What this has in common with the pastoral ideal is that it too is also a kind of uncritical worship of the past, and as such it is equally wooden and unreal. Rather, only the gradual change of the given past by the action of the social community working through time can produce and shelter life: 'Change begets change', as Dickens observes at the opening of Chapter xviii (298). And by now, Dickens intuitively had understood that such a process could be furthered only in the living centres of human society, cities. Here human society now was, and here human life must be lived.

A key example of how the force of life can be generated in an urban environment of age and gradual decay is the fountain of Fountain Court, in the Temple, one of the very oldest parts of London. It is a kind of urban garden, and under its benevolent influence the marriage of Ruth Pinch and John Westlock is fostered, nurtured and agreed, and however cloying Dickens' prose becomes while describing it, the marriage is intended to be a significant and hopeful part of the novel's resolution.

Because of the importance of the marriage which will be arranged within it, Fountain Court becomes a centre of moral value for the novel. Like the neighbourhood surrounding Todgers', Fountain Court is old, dull, dark, grimy and worn, and in it grows the same sort of 'slow vegetation' that is found in the churchyards near Todgers'. But it reacts vigorously enough to the presence of Ruth Pinch:

> The Temple fountain might have leaped up twenty feet to greet the spring of hopeful maidenhood, that in her person stole on, sparkling, through the dry and dusty channels of the law; . . . old love letters, shut up in iron boxes in the neighbouring offices . . . might have stirred and fluttered with a moment's recollection of their ancient tenderness, as she went lightly by. Anything might have happened that did not happen, and never will, for the love of Ruth. (687–8)

The excitement of the fountain is quite openly sexual, and like the treasure buried beneath Todgers', related to and perhaps even engendered by the process of slow ageing and decay around it. The presence of Ruth is so electric that even the dead love letters locked away in the law offices of the Temple are momentarily stirred to life. The very next moment, Ruth meets John Westlock; and here, by silent agreement, they return after the reunion scene orchestrated by Old Martin, and again under the influence of the fountain realise their mutual love.

The meaning of all this is clear. Locating the hope for the future and even the spirit of life among the oldest artifacts of the city, Dickens is reaffirming his belief that the only road to human regeneration is within society. The very age of society's institutions, rather than being cause for giving way to despair at reforming them, itself has become a sign of hope. It can be said that this impulse is basically conservative, and it is true that much of the old in the novel—like Todgers' and the Temple —is affirmed, and whatever is new—like the flashy and ostentatious house of Ruth's *nouveau riche* employer or the Anglo-Bengalee's offices—often is rejected. But this is not entirely just. The spirit of accommodation which informs the novel rejects what is wholly new *and* wholly old. Only a judicious admixture of the two results in structures, both physical and social, which fulfil human needs.

IV

The word 'mystery' occurs with surprising frequency in *Martin Chuzzlewit*. It is used in connection with Todgers', and the buried wealth in its cellarage, and to describe Fountain Court as well. There is also a figure in the novel who is a living mystery— Nadgett, the detective.

Nadgett appears at first in the employ of the Anglo-Bengalee as their confidential investigator. He is the perfect man for the job:

> ... for he was born to be a secret. ... How he lived was a secret; where he lived was a secret; and even what he was, was a secret. In his musty old pocket-book he carried contradictory cards, in some of which he called himself a coal-merchant, in others a wine-merchant, in others a commission-agent, in others a collector, in others an accountant: as if he really didn't know the secret himself. (447)

His habits, origins, family, wealth, are all secrets to everyone, perhaps even to Nadgett himself. But he is also a collector of facts and an observer of details, and by using the vast amount of information he has quietly assembled, Nadgett pieces together the mystery of Montague Tigg's murder and discovers the identity of the perpetrator, Jonas Chuzzlewit.

Nadgett's role becomes more and more important in the plot of the novel as it progresses, with Dickens obviously becoming more interested in the idea of detective work as he wrote. (The modern detective had only been on the scene for a very few years, in effect created first in fact and then in fiction by the French thief turned policeman, François-Eugène Vidocq, whose popular *Memoires* were published in 1828–9.) Dickens found in Nadgett a sympathetic character, and his work analogous to that of his own—not only in so far as Nadgett was a patient observer, but that his awareness and solution of a mystery manifested Dickens' growing awareness that at the centre of the society he was trying to analyse lay a mystery. Dickens had begun the novel in a mood of supreme confidence, with the ambition of laying bare the essence of an entire society, and later, two entire societies. Now, however, in midstream, he saw additional complications. For every human relation, even the most commonplace and acci-dental, could no longer be viewed in isolation, but was involved with, and to a certain extent drew its significance from, this central mystery. Only by penetrating this mystery and by making it explicit, aided in this process by his infinite patience and powers of observation, could the writer make sense of the world he saw.

The links between the deeper mysteries of the novel and Nadgett's detective work are not fortuitous. As a number of critics have noticed, detectives are prominent characters in Dickens' mature novels, and their activities have more than a surface relation to Dickens' own fictional detective work. Donald Fanger writes: 'Each of these novels [after *Martin Chuzzlewit*] will involve detective work, not simply to unravel the mysteries of plot but, more importantly, to lay bare the subterranean network of social relationships.'[11]

There is a moment in the novel when this discovery—the discovery that there was what he would now call a social *system*—bursts into consciousness. It is, appropriately enough, in the Chapter entitled 'Secret Service' (Chapter xxxviii). Walking by him in the street, Tom Pinch has just looked at Nadgett (who, unknown to him, is his landlord) and brushed his sleeve. But, of course, they do not recognise each other:

> Mr. Nadgett naturally passed away from Tom's remembrance as he passed out of his view; for he didn't know him, and had never heard his name.
>
> As there are a vast number of people in the huge metropolis of England who rise up every morning not knowing where their heads will rest at night, so there are a multitude who shooting arrows over houses as their daily business, never know on whom they fall. Mr. Nadgett might have passed Tom Pinch ten thousand times; he might even have been quite familiar with his face, his name, his pursuits, and character; yet never once have dreamed that Tom had any interest in any act of mystery of his. Tom might have done the like by him, of course. But the same private man out of all the men alive, was in the mind of each at the same moment; was prominently connected . . . with the day's adventures of both; and formed, when they passed each other in the street, the one absorbing topic of their thoughts. (589)

That two men, completely unknown to each other, can pass each other in the street, briefly touch, and yet without realising it be intimately involved with each other and the same individual, Jonas Chuzzlewit, and even more remarkably, both be thinking of him at that precise moment, and furthermore that all this should *not* be a mere coincidence, is the substance of the great discovery Dickens has made.

This passage stands in sharp contrast to Dickens' earlier descriptions of the alienation and isolation of urban life, like that of 'Thoughts About People,' where he had noted 'with how little notice, good, bad, or indifferent, a man may live and die in London' (SB, 215). Here too he is describing the disconnectedness of city life, but as a simple, matter-of-fact statement of observed social fact. While the view of society in 'Secret Service' does not negate this observation about alienation, it sees through it and beyond it to search out the underlying social relations it has heretofore obscured.

Observations like this, about the isolation imposed by life in London were frequent in the literature of the first half of the nineteenth century. One which dates from the time at which *Martin Chuzzlewit* was being written was made by the young Frederick Engels. Engels also was particularly disturbed by the way Londoners were so indifferent to each other, as well as isolated and alienated. But he too, like Dickens, saw that a general principle lay behind this apparent randomness: 'this narrow self-seeking', he wrote, 'is the fundamental principle of our society everywhere, . . . nowhere so shamelessly barefaced, so self-conscious as just here in the crowds of the great city.'[12] Engels had also discovered that the social body was a system, one which gave meaning to every casual action and interaction of urban life. Furthermore, he too realised that it was the city which revealed modern society most completely, and in its most advanced form.

The structure of *Martin Chuzzlewit*, which used the cash nexus and selfishness as the centre of Dickens' analysis of English society, was fixed too firmly by the close of the novel to be changed, and did not allow him to use to full advantage this important perception. The novel reverts to a comic pattern, and so ends with the exposure of Pecksniff as a fraud, as if this somehow could set all things right again. But as was often the case, what occurred to him toward the end of one novel provided the organising focus of the next. Though it was fully two years before he began *Dombey and Son*, it was in that work that Dickens did seize and elaborate the notion of a social system to create a more profound and accurate novelistic critique of contemporary English life than he, or indeed anyone else, had heretofore achieved.

CHAPTER FIVE

Dombey and Son: The World Metropolis

Dombey and Son is a wide-ranging novel, embracing locales as diverse as Leamington Spa, Brighton and Dijon. But for all that, we never doubt that the source of the novel's action, and the place to which it must return, is London. London pervades the novel, not only as setting, but in many ways as much a part of the plot as the leading characters. Yet despite its dominance, the metropolis is not given precisely the same kind of particularity that is evident in Dickens' London in *Martin Chuzzlewit*. There is in *Dombey and Son* no passage at all like that in *Martin Chuzzlewit* which placed Todgers' so concretely inside the metropolitan scene. One senses that Dickens, far more and far more consciously than in the earlier novel, was now using London not so much as *a* city, but as a general type for *the* city. The London of the Chuzzlewits had been the centre of a nation; the London of Dombey is the centre of the world.

This process of generalisation reflects the organisation of the novel as a whole. It is the first of Dickens' novels which can be said without qualification to be a social novel; that is, its primary goal is to depict directly society and social relations. As the previous chapter demonstrated, this was true to a certain extent of *Martin Chuzzlewit*, and indeed such an aim can be traced in the fiction as far back as *Nicholas Nickleby*. That novel had extended Dickens' previously limited social range of fictional characters to embrace all classes, from Members of Parliament and industrial capitalists to lowly drudges like Smike and Newman Noggs. Dickens here was more or less following the eighteenth-century model, depicting society by depicting characteristic members of each class and rank, especially from the social extremes. But it was a model not particularly suited to nineteenth-century experience; and it was later in *Barnaby Rudge* that Dickens seized what would develop into his most effective device for approaching social questions. That novel deals with the problem of the nature of social authority, but as we have seen does so most successfully by considering the relations of individuals in the many variations on the theme of the rebellious son versus tyrannical father. This technique is essentially Shakespearian, for in Dickens' mature novels, as in Shakespeare's mature plays, the principal themes are reflected in every part of the whole, giving them an incomparable unity of incident, theme and language. From 1841–2, after completing *Barnaby Rudge*, Dickens was increasingly preoccupied with social questions; and though *American Notes* and *Martin Chuzzlewit* both do address themselves to such matters, only with *Dombey and Son* did Dickens master the technical problems of adapting the novel to such a purpose.

In writing it, Dickens wanted to emphasise two things he had come to believe very strongly in 1846: first, that despite appearances of vitality and prosperity, there was something very wrong with contemporary English society; and second, that whatever it was that was wrong, its corrupting influence had spread to all social classes, from the very highest to the very lowest. The technique Dickens chose was to depict the whole of society through some small, representative part of it, that part being the establishment of Dombey and Son. It was a most brilliant solution to the technical problems of the social novel: subject and technique efficaciously coalesce in these 'Dealings with the firm of Dombey and Son'—the family, the home, the 'house', and the novel itself.

How successful *Dombey and Son* was in this respect can be seen more clearly from a comparison with the two earliest Christmas books, *A Christmas Carol* (1843) and *The Chimes* (1844). They too reveal an increasing social awareness, and concentrate upon the problems of poverty, class division and class responsibility, but in a much less effectual manner. In these two short books, Dickens seemed to be struggling to find a way to express his perceptions about the 'Condition of England' question. Both, but especially *The Chimes*, show the still growing influence of Carlyle, though this influence was more general than specific.[1] In these short works, Dickens strongly implies that social problems are not individual anomalies, but exist because of the way society as a whole is constituted. Thus, in *A Christ-*

mas Carol, Scrooge's avarice blights not only the lives of his employees but his own existence too: the rich, then, suffer in some way from poverty as well as the poor. In *The Chimes,* Dickens is more explicit about the interrelatedness of social vices. The horrifying vision which Dickens places in poor Trotty Veck's head—in which he sees how a mother, his own daughter, could be led to commit the unnatural act of infanticide out of love, in order to spare her child death by starvation—melodramatically demonstrates that it is society itself that has become unnatural.

The advance of *Dombey and Son* over these works is dramatic and substantial. For example, Dombey believes he is immune to any adverse effects of the social system; and furthermore that he is isolated from the lower classes. His personal and business lives are based on the firm assumption that he and his class have and can have no relation to the lower orders of society but that of employer and employee. Dickens points out not only the personal consequences of such a position—Dombey is dehumanised, cold, hard and impotent—but that it is an impossible denial of social actuality. Dombey lives on money the Toodles of the world have earned for him, travels on trains they drive, faces the same inexorable realities of human experience, and must do so under the influence of the same social laws. The story of the firm and family prove this ineluctably to be so.

Such is Dickens' skilful economy in *Dombey and Son* that even the most casual asides seem to reinforce this perception of the social fabric as a social system. At times, in fact, Dickens is guilty of over emphasis. A passage like this, which closes Chapter xxxiv, may seem far too portentous: 'In this round world of many circles within circles, do we make a weary journey from the high grade to the low, to find at last that they lie close together, that the two extremes touch, and that our journey's end is but our starting-place?' (495–6) But certainly this could not be said of this description of Sir Barnet Skettles: '. . . like a sound in the air, the vibration of which, according to the speculation of an ingenious modern philosopher, may go on travelling for ever through the interminable fields of space, nothing but coming to the end of his moral tether could stop Sir Barnet Skittles in his voyage of discovery through the social system' (341). The effortlessness of allusion in this apparent digression is truly remarkable.

II

If, *Dombey and Son* was intended to be a novel about society as a whole, there was undoubtedly only one place in England where it could be set, the one place where the world could be seen to exist in microcosm—the world's metropolis. London.[2] One traditional literary view of the large city had, of course, always been as the epitome of the world at large, containing every human type or, more usually, every human vice. It was the world writ small. John Gay's *Trivia: Or, the Art of Walking the Streets of London* (1716), offers an excellent example of this view of the city, surveying with ironic detachment every sort of person, profession and pastime (especially the wicked ones) the metropolis contains. Walking through it was a particularly good way to appreciate this, as if one were window shopping in some 'great emporium', as Wordsworth had called London in *The Prelude* (Book VIII, 1.594). Dickens had used the stock device many times himself, as in Chapter xxxii of *Nicholas Nickleby*, where the goods of the city are displayed in 'rich and glittering profusion' (409), side by side with all the vices.

But in *Dombey and Son*, this conventional view has taken on an entirely new meaning. In the mid 1840s London had become the economic nerve centre of the world, and it was now not only a national but a global emporium. The opening of China to British trade in the Opium Wars and the repeal of the Corn Laws in 1846 were only two great signals of the inauguration of a truly global economic and political system. And as surely as that international system was British, London was its capital. Henry Mayhew summed up London's new position in 1849: 'the metropolis . . . constitut[es] not only the densest, but the busiest hive, the most wondrous workshop, and the richest bank in the world. . . . [One] could not help feeling how every power known to man was used to bring and diffuse the riches of every part of the world over this little island.'[3]

As if to emphasise the point, the firm of Dombey and Son is placed at the centre of this bustling global storehouse:

Though the offices of Dombey and Son were within the liberties
of the City of London ... there were hints of adventures and
romantic story to be observed in some of the adjacent objects.
Gog and Magog held their state within ten minutes' walk; the
Royal Exchange was close at hand; the Bank of England, with
its vaults of gold and silver ... was their magnificent neighbour. Just round the corner stood rich East India House,
teeming with suggestions of precious stuff and stones.
 ... Anywhere in the immediate vicinity there might be seen
pictures of ships speeding away full sail to all parts of the
world.... (32)

This is the capital of an Empire, and a palpable smell of Imperial
power pervades the city. There are numerous other allusions to
the Empire in the novel, including the Dombey firm's trade,
Captain Cuttle's profession, Major Bagstock's past exploits in
both Indies, Mrs Pipchin's dead husband in South America,
young Bitherstone who has been sent from India to school in
England, and so on.

There was yet further reason for choosing London to be the
focal point of *Dombey and Son*, for the novel was not only to be
about the present state of contemporary society, but about the
direction in which that society was moving: a direct confrontation with the modern. His experiences in America had convinced
Dickens that the new age was going to be an urban age, and
London was the most advanced of all the world's cities.[4] As the
novel was being written, the population of England was just
shifting toward being predominantly urban, as the census of
1851 would reveal. The emphasis on the city here cannot be too
strongly stressed, for while Dickens' recognition of the revolutionary social importance of the railway and the developing
industrial technology it symbolised in *Dombey and Son* has long
been acknowledged, his understanding of the equally revolutionary modern development of the city has not.

Indeed, Dickens intuitively had grasped that it was the city
which had made the railways possible. It was the Toodles of the
city who furnished the raw labour to construct and operate them,
and the Dombeys of the City who raised the capital to finance
them, and both in immensely large quantities: about 200,000

navvies were working on railways at any one time in the 1840s, and between 1839 and 1848, a staggering total of £224,000,000 capital was raised for them.[5] And, one might add, it was the city as political capital which had made railways possible. Not only did the construction of each and every line require an additional Act of Parliament as authorisation, but in many cases it was only because railway development had the force of law that substantial opposition to it could be overcome.

This sense of modernity in the novel is underscored by the large number of characters who are embodiments of the past, frozen odd bits and pieces of another age vainly coping with the new. Mrs Skewton is the most memorable of these Regency relics, whose decrepit body is a constant mockery of the trappings of youth it affects to carry. Sol Gills' constant lament is that 'the world has gone past me' (38) (though he is in some measure redeemed by his recognition of the fact, and his efforts to ensure that his nephew does not share the same fate). Other similar figures include Mrs Pipchin, whose humanity was buried along with her husband in the Peruvian mines; Dr Blimber, passionate only about the ancient world; his daughter, a student of dead languages; Cousin Feenix, a feeble shadow of a Regency rake forever tottering into wrong places and improper anecdotes; and yet another antique Regency survivor, the Game Chicken.

For that matter, so is Dombey a relic of the past. The origins of the Dombey fortune are mercantile, placed squarely in the eighteenth century. He is, therefore, not a parvenu industrialist, but a merchant prince of the thoroughly respectable sort who has inherited, not earned his money. And though he knew the Dombeys of the City initially financed industrial ventures like the railways, Dickens does show an instinctive awareness that their day was also passing. The trade boom of the last two thirds of the 1840s[6] and the prosperity it brought to the Dombeys in some respects masked the dramatic nature of the changes being wrought in the nature of capitalism by the railways. We now recognise this as a crucial period in the development of the English economy, the beginning of the second phase of industrial capitalism, and the take-off into self-sustained growth.

What this means is that the first age of industrial capitalism in England, centred around the textile industry, was closing.

Industrial production hitherto had tended to meet existing needs, making clothing and cutlery for example, but doing so more cheaply than had been possible before. But now the development of the railways was stimulating the unprecedented and rapid growth of the iron and coal and related industries, which met no existing needs. They created needs and then filled them: production whose result was greater production. The cotton mills took fifty years to change England; the railways did so overnight. When Thomas Arnold saw the first railway train passing through Rugby, he recognised what had happened: 'I rejoice to see it', he wrote, 'and think that feudality is gone for ever.'[7]

To return to the world of the novel, we can see that Dombey's wealth is not in doubt, but what had happened was that the stewardship of the economy had passed from the hands of his class into those of the great industrial entrepreneurs, men like the railway king, George Hudson.[8] And later on the personal level, when a crisis in the firm of Dombey and Son is caused by the death of Son, Dombey turns the wrong way: not to the dynamic and irresistable force of the future, the fiery railway, but instead to the aristocracy, a sterile and powerless remnant of the past. Dombey's collapse dates from his rejection of Toodle on the platform of Euston Station and his introduction to Edith Granger, his future wife, in Leamington Spa the next day. The irony of the situation is multiplied by the fact that it is the railway which carries him to his doom, far faster than he could move to it himself.

III

While *Dombey and Son* attempts to describe and comment upon the dramatic changes being wrought upon English society by the processes of industrialisation and urbanisation, it is wholly in keeping with its overall method that it does so by examining specific individuals and incidents. For example, English society is represented by London, the preeminently modern metropolis. It contains virtually every order of person, house (residential and commercial) and material object of significance in that society. The people range in station from the blue blooded aristocracy (Edith and Cousin Feenix) to the merchant aristocracy (Dombey) to self-made businessmen (Carker the manager) to the several grades of white collar middle class (Morfin and the other Carker), the trading middle class (Gills), the upper reaches of the working classes (Mrs MacStinger) and both the deserving and the undeserving poor (the Toodles and the Browns). The houses and their neighbourhoods, always matched with Dickens' unfailingly precise eye for social nuance, range from the elevated surroundings of Bryanstone Square (near Dickens' own Devonshire Terrace house) down to humble Staggs' Gardens in 'Camberling Town'. There are even two vastly different suburbs, Norwood, new and glamorous, and the other near the Finchley Road, perched on the edge of a manmade morass of brickfields and refuse. The goods traded in by these many characters in these varied locations also encompass the widest possible range, including everything from rags and bones to pigeons to fruit and vegetables (Towlinson, the butler, resolves to set up as greengrocer when Dombey and Son breaks up below stairs), to nautical instruments, and even to human milk. The range extends by implication to human life itself, for Dombey and Son maintain a counting house in Barbados; therefore they must be involved in the triangular trade of rum, cotton, and slaves. While it is true that slavery in the Empire was abolished in 1833, a few years before the beginning of the novel's action, it still flourished in America where the cotton was grown. (Knowing Dickens' views on slavery, we can say that this could not have been an accidental detail.)

In some way, no matter how slight their relation to the plot, all of the characters of the novel, and the classes they represent and houses they inhabit and goods they trade in, are affected by the tumultuous arrival of the railway. One of the more forceful incursions of the railway into the novel is its role in the death of Carker. One even wonders if Sol Gills' mysterious investments, which flourish unexpectedly and so provide something of a fortune for Walter despite the collapse of his marine instrument trade, were railway shares. Most instructive of all, however, is the arrival of the railway at Staggs' Gardens, by which Dickens links the city with the advance of industrialisation.

The event is described as a natural cataclysm:

The first great shock of a great earthquake had, just at that period [ca. 1836], rent the whole neighbourhood to its centre. Traces of its course were visible on every side. Houses were knocked down; streets broken through and stopped; deep pits and trenches dug in the ground; enormous heaps of earth and clay thrown up; buildings that were undermined and shaking, propped up by great beams of wood. . . . There were a hundred thousand shapes and substances of incompleteness, wildly mingled out of their places, upside down, burrowing in the earth, aspiring in the air, mouldering in the water, and unintelligible as any dream. . . .

In short, the yet unfinished and unopened Railroad was in progress; and, from the very core of all this dire disorder, trailed smoothly away, upon its mighty course of civilisation and improvement. (62–3)

The metaphor of the earthquake is hardly casual, for it says much about the way in which social changes like the railway were being perceived. The traditional view of revolutionary social events was as of a natural disaster upsetting the normal, continuing steady state of the social organism. Events like the arrival of the railway demanded a new consciousness of the nature of change, for it did not mean a temporary imbalance in an ongoing equilibrium, but a transformation of that equilibrium.[9] The people of Staggs' Gardens have not yet become aware of this, and refuse to change their own lives to accommodate the railway: 'as yet, the neighbourhood was shy to own the Railroad' (63). They are confident the railway will eventually leave Staggs' as it had always been.

While Dickens' remark that the railway's course is one 'of civilisation and improvement' may at first be seen as ironic in tone, or at least arguably so, the novel's second encounter with Staggs' Gardens proves this not to have been the case. Now, some time later,

There was no such place as Staggs's Gardens. It had vanished from the earth. Where the old rotten summer-houses once had stood, palaces now reared their heads, and granite columns of gigantic girth opened a vista to the railway world beyond. The miserable waste ground, where the refuse-matter had been heaped of yore, was swallowed up and gone; and in its frowsy stead were tiers of warehouses, crammed with rich goods and costly merchandise. . . .

To and from the heart of this great change, all day and night, throbbing currents rushed and returned incessantly like its life's blood. (217–18)

The poverty and squalor is gone forever, replaced by an entirely new way of life—'the railway world'. It has changed human experience even to the perception of time, for now there is 'railway time' (218). What is most apparent here is that the change, however sudden and complete, is wholly for the good. The lives of Staggs' residents are now pleasant, productive and lively. Like Toodle, whose social rise is also literal, from the mines up into the railway world, the entire neighbourhood has 'come up' in the world.

The essence of the railway, then, is its potential for benefiting all social classes by making mere change into progress. When Dombey and Major Bagstock pass through a slum exposed by the railway *en route* to Leamington Spa, Dickens abates none of the squalor in his description, but is careful to say that the railway 'has let the light of day in on these things: not made or caused them' (282). The railway, and the economic change it symbolises, are forces of great power than can be used for the good: 'Night and day the conquering engines rumbled at their distant work . . . like tame dragons . . . as if they were dilating with the secret knowledge of great powers yet unsuspected in them, and strong purposes not yet achieved' (219). This great potential of the railway is what links it to the city. For if the most salient feature of the railway is its power, its ability to cause change, that of the city upon which it works is its potentiality, the ability to be made into something better than it now is.

Looking more closely at the many houses of the novel affords an opportunity to gauge more finely Dickens' attitude toward the city. Several critics have noted that houses in the novel tend to mirror their inhabitants; Dombey's most noticeably, but others as well, such as Cousin Feenix's and Carker's.[10] This is certainly true, but it should be noted that the phenomena seem purely local: the city itself remains immune to the corrupt houses it contains. Several times Dickens points out that Dombey's house is isolated from the others in the street, about which Dickens really has nothing to say. Clearly, if Dombey is representative of a class, his house is not. And, in addition, while Dombey's house passes from gloomy mourning to abandonment to gaudy display to the auction block, it remains 'dumb to all that had been suffered in it' (846). That is to say, the house itself seems to have no basic identity, and can be anything in turn.

Similarly, Dombey's offices in the City do not seem meant to be a comment upon the City itself, nor Carker's house on the villas of Norwood, and so on. In fact, these houses, and the world of objects as a whole, are curiously altogether indifferent to human existence. We can see this quite markedly in the description of the church where Florence and Walter are married:

> Youthful, and how beautiful, the young bride looks, in this old dusty place, with no kindred object near her but her husband. There is a dusty old clerk, who keeps a sort of evaporated news shop . . . a dusty old pew opener who keeps only herself . . . dusty wooden ledges and cornices . . . dusty old sounding-boards . . . (807)

and so on. What is striking here is the absence of any reflection of the joy of the married couple which we would expect from Dickens in such a scene: these objects and the people who are like objects, are silent, aloof and indifferent.

This is not simply an isolated incident: it indicates on a local scale what is true of the city as a whole, that it is indifferent and neutral to the people it contains. To emphasise this is, I think, Dickens' intention in having Florence retrace her childhood flight through the London streets on the morning of her wedding. The first of these passages which describes Florence alone in the city is a transport of terror, anxiety and fear. What we are seeing are ordinary and harmless sights transfigured by the mind of a terrified child: in sharp contrast are similar scenes in *Oliver Twist* where the city is bewildering and genuinely frightening not only to Oliver but to the reader and even the author. But when Florence, now grown up, and on the arm of her intended husband, walks the city streets from the church where Paul is buried to the church where she will be married, Dickens emphasises the absence of fear:

> It is a fair, warm summer morning. . . . Riches are uncovering
> in shops; jewels, gold and silver flash in the goldsmith's sunny
> windows. . . . Lovingly and trustfully, through all the narrow
> yards and alleys and the shady streets, Florence goes. . . . (806)

On Walter's arm, Florence sees nothing to fear.

The waves in *Dombey and Son*, Denis Donoghue has remarked, 'say whatever the listener is capable of hearing.'[11] The
city, like them, is equally malleable and can be whatever those
who live in it make of it. As the frequent references to gold,
silver and jewels reiterate, the London of *Dombey and Son*, if
indifferent to its inhabitants, is nevertheless an incarnation of
boundless wealth and potentiality which they can turn to any
account they will, good or bad. Dickens' attitude towards the
city, indeed towards the modern industrial world it represents, is
not one of total rejection or total acceptance, but rather a
thoughtful ambivalence. This consists first of all in a recognition
of the inevitability of the advent of this modern world, which is
itself indifferent to its own progress, whether for the better or the
worse. Balancing this attitude is Dickens' mistrust of the past
and current direction of English society.

The deepest roots of mid-Victorian optimism were to be found
in the belief that progress was possible. This was above all a faith
that the ancient crippling constants of human existence, suffering and death, could be overcome—even raw Nature itself was
controllable. This was a credo Dickens held himself. Dombey too
is a firm proponent of this belief, and paradoxically, his fall
demonstrates nothing if not that Dickens could see its futility
as well as its virtues. It has been suggested that this attitude in
Dombey and Son shows Dickens wanting to have it both ways,
criticising society but affirming the forces it has created.[12] Perhaps
this is so, but I think it can better be characterised as the result
of a struggle between two of the strongest of Dickens' beliefs, his
faith in progress, and his doubts about the English social system.

This dichotomy becomes apparent in the novel in a number of
ways, one of the most striking of which is the way in which
Dickens divides certain of his beliefs between two of his characters, Carker and Dombey. Carker, in this respect like Dickens,
sees through the pretences of the society around him with

unflinching accuracy, and is the only character to understand how vulnerable Dombey actually is. But this does not prevent Dickens from having Carker die a horrible death, run down by a locomotive engine. Dombey is quite obviously pilloried in the novel, yet at the very same time Dickens could express himself in straightforward Dombeyan terms, espousing the doctrine of progress and extolling the benefits of modern society. He did so quite unabashedly in an essay, 'The Chinese Junk', for *The Examiner* (24 June 1848, MP, 102–5), as *Dombey and Son* was winding to a close. In it, stimulated by the exhibit of a Chinese junk in London, Dickens characterises Chinese society as stultifying because it is timebound, paralysed in the past. European civilisation, by contrast, is dynamic and for that reason far, far superior. Perhaps unconsciously mirroring his deep sympathy with Dombey, Dickens even gave him some of his personal qualities as well, including his own inability to express emotion in the presence of his children.[13] One should note too that Dickens was the merchant prince of novelists: he earned roughly £10,000 from the serialisation of *Dombey and Son*, a sum which even today most writers would be proud to have earned on a single book. (Not long afterwards, he became a successful magazine publisher as well.)

Other signs of his deeply divided feelings are perhaps the facility with which Dickens had Walter Gay turn out for the good, though he had intended him to go bad; or the rehabilitation of Cousin Feenix at the end of the novel, when Dickens allows him to stand forward as a true gentleman, as if to say the Regency past was perhaps not so terrible after all, at least in comparison with the present. One may similarly construe the end of the novel, when, though one house of Dombey and Son has fallen, a new firm is foreshadowed, 'perhaps to equal, perhaps excel' the old (877).

I think that word—'perhaps'—sums up Dickens' attitude toward modern society at the novel's end. Society as it is, is rotten; but with the power of the railway, and all it represents, change may yet be possible. The railway universe that replaces Staggs' Gardens may be for the best after all—perhaps.

CHAPTER SIX

Bleak House: Homes for the Homeless

The London of *Bleak House*, on the surface, is in many ways like the city of *Dombey and Son*. It contains a large variety of characters who represent the entire range of the social system; it encompasses a great diversity of metropolitan locales within its boundaries; and it is the setting of the novel's key events. But while the city of *Dombey and Son* was the centre of a world of unlimited potentiality, which the dynamic power of industrial technology might harness to transform human life permanently for the better, the city of Jarndyce and Jarndyce is a cancerous wen, which threatens to engulf the world and perhaps extinguish human life altogether.

The actual city was becoming intolerable to Dickens, too. At about the time he began planning the novel, he had written to Bulwer Lytton: 'London is a vile place, I sincerely believe. I have never taken kindly to it, since I lived abroad. Whenever I come back from the country now, and see that great heavy canopy lowering over the housetops, I wonder what on earth I do there except on obligation' (10 February 1851; NL, II, 272). This letter exhibits the same tone which colours the city of *Bleak House*: it is indeed 'a vile place'.

Dombey and Son had been completed in March 1848; Dickens began working seriously on *Bleak House* in the summer of 1851 (though he did not begin writing until November). Yet, the London of *Bleak House* is so problematic, and in this so far removed from that of *Dombey and Son*, that an account of what had caused such a change in Dickens' attitudes in the few years that separate them appears necessary. Certainly, the novel between them *David Copperfield*, offers little in the way of explanation. The impulse of that novel, at least at first, had been primarily autobiographical, and it seems more than any other of Dickens' novels to this date to be set quite securely in the historical time (ca. 1825–35) in which it nominally takes place.

Plates

1. NEWGATE PRISON. From *L'Illustration* (Vol. 15, 1850); M. G. Thomas.

Newgate, and the 'Debtors Door' through which the condemned prisoners were taken to the gallows, terrified Dickens as a boy and fascinated him all his life. 'We have never outgrown the rugged walls of Newgate', he wrote: 'All within, is still the same blank of remorse and misery' ('Where We Stopped Growing', *HW*, 1 January 1853).

2. HOMELESS LONDONERS. From *L'Illustration* (Vol. 17, 1851); 'Gavarni', pseud. of Sulpice-Guillaume Chevalier.

Covent Garden and its surrounding slums fascinated Dickens as much by its squalor as its excitement—what he called its 'profound attraction of repulsion'. When Amy Dorrit and Maggie walk through Covent Garden at night, it is figures such as these they see: 'homeless people, lying coiled up in nooks' (*LD*, 174).

3. COVENT GARDEN. Watercolour; George Scharf, 1824.

After the move to London, walking through Covent Garden was one of the young Dickens' favourite pastimes. After he began working at nearby Warren's Blacking, its variety and excitement provided him with almost his only source of amusement and relaxation. Forster wrote of this time: 'To be taken out for a walk into the real town [from Camden Town]; especially if it were anywhere about Covent Garden or the Strand, perfectly entranced him with pleasure' (*Life*, 1, 14).

4. THE STRAND FROM VILLERS STREET. Watercolour: George Scharf, 1824.

This view of a crowd gathering to watch a fire in a house in the Strand was taken from Villiers Street, which led down toward Hungerford Stairs and the site of Warren's Blacking Warehouse where Dickens worked at about this time.

5. WATERFRONT, LAMBETH RIVERSIDE. Photograph; unknown photographer, ca. 1860s.

Until the great embankment projects of the 1850s and 1860s, both banks of the Thames from Millbank to Rotherhithe looked much like this. Dickens' description of Warren's Blacking Warehouse might easily fit any of these collapsing structures: 'a crazy, tumble-down old house, abutting of course on the river, and literally overrun with rats' (*Life*, I, 21). Such houses recur as central images in the novels, from *Oliver Twist* to *Our Mutual Friend*.

6. BIRMINGHAM AND LONDON RAILWAY IN PROGRESS. Pencil sketch; George Scharf, 1836.

This view, taken from Hampstead Road in Camden Town, is of the works described in Chapter vi of *Dombey and Son*: 'The first shock of a great earthquake had, just at that period, rent the whole neighbourhood to its centre. Traces of its course were visible on every side. Houses were knocked down; streets were broken through and stopped; deep pits and trenches dug in the ground; enormous heaps of earth and clay thrown up; buildings that were undermined and shaking, propped up by great beams of wood' (*DS*, 62).

7. THE THAMES. Engraving; George Cruikshank, 1830.

This portrayal of the Thames as an open sewer, condemning a private water supply company (there were several in London) for drawing untreated water from it, dates from 1830, but the situation remained much the same through the 1860s. Every year, tens of millions of tons of raw sewage were discharged into the river, which supplied the drinking water of most poor Londoners. The foul and corrupted river emerges as a central leitmotif in Dickens' mature novels, beginning with *Bleak House*.

8. MR DODD'S DUSTYARD. From *Illustrated Times*, 23 March 1861.

This famous mid-Victorian dustyard and its dust mounds (reputed to be a source for the Harman mounds in *Our Mutual Friend*) exhibits part of London's literal underworld. The people shown sifting through the dust in this sketch were a few of the many thousands who made livings—some even fortunes—collecting and sorting the city's immense daily production of waste matter. The industry disappeared in the years after the opening of Sir Joseph Bazelguette's great sewage system late in the 1860s.

9. A DISUSED SHOPFRONT IN THE STRAND. Pencil sketch; George Scharf, 1828.

Walking through the city streets, reading advertising bills like these, and looking in shop windows, was one of Dickens' greatest pleasures. (Among these posters can be seen a notice for Warren's Japan Blacking.) In March, 1870, a few months before his death, Dickens told Forster, with what sadness can only be imagined: 'walking up the length of Oxford Street ... [I] had not been able to read, all the way, more than the right hand half of the names over the shops' (*Life*, II, 411).

2. Homeless Londoners

1. Newgate Prison

3. Covent Garden

4. *The Strand from Villiers Street*

5. *Waterfront, Lambeth Riverside*

6. *Birmingham and London Railway in Progress*

7. *The Thames*

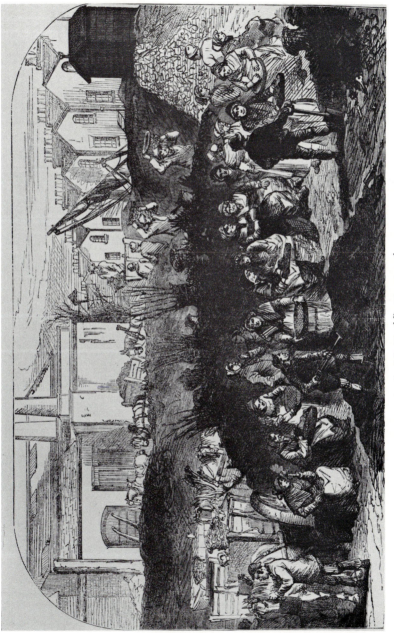

8. *Mr Dodd's Dustyard*

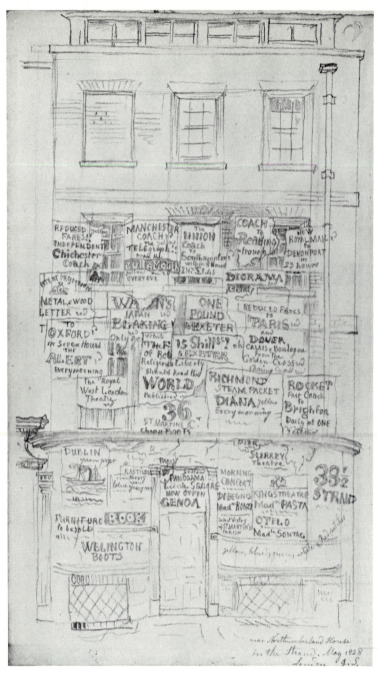

9. A Disused Shopfront in the Strand

In it London is, quite definitely, the city of the 1820s and 1830s, not that of the late 1840s. In a sense, the overall structure of the novel is retrospective, too, looking backward to the early novels in its ultimate retreat from London. So, rather than seek an explanation in the dynamics of his fictional development, I shall argue that Dickens' changed view of London in *Bleak House* was the result of an overall change in his thinking about social questions. This was evident first in Dickens' commitment to several practical social projects, then in his new magazine, *Household Words*, and finally in his fiction, in *Bleak House*.

During the late 1840s, Dickens had turned more and more toward the careful consideration of certain fundamental social ills that previously had not particularly interested him. Those upon which he concentrated previously had tended to be clearly identifiable institutions or abuses that could be dealt with simply by abolishing them. Among these were the debtors' prisons, the workhouses, Yorkshire schools, or, in *Dombey and Son*, the Charitable Grinders' school. What distinguished Dickens' new concerns were their general nature and the fact that they could not be dealt with in this simple, negative manner, but required more complex positive action. One of the chief among these new concerns was public sanitation. Edwin Chadwick's graphic and shocking report, *The Sanitary Condition of the Labouring Classes*, had appeared as long before as 1842, yet it was only in 1848 that Parliament belatedly established the General Board of Health. Dickens' brother-in-law, Henry Austin, was an employee of the Board. Some years previously, as an engineer on the Blackwell railway, Austin had been appalled at seeing the living conditions in the slums through which the railway passed, and devoted his energies from that time to ameliorating the dwelling places of the poor.[1] At least in part as a result of his persuasive efforts, Dickens became engaged in the public struggle to improve sanitation, and was brought round to support Chadwick, a man for whom he had little personal regard.

Yet by the time *Bleak House* was being written, virtually nothing had been accomplished in London. The General Board had proved inefficient, and its members had become involved in petty squabbling and administrative infighting, and the cholera threat remained. Indeed, the epidemic of 1848 eventually had

proved the worst so far, for unknowingly, the Board had exacer-
bated the outbreak by flushing the drains, making a limited local
infection waterborne and epidemic. Three years later, in 1851,
the problem of sanitation remained as bad as ever before.

Dickens' involvement in the sanitary movement took the form
of a series of articles on social matters published in *The Examiner*,
and after 1850, in his own *Household Words*. But his frustration
at the failure of sanitary reform must have been all the more
violent because he had for several years himself been involved in
a more practical venture to deal with a pressing social problem
that was successful—his close friend Angela Burdett Coutts'
home for fallen women.

Miss Coutts had first asked him, in the Spring of 1846, for
advice and information about aiding fallen women through
existing institutions, but by mid 1847 she and Dickens had
determined to establish a completely new institution, with
Dickens having placed himself in full control of it.[2] He not only
selected and furnished a suitable house in Shepherd's Bush,
which he renamed Urania Cottage, but also personally selected
the staff, searched the streets and prisons for suitable inmates,
worked out a detailed set of rules and regulations for its daily
operation, and even had a hand in choosing the fabrics the
women would use to make their dresses—he preferred bright,
lively colours.

But most important of all his decisions was that concerning
what would happen to the women once they had left Urania
Cottage. Unlike graduates of existing shelters, they would not
be required to bear their shame permanently by avoiding
marriage: they were to be taught useful domestic skills, shipped
out to the colonies (Australia, as it turned out) and there married
to honest settlers. They would be allowed to reenter society, even
if it were one 10,000 miles away.

As he grew more and more involved in the work, Dickens
became increasingly preoccupied with the causes of the women's
distress. Why had they been on the streets in the first place? The
uncomfortable answer was, they had no alternative. 'It is dreadful', he wrote to Miss Coutts on 3 November 1847, 'to think
how some of these doomed women have no chance or choice. It is
impossible to disguise from one's self the horrible truth that it

would have been a social marvel and miracle if some of them had been anything else but what they are' (*Coutts*, 105). Slightly earlier, in September, he had reacted strongly to George Cruikshank's experimental Temperance propaganda work, *The Bottle*,[3] in a letter to Forster: 'The philosophy of the thing . . . [was] all wrong; because to be striking, and original too, the drinking should have begun in sorrow, or poverty, or ignorance—the three things in which, in its awful aspect, it *does begin*' (*Life*, II, 12). The point is much the same—poor people are not inherently evil but they are driven by their poverty to commit social crimes.

By the time he came to write a critique of Cruikshank's sequel to *The Bottle*, *The Drunkard's Children*, for *The Examiner* the following year (8 July 1848, *MP*, 105–8), these vague but strong sentiments had become more precisely focussed by his experiences at Urania Cottage. Cruikshank apparently believed drink alone caused poverty, Dickens complained, but this was to ignore the real causes of drinking:

> Foul smells, disgusting habitations, bad workshops and workshop customs, want of light, air, and water, the absence of all easy means of decency and health, are . . . its common, everyday, physical causes. The mental weariness and languor so induced, the want of wholesome relaxation, the craving for *some* stimulus and excitement . . . and, last and inclusive of all the rest, ignorance . . . are its most obvious moral causes. (*MP*, 105)

To Cruikshank's work, Dickens contrasted Hogarth's famous engraving 'Gin Lane', a work which demonstrated that drunkenness does not originate in gin-shops:

> Drunkenness does not begin there. It has a teeming and reproachful history anterior to that stage; and at the remediable evil in that history, it is the duty of the moralist, if he strikes at all, to strike deep and spare not. (*MP*, 106)

The undefined 'sorrow, or poverty, or ignorance' of the earlier letter have hardened into a distinct causal relationship, with an impressive attention to detail. Now, according to Dickens, there were primary moral causes, above all ignorance and the mental starvation of the working classes; secondary physical causes, poor working conditions and unsatisfactory housing; and at the end of the chain, drink. This change in emphasis had affected the operation of Urania Cottage too: at first it admitted only prostitutes, but quickly Dickens began to allow in honest poor women, like needlewomen or domestic servants, whose inability to earn a living wage by their trades would soon compel them to supplement their earnings by selling themselves. The evil was not prostitution itself, but the intolerable social conditions oppressing poor women.

II

This development in Dickens' social thought was not long in surfacing in the fiction. While it has been argued convincingly that one cannot find a direct influence of the work at Urania Cottage in Dickens' writing,[4] it is clear that the experiences there changed his views on important social questions, and this in turn indirectly affected his art.

This change in part took the form of a new attitude toward the uses and functions of literature. Dickens was calling attention to this when he closed the Preface to the first book edition of the novel by stating: 'In *Bleak House*, I have purposely dwelt upon the romantic side of familiar things.' This statement has always been puzzling, for it is not really clear what 'romantic' might refer to in a novel about the law and death, nor what 'familiar' might refer to in a novel in which it is said it would not be strange to encounter a dinosaur on a public street. Nevertheless, I think we can ascertain what Dickens was pointing toward. In fact, one of the difficulties is that he seems to have meant two quite different things.[5]

Part of his meaning is involved in his growing conviction that the imaginative, entertaining—i.e. 'romantic'—aspect of literature was one important means of combating what he had earlier called the 'mental starvation' of the working classes. The value of literature as entertainment was under strong attack in mid-Victorian England, both from earnest Evangelicals who called it immoral, and latter-day Utilitarians, who thought it insufficiently serious. Throughout his career, Dickens had considered fiction to have the dual functions of amusement and instruction, but in the early 1850s, with the establishment of *Household Words*, he became especially concerned to stress the value of entertainment *per se*.[6] 'A Preliminary Word', the announcement heading the first issue of the magazine, proclaimed it would contain 'knowledge' but still not be bound 'to grim realities'. It would show instead 'that in all familiar things, even in those that are repellant on the surface, there is Romance enough, if we will find it out' (HW, 30 March 1850; MP, 167–9).

This theme of the remark, the importance of the imagination and the value of fancy and romance, later would be developed as the central message of *Hard Times*. But the statement also suggests another meaning, involving the nature of the relationship between art and reality. In this statement, Dickens was trying to express a belief that certain aspects of the real world had become remote to our sensibilities, and that it was the role of art to make us aware of them. Somehow, we had come into the position of not fully knowing what the world we live in is actually like; it was the function of art and the duty of the artist to change this. What we were not seeing, Dickens told his readers, were those things around us that indicated the gravity of fundamental social problems and how little was being done to solve them. Whatever was ugly was being ignored: if important aspects of social reality were ugly, they simply would not be allowed to exist.

Throughout Europe at mid-century, writers were sensing that a dramatic reversal in the traditional relationship between fiction and fact had occurred. Earlier in the century, fact and reality often were considered to be inherently dull or downright unpleasant; therefore it was necessary to embellish reality to make it interesting. So while Dickens had tried in *Sketches by Boz* 'to present little pictures of life and manners as they really are',[7] he had given the pictures fanciful flourishes of wit and style, and included his patently unrealistic short stories as well. But increasingly writers were perceiving reality as anything but dull— it was becoming so fantastic, and even horrifying, that it was surpassing the boundaries of fiction. Donald Fanger notes Balzac writing that, 'The reality of social life . . . "especially in Paris," is such that it is constantly outstripping "the imagination of inventors." In short, "the boldness of reality rises to combinations so implausible or indecent that they are forbidden to art

unless the writer soften them, prime them, expurgate them." '⁸
Dickens was already writing in the same vein in 1841, when he
defended in the Preface to *Oliver Twist* the character of Nancy
against charges of unreality: 'It is useless to discuss whether the
conduct and character of the girl seems unnatural, probable or
improbable, right or wrong. IT IS TRUE' (OT, xvii).

Now, however, Dickens' revelations about reality were not
casual, but programmatic. As we have seen, Dickens, from the
time of *Oliver Twist*, had always felt it a duty to acquaint his
reading public with unpleasant but serious social problems,
revelations of harsh fact impossible to believe, yet true. But in
Bleak House, we are no longer dealing with specific problems,
but a society which is problematical—in fact, it is the city itself
which has become the problem.⁹ And it is a problem so complex,
so convoluted, and so very unpleasant, that only through extreme
measures can the novelist compel his audience to confront it.
This was the second motive for presenting the romantic side of
familiar things—to force readers to see a truth far stranger and
far more horrifying than any possible fiction.

III

This intention is evident from the very first words of the novel:

> London. Michaelmas Term lately over, and the Lord Chan-
> cellor sitting in Lincoln's Inn Hall. Implacable November
> weather. As much mud in the streets, as if the waters had but
> newly retired from the face of the earth, and it would not be
> wonderful to meet a Megalosaurus, forty feet long or so,
> waddling like an elephantine lizard up Holborn Hill. Smoke
> lowering down from chimney-pots, making a soft black drizzle,
> with flakes of soot in it as big as full-grown snow-flakes—gone
> into mourning, one might imagine, for the death of the sun.
> Dogs, undistinguishable in mire. Horses, scarcely better;
> splashed to their very blinkers. Foot passengers, jostling one
> another's umbrellas, in a general infection of ill-temper, and
> losing their foothold at street-corners, where tens of thousands
> of other foot passengers have been slipping and sliding since
> the day broke (if this day ever broke), adding new deposits to

the crust upon crust of mud, sticking at those points tenaciously to the pavement, and accumulating at compound interest.

Fog everywhere. Fog up the river, where it flows among green aits and meadows; fog down the river, where it rolls defiled among the tiers of shipping, and the waterside pollution of a great (and dirty) city. Fog on the Essex marshes, fog on the Kentish heights. Fog creeping into the cabooses of collier-brigs; fog lying out on the yards, and hovering in the rigging of great ships; fog drooping on the gunwhales of barges and small boats. Fog in the eyes and throats of ancient Greenwich pensioners, wheezing by the firesides of their wards; fog in the stem and bowl of the afternoon pipe of the wrathful skipper, down in his close cabin; fog cruelly pinching the toes and fingers of his shivering little 'prentice boy on deck. Chance people on the bridges peeping over the parapets into a nether sky of fog, with fog all round them, as if they were up in a balloon, and hanging in the misty clouds.(1)

The details of the descriptions are concrete: the weather, the places, the people and animals, even the fog and the mud, are all commonplace and to a Londoner of 1851, part of his everyday experience. Yet the overall effect of the passage is one of estrangement: the individual components are ordinary but they are so coloured by the strange atmosphere of the passage that they are transmuted into an alien cosmos. The mud threatens to dissolve everyone or everything that touches it; smoke becomes a threatening rain of blackness, blotting out the sun; fog isolates people from the city around them as if each were in separate balloons. The odd syntax heightens the dislocating effect. Before us as we read, these ordinary objects are being endowed with striking new meanings. The familiar elements of the London cityscape have been assembled into a terrifying atmosphere of darkness and stagnation.

The opening pages of the novel represent the beginning of a deliberate campaign by Dickens to force his audience to see and understand the hidden, problematic nature of their familiar environment. So far, the effect is one only of strangeness. But as the novel progresses, the problems of sanitation and disease will be seen to make up the substance of the hidden connections that exist in this bewildering urban scene. We can begin to approach Dickens' meaning by examining some of the important elements of the opening passages, beginning with the mud.

The mud of mid-century London was, after all, quite different from the harmless if messy stuff children today make into pies. It was compounded of loose soil to be sure, but also of a great deal more, including soot and ashes and street litter, and the fecal matter of the legion horses on whom all transport in London depended. In addition, many sewers (such as they were) were completely open, and in rainy weather would simply overflow into the streets. Dogs, cattle in transit either to Smithfield or through the town (many dairies were still inside the city), and many people as well as used the public streets as a privy, but then even most privies were simply holes in the ground with drainage into ditches or another part of the street. (London was still a good fifteen years away from having an effective drainage system.) The mud must at times have been nothing less than liquid ordure.

Millions of people who walked through it daily, it seems, in some important sense were unaware of this simple fact. Though at every street corner, a waif like Jo might be standing, waiting to sweep a relatively clean path through the mud (perhaps six inches deep at the centre of the road according to one estimate) for well dressed pedestrians, somehow the fact of his existence or that of the mud itself was not 'real' Jo swept the mud, but beyond his sweeping he could be ignored. Even so, occasionally women still wore pattens, elevated wooden outer shoes, to traverse the streets, to keep their feet out of the mud. The boot scrapers one still sees outside older London houses and public buildings are additional indications of the condition of the streets, yet rarely does one find them mentioned in the literature of the period.

This insensitivity, then, is what Dickens felt he must assault—the sensibility of an audience cut off from their perceptions of the actual world in which they lived. One of the great mysteries of the Victorian period is how stark realities such as this needed to be 'discovered' by people who could hardly avoid daily contact with them. Yet such discoveries nevertheless were frequent: how

often in Victorian letters, diaries, articles or novels do we come across the horrified confession, 'I had not known such things existed'? In *Bleak House*, Dickens even provides us with a classic and no doubt typical instance of this experience, that of Mr Snagsby, who is taken on a tour of Tom-all-Alone's by Inspector Bucket. He finds there 'such smells and sights that he, who has lived in London all his life, can scarce believe his senses' (310). And in the end, he does disbelieve his senses, becoming 'doubtful of the reality of the streets through which he goes' (317). It is the 'romance' of *Bleak House* which makes the necessary connections for him and for the reader: Jo, the crossing sweeper whose existence society refuses to acknowledge, spreads the infectious disease engendered by the foul material in which he must work and live.

The novel's fog is an even more compelling example of the insistence on the *real*, in all its fantastic aspects. The key to understanding the deeper significance of the fog is the East Wind. This can be mistaken for a somewhat clumsy and transparent device Dickens invents to image John Jarndyce's 'split' personality. (There are several characters in the novel who similarly divide and isolate their public and private selves in an attempt to cope more easily with the unavoidable tensions of urban living.) Whenever Jarndyce is confronted by an uncomfortable situation—made angry by a friend, embarrassed by an expression of gratitude for his largesse, or frustrated by a social evil he cannot alter—he externalises the emotion, transforming it into the East Wind, and retreats into the Growlery, the private sanctuary where he indulges in appropriate activity until his usual good spirits return. (The East Wind was in the eighteenth century often linked with splenetic humour, associated with ill temper, depressed feelings, and spite.)

However, Dickens' insistent use of the device—and the fact that three of the dozen titles he toyed with for the novel refer directly or indirectly to it—suggest he intended it should have a greater significance. And as a simple meteorological phenomenon it would have conveyed just that. Today, when there is relatively little pollution visually apparent in London, the fact that the prevailing winds over the metropolis are westerly, that is blowing from west to east, is of little importance. However, when

London was heated and powered by some million coal fires and before there was any effective sewage disposal system, this insured that the smoke and smell produced in the city normally would be blown down the Thames Valley to the sea. Chiefly for this reason, since medieval times the better residential suburbs of London have always been built farther and farther westward, so that airborne pollutants would be carried away from them and out of harm's way, or, in what amounted to the same thing, toward the eastern part of the city where the poor generally lived. (This pattern also exists in many other large English cities.)

But the weather of England, is of course, very uncertain, and frequently the wind blows the 'wrong' way. The result, in the 1850s, was one of Mr Guppy's 'London particulars'. Some years later, a London guidebook described what happened thus:

> As the east wind brings up the exhalations of the Essex and Kentish marshes, and as the dampladen winter air prevents the dispersion of the partly consumed carbon from hundreds of thousands of chimneys, the strangest atmospheric compound known to science fills the valley of the Thames. Not only does a strange . . . darkness hide familiar landscapes from the sight, but the taste and smell are offended by an unhallowed compound of flavours, and all things become clammy to the touch.[10]

Recalling again the absence of a sewage system, and that whatever refuse did not stagnate and rot where it fell ended up in the Thames, to be carried downstream to those same Essex and Kentish marshes, we begin to get an idea that the word 'unhallowed' was hinting at. As a writer in *The Lancet* put it, 'The waters of the Thames are swollen with the feculence of the myriads of living beings that dwell upon the banks'.[11] The river was an open sewer, a festering breeding ground of fever and disease. And when its gaseous effusions (which were generally believed to be the actual causes of disease) mixed with smoke to form a fog, life in every part of the city was in danger.

We can safely conjecture, then, that the connection between the fog of the novel and the East Wind eventually would have been seen by Dickens' audience. The connection certainly was in Dickens' mind, for he had mentioned it in a speech given to

the Metropolitan Sanitary Association a few months before
beginning *Bleak House*, as follows:

> That not one can estimate the amount of mischief which is
> grown in dirt . . . is now as certain as it is that the air from
> Gin Lane will be carried, when the wind is Easterly, into May
> Fair, and that if once you have a vigorous pestilence raging
> furiously in Saint Giles's, no mortal list of Lady Patronesses
> can keep it out of Almack's. (*Speeches*, 128)

The diseases produced by the accumulation of raw sewage not
only affect the poor of the East End, but inevitably are borne
by the wind to the West End, as well. The very same idea becomes one of the most important thematic devices of *Bleak
House*. The rotting, half-buried corpse of Lady Dedlock's lover
gives off noxious emanations which infect Jo with a fever, which
he in turn passes to Esther, Lady Dedlock's daughter, disfiguring
her for life. Lady Dedlock may visit Tom-all-Alone's if she wishes,
but Tom will repay the call with deadlier intentions. It is the
foggy East Wind, then, which guarantees that all classes of
society will be linked by death, if not by their mutual responsibility.[12]

The technique is that of the novel as a whole. The familiar
things—closely observed, carefully described—form the basis
whence proceed by incontrovertable logic their 'romantic',
visionary, ultimately even apocalyptic, aspects. Nothing, in the
end, no matter how fantastic, seems out of place: as Forster wrote,
'Nothing is introduced at random, everything tends to the
catastrophe, the various lines of the plot converge and fit to
its centre, and to the larger interest all the rest is irresistibly
drawn' (*Life*, II, 114). The final result is to rescue reality from
obscurity.[13]

But in addition to the general influence of Dickens' changing
social ideas on the shape and substance of *Bleak House*, there is
also in the novel a more specific emphasis upon one particular
social problem—housing. Increasingly, during the early 1850s,
Dickens was coming to believe that the housing issue was crucial,
for above all it was poor housing which directly caused the illness
—physical and mental—that crippled the poor.

This concern was evident first in *Household Words*, which

from its inception in March 1850, became a platform for various reforms related to housing. As editor, Dickens put forward articles which advanced the related causes of inner city parks ('Lungs for London', *HW*, 3 August 1850), stricter building codes ('The Great Invasion', *HW*, 10 April 1852), and in many, many pieces, sanitary reform. It was here, to use Dickens' own words, that he had come to feel it was 'the duty of the moralist ... to strike and spare not.' And it was here as well that the most immediate and lasting good might be effected. The Shepherd's Bush institution, as it had developed, was a case in point. As he wrote to Miss Coutts about her sponsorship of Urania Cottage (which significantly he later called a 'Home for Homeless Women'): 'Imagining backward to what these women were and might have been, and forward to what their children may be, it is impossible to estimate the amount of the good you are doing' (21 March 1851; MS., PML). And as Dickens was beginning *Bleak House*, he became involved in another social venture with Miss Coutts, this not related merely indirectly to housing, but a project to *build* housing.[14]

During the early months of 1852, Miss Coutts became interested in erecting workmen's housing herself. The tone of her letters imply that it was Dickens who had suggested such a project to her; perhaps he did so while discussing his plans for the new novel. (No doubt, both she and Dickens had seen and been impressed by several model workmen's cottages, built under the aegis of Prince Albert, which had been shown at the Great Exhibition the year before and which had attracted much public notice.) She wrote to him about it early in January, and on 13 January 1852 he answered enthusiastically 'I believe it to be *certain*, that a scheme like yours is the only hopeful way of doing lasting good, and raising up the wretched' (*Coutts*, 191; Dickens' italics).

With the help of several friends and associates, among them police Inspector Field and Dr Southwood Smith, Dickens selected a suitable site in Bethnal Green, known as Nova Scotia Gardens. A professional architect, Philip Hardwick, and Henry Austin were asked to work on the building plans; by March, when the first number of *Bleak House* was in print, Miss Coutts had already purchased the land. Dickens worked seriously on the

project through the month of May.[15] Thus, the opening numbers
of *Bleak House* were written, perhaps even conceived, in con-
junction with this work on a practical project to build clean,
sound, healthy and inexpensive housing for the poor.

IV

The image of the decaying house not only provides the title but
is one of the principle elements organising and informing *Bleak
House*. Dickens' attention to housing in the novel is suggested
merely by the impressive range of houses he describes in it:
Chesney Wold, Bleak House, Boythorn's house, Tulkinghorn's
chambers, Snagsby's shop, the Jellyby house, the Bagnet's shop,
Krook's shop and the rooms above it, the brickmakers' shanties
and Tom-all-Alone's, to name but a few.[16]

The very first house which we are shown makes most of the
relevant points. This is Chesney Wold, which is seen dissolving
into the leaden landscape of its park under the assault of torren-
tial rains which bring no renewal of fertility, no hope of
regeneration, but only the stench 'of the ancient Dedlocks in
their graves' (9). The house itself is 'like a body without life'
(564). The Dedlock town house in London is little better, a
'Fairy-land to visit, but a desert to live in' (11). These are bleak
houses indeed. That of the Jellyby household, which we see next,
is no less so: Thavies Inn where it is located is described as 'a
narrow street of high houses, like an oblong cistern to hold the
fog' (35). The vast majority of the novel's other houses are hardly
any different. The Smallweeds dwell 'in a little narrow street,
always solitary, shady, and sad, closely bricked in on all sides
like a tomb' (287). When Richard and Ada marry, they set up
their home above Mr Vholes' office in Symond's Inn, a 'dingy
hatchment' which 'looks as if Symond were a sparing man in
his way, and constructed his inn of old building materials, which
took kindly to the dry rot and to dirt and all things decaying
and dismal, and perpetuated Symond's memory with congenial
shabbiness' (547). All of these places smack more of the tomb
than the hearth. They are, moreover, all houses of the respectable
middle classes and of the gentry, not of the impoverished or the
indigent.

The message borne by these houses is all the clearer for that. Society has as its first responsibility to its members the provision of shelter, warmth, light and food—in short, the provision of a home. Even here, in the houses of those who in Victorian England could surely afford to buy all of these things, they are still lacking. The fires of Chesney Wold can never dry it out; Grandfather Smallweed is forever squirming before fires, forever cold; in the Jellyby house, the fire is always out, and consequently food and hot water are never available when they are needed. All of these places may be houses—they are most certainly not homes.

In the houses of the poor, the social failure is that much more obvious. In Miss Flite's room, Esther notes 'neither coals nor ashes in the grate, and I saw no articles of clothing anywhere, nor any kind of food', only 'an open cupboard . . . dry and empty' (54). Captain Hawden's rooms below are equally bare, but here in addition 'the air . . . is almost bad enough to have extinguished [the candle] if he had not' (136). The brickmaker's hovel lies 'in a brick-field, with pigsties close to the broken windows, and miserable little gardens before the doors, growing nothing but stagnant pools' (105–6).[17] Inside is a 'damp offensive room' (106) whose 'nature [was] almost hopeless of being clean' (110), and where it is no surprise to anyone that Jenny's baby son dies.

The bleakest of these bleak places is Tom-all-Alone's, the 'black, dilapidated street' of 'tumbling tenements' and 'crazy houses' (220) where 'Jo lives—that is to say, [where Jo] has not yet died' (219). The very word is unknown to Jo—'What's home?' he asks at the Inquest (148). The people who live in this slum are 'a swarm of misery'; but clearly it is the slum environment that has 'bred a crowd of foul existence that crawls in and out of gaps in walls and boards; and coils itself to sleep, in maggot numbers, where the rain drops in' (220). Not a word of the carefully modulated prose indicates that this is a crowd of humans and not worms. Once, and only once, do we penetrate to the inside of one of these rooms, and are told, 'It is offensive to every sense; even the gross candle burns pale and sickly in the polluted air' (312). More than this Dickens will not say. But even this foul habitation eventually is denied to Jo, who is compelled like 'other lower animals' (221) to move on every moment of his brief and miserable existence.

Though the bleakest, Tom-all-Alone's is not the largest of these houses. Metaphorically speaking, that is London itself. To Esther, seeing it for the first time, buried in fog, it seems a place totally unfit for human habitation: 'We drove slowly through the dirtiest and darkest streets that ever were seen in the world (I thought), and in such a distracting state of confusion that I wondered how the people kept their senses' (28). (As the novel will demonstrate, usually they do not.) The only peace and quiet in London, the rest of the paragraph intimates, is to be found in the tomb.

What makes the London of *Bleak House* even more horrific is its size. It is not only so much a microcosm of the world, but a malignant part of it threatening to consume and appropriate the whole. Its 'lurid glare' (429) overhangs distant St Albans and even Bleak House. Its foul influence extends to Chesney Wold and Deal. The countryside around the city is filled not with lush green vegetation, but with the barren waste of the brick-fields, which are the stuff of which more of London's bleak houses will be built. He wrote to Miss Coutts, at about this time, noting the destructive effects of this growth: 'If you go into any common outskirts of the town now, [you will] see the advancing army of brick and mortar laying waste the country fields and shutting out the air' (18 April 1852; *Coutts*, 199).[18] The urban fog and mud, metaphorical and literal, are threatening to poison all of England.

What is wrong with these houses? Why are they so bleak? Dickens begins to sketch out an answer to this question from the earliest chapters. The Jellyby household affords another example of this social infection, but more clearly suggests what is behind it. It is both 'very untidy' and 'very dirty', domestic disorder that creates, as Forster put it, 'a household muddle outmuddling Chancery itself' (*Life*, II, 116). Mrs Jellyby wastes her time and energies on wholesaling the trappings of Western civilisation to African savages who couldn't care less for them, without caring that her domestic mismanagement has reduced her own children to a state of savagery. The message is clear: by refusing to accept her primary social responsibilities, which are domestic, Mrs

Jellyby creates chaos and confusion that threatens to destroy her entire family, and infects all the servants, corrupting them as well. A number of other women in the novel demonstrate a similar point. The case of Miss Wisk, whose mission 'was to show the world that woman's mission was man's mission' (422), or her colleague, 'an extremely dirty lady . . . whose neglected home . . . was like a filthy wilderness' (422), underline the same moral. The first duty of a woman was her home and family, and if this were neglected, the social consequences would be overwhelming.[19]

This is not a cut-and-dry case of sex bias, for Dickens was well aware that men as well as women have domestic responsibilities, and where they neglect them Dickens comes down upon them with equal rage. If anything, Skimpole's neglect of his household is presented as even more insidious than Mrs Jellyby's, and even more damning in that his abdication from responsibility is based in selfishness and not a laudable but misguided zeal to help others. His house is predictably bare and filthy; but even more hurtful is his boast that, ' "In this family we are all children, and I am the youngest" ' (597). This, his refusal to be a father, has doomed his children to lead lives as useless as his own: they cannot cook, they cannot sew, they cannot keep house at all. And again, the moral infection spreads: Skimpole's improvidence is passed on to Richard Carstone, who is goaded by him into spending money he does not have.

It is possible to read this as a plea to keep women in the home and conjugal bed, where they belong, and out of politics and all other serious intercourse with the world. Certainly, a remark Dickens wrote to Miss Coutts, commenting on a religious institution for fallen women, can so be taken: 'The suggested place is but a kind of Nunnery . . . of a . . . pernicious and unnatural nature. As if every home in all this land were not a world in which a woman's course of influence and action is not marked out by Heaven' (17 May 1849; MS., PML). Or as he wrote to a young woman seeking advice about her future, 'In your small domestic sphere, you may do as much good as an emperor can do in his' (To Emmely Gotschalk, 1 February 1850; NL, II, 203). But Dickens did not intend that women should never leave the home. In *Bleak House*, for example, we see Esther constantly engaged in charitable missions, and Mrs Bagnet running the family business. Dickens also encouraged several young women writers, and published their work in *Household Words*. What he did believe was that the first and most important duty of any individual—regardless of sex—was to the family and the home. For whatever happens in the home will determine the quality of the social life of the nation. And if society fails at that level, so too will it fail at all levels.

Chapter xl, 'National and Domestic', makes the point explicitly. What is literally true of each of the novel's residential houses is true metaphorically of *the* House, the House of Commons. As on the domestic level, those in positions of national responsibility have ignored their duties, and chaos and confusion result. To the -oodles and -uffies, the 'People' to whom they are nominally responsible are 'a certain large number of supernumararies, who are to be occasionally addressed, and relied upon for shouts and choruses, as on the theatrical stage' (161). Their interests lie elsewhere; like Mrs Jellyby, who rides through London's East End with her mind on the Far East (Chapter xxix), blind to the squalor before her very eyes, they cannot see the diseased state of the nation they govern. The moral was this: '. . . I have grave doubts whether a great commercial nation . . . can better Christianize the benighted portions of [the world] than by the bestowal of its wealth and energy on the making of good Christians at home, and on the utter removal of neglected and untaught childhood from its streets, before it wanders elsewhere' (To Rev. Henry Christopherson, 9 July 1852; NL, II 401). For home and nation, the warning was the same— put your own house in order first.

The same domestic analogy applies to the novel's greatest muddle, Chancery. Here again it is the failure of those with primary responsibility to act that causes the rot. It is located from the very first at the heart of the fog and mud of the city, and called the source of 'the groping and floundering condition' (2) of the body politic. (Even its location is symptomatic of governmental incompetency, for it sat in Lincoln's Inn out of term because the 'new' law courts at Westminster [built in the 1820s] were too small to house all the important juridical bodies that administered the law.) Chancery is important in the novel for a number of reasons. Its metaphorical jurisdiction is cosmic, involving 'the round of every man's acquaintance' (3) in a suit one is born into and can only escape in death, and which deals with questions of ultimate equity and justice—in short, to be alive at all is to be in Chancery.[20] And as one perceptive critic has noted, according to Blackstone, the Lord Chancellor was 'the general guardian of all infants, idiots and lunatics; and has the general superintendence of all charitable uses in the kingdom.'[21] The Lord Chancellor, by definition then, stands *in loco parentis* to the entire nation, but like the other defective parents of *Bleak House*, abdicates from his social responsibilities. The results are devastating.

The purely legal abuses of Chancery, its interminable delays and prohibitive costs, were equally perversions of its original purpose. It had originated in the Middle Ages as a means of speeding and mitigating the King's justice, as it were to cut 'red tape'.[22] Even more to the point, however, was its jurisdiction over matters of wills and testaments, and it is here that we can begin to see its most intimate connections to the rest of the novel.

If *Bleak House* was meant to attack the governing classes for their abdication from responsibility, the focus on Sir Leicester Dedlock could not have been more apt. Despite the Reform Bill, now some two decades old, political power in England still lay firmly in the hands of the three hundred or so great landed families. The -oodle and -uffie factions, and their stooges, dominated the two political parties. Even the economic revolution of the railways had not weakened their influence. In fact, their position had never been stronger, at least financially: the burgeoning demand for fuel and iron to make steel and power locomotives made them richer from the royalties paid for the coal and ore lying under their estates, and other pieces of those estates which had only a few decades before been farmland, but were now part of large cities, yielded greatly increased rents. Property was still, as it had always been, power.[23]

One can understand why Chancery's jurisdiction over many questions of title and ownership, often perplexingly difficult to ascertain after a series of complicated bequests and entails, was not only of personal, but of great economic and political importance. When Dickens writes that Chancery 'has its decaying houses and its blighted lands in every shire', the allusion is precisely literal as well as metaphorical: its stranglehold over property was as serious an impediment to the economic development and prosperity of the nation as was its moral iniquity. One can understand further now why Tulkinghorn plays such a crucial role in the novel. For in this economic system, writes one historian, it was lawyers who 'were the investment counsellors of the day, guiding the mortgages that made property development possible, channelling the investments that produced returns "safe as houses".'[24] When Dickens shows us Tulkinghorn walking the streets of London 'in the confidence of the very bricks and mortar' (662), he is not creating a fantastic metaphor, but merely elucidating the fantastic truth.

V

The implication of the series of bleak and corrupt houses we are shown, from Tom-all-Alone's to Chancery to London itself, is that the nation is on the verge of total paralysis, and perhaps to follow, a violent, apocalyptic explosion. Moreover, no one can escape the imminent destruction: the infection which begins in the fetid and putrescent graveyard where Lady Dedlock's lover lies first strikes Jo, but then Esther Summerson, Lady Dedlock's illegitimate daughter. The ruling classes are not immune to the consequences of their social failures.

The question that immediately arises is how the situation is to be set right. The answer mentioned above, to put one's own house in order first, sounds ridiculously simpleminded. Nevertheless, it is the key to unlocking the paralytic stranglehold afflicting the novel's many bleak houses. On every level, one must accept appropriate duties and responsibilities—women should be good housekeepers, wives and mothers, and men good providers, husbands and fathers. Both should practise charity (though with humility and compassion) among the less fortunate. Thus, the home becomes a radiant centre of active virtue and human affection whose influence spreads ever outward into society. As John Jarndyce advises his ward, Richard, he must love Ada, his bride, ' "in your active life, no less than in her home when you revisit it, and all will go well. Otherwise, all will go ill" ' (180).

The most instructive case is that of Esther Summerson. Esther's situation—she is a bastard and has had an awful childhood—is extreme, but still typical, for very few of the novel's characters about whom we have full information have avoided childhood deprivation of some sort, whether psychic, physical, or both. As for all the novel's people, Esther's risk in the world is losing her identity, dissolving like the first paragraph's horses and dogs, 'indistinguishable in mire' (1). Esther is always being told what she must be like, and what role she must assume, even by her friends. All of her dreams (there are several) enact fears of precisely this nature, as does the one that occurs the first night she is in London:

> I began to lose the identity of the sleeper [Caddy Jellyby] resting on me. Now it was Ada; now, one of my old Reading friends from whom I could not believe I had so recently parted. Now, it was the little mad woman worn out with curtseying and smiling; now, some one in authority at Bleak House. Lastly, it was no one, and I was no one. (45)

The threat here is total dissolution, yet ironically, in a sense Esther really is 'no one' because her father, unknown to her, is Nemo, the man with no name.[25] But this is not all Esther must bear. Her act of kindness in nursing Jo when he is dying is rewarded by her infection with smallpox and her subsequent disfigurement. However, her suffering is not in vain. During her illness and delirium, she is forced to confront all of her previous selves: 'At once a child, an elder girl, and the little woman I had been so happy as, I was not only oppressed by cares and difficulties adapted to each station, but by the great perplexity of endlessly trying to reconcile them' (488). Once her 'old face' is gone (491), she can see herself and allow herself to be seen by others as what she was never before allowed to be—her true self. And once she has had this harrowing experience, her true identity is revealed to her, for she discovers she is Lady Dedlock's daughter.

What sustains Esther through her many trials is her unfailing sense of duty. Dickens was wont to combat his own 'morbid' thoughts by throwing himself into 'action, usefulness . . . doing something' however small and unimportant it might seem (To

Emmely Gotschalk, 17 February 1850; NL, II 203). Thus, Esther's constant admonition to herself to remember her duty similarly serves as a variety of therapy, firm action resolving her self-doubt and depression.

What is most important about active charity is not, however, the personal reward, substantial though it be. It is worth noting that the reward can be quite substantial: Esther is illegitimate, but she overcomes this disability through her sense of duty, going on to marry Allan Woodcourt, whose family even has somewhat obscure and comic claims to gentility. But more important than his ancestry is his profession, medicine. Together, Allan and Esther as doctor and nurse will extend their circle of benevolent influence to many of the poor and suffering. John Jarndyce explains: ' "I mean, [Woodcourt is] a man whose hopes and aims may sometimes lie (as most men's sometimes do, I dare say) above the ordinary level, but to whom the ordinary level will be high enough after all, if it should prove to be a way of usefulness and good service leading to no other" ' (816). That Richard Carstone does not follow this simple advice is at least in large part the reason for his entrapment in Chancery and his destruction by it.

Jarndyce himself is the other chief incarnation of this spirit of selfless generosity in the novel, acting as the unknown benefactor of Miss Flite and Neckett's orphaned children, and going far beyond the bounds of family ties to aid his young wards. The most exceptional manifestation of his spirit and deeds is what he has done with his home, Bleak House, for it is the only house in the novel which is most definitely not bleak.

Like Esther, he is gifted with the ability to turn any 'house [into] home in a moment' (609), and the chapter in which Esther and the Chancery wards arrive at Bleak House is named, appropriately, 'Quite at Home' (Chapter vi). His greeting to them is simply (and effectively), ' "You are at home" ' (63). A blazing, warm fire in a snug room completes the welcome. Later, as Esther explores the house, its other characteristics become apparent. It is old, and its rooms are irregular in size and shape, and connected by odd, labyrinthine hallways. But this is not, like London, a terrible labyrinth. Rather, it is 'pleasantly irregular' (66), its oddness compounded of long use and gentle accommodation to the needs of its inhabitants: 'light, and warmth, and comfort' (67). Bleak House, then, is 'a dreary name, . . . but not a dreary place' (31), entirely because of the efforts of Jarndyce, for when he inherited it, it had been 'shattered and ruined' (96) by its involvement in Chancery.[26]

But very few people in the novel other than Esther, her husband and her guardian respond adequately to their social and personal obligations. Those characters who entirely abdicate their responsibilities are granted no reprieve by Dickens, no matter how personable or pathetic they may be. Sir Leicester Dedlock is an excellent example of this group, for he is not consciously malevolent. He appears first as stiff and stupid, but one senses that as the novel progressed, Dickens warmed to him. But even the flood of sympathy later generated on his behalf does not save him from his deserved fate, the literal paralysis which metaphorically he is in part responsible for bringing upon the nation. One of the most moving scenes of the novel summarises with magnificent economy Sir Leicester's blind but noble life, as Tulkington arrives to announce that Rouncewell's candidate has won a seat in Parliament; Sir Leicester grandly orders the lights removed, to listen to the foreshadowing of his doom while night falls on Chesney Wold.

There is yet another group of characters in the novel, who are neither victims or exploiters but fall somewhere between. These are people who have coped with the struggle of survival in London seemingly by dividing themselves in two, into public and private selves.[27] The private self has no contact with the world of mud, fog and law, and so retains its integrity. The public self, which does, absorbs all the moral taint such contact carries with it. Thus, Skimpole can advise the man arresting him for debt not to ' "be ruffled by your occupation. We can separate you from your office; we can separate the individual from the pursuit. We are not so prejudiced as to suppose that in private life you are otherwise than a very estimable man" ' (75), as in fact he is. And so for that matter is the Lord Chancellor, who is 'legally ignorant' of the lives he has ruined in his public capacity, though outside the Court he is a very pleasant, kindly old man.

The most carefully drawn of these characters is Inspector Bucket, who is in large part based on Inspector Field of the

Metropolitan Police, about whom Dickens wrote a number of laudatory articles in *Household Words*.[28] Bucket appears as an equally praiseworthy personage in the novel as Field had in the magazine, and there can be no doubt that Dickens had nothing but admiration for his detective skill and *savoir faire* in the criminal underworld. (And as with Nadgett in *Martin Chuzzle-wit*, Bucket's work, piecing together a meaningful narrative from isolated signs and clues, is not unlike that of the novelist.) But if one reads carefully enough, one can see that Dickens was not blinded by his admiration to Bucket's compromised moral position. The Inspector does try ' "to make things as pleasant as is consistent with my duty" ' (678), and offers the distressed he encounters genuine sympathy and consolation when necessary. But his duty always comes first, and if personally he is devoted to the truth, the Law which he serves so professionally is not—it is an institution for which 'the mere truth won't do' (704). Bucket is not above arresting an innocent man, so that should he turn out to be guilty, Bucket will be the one to collect the reward of a hundred guineas, doing so with the remark, ' "it may as well be made by me as any other man" '(678). The most one can say for Bucket is that this strategy for survival does work, even if he is left morally compromised, and so he makes the near best out of the almost impossible situation in which the people of *Bleak House* find themselves.

VI

The London of *Bleak House* is paralysed by oceans of mire, isolated and corrupted by fog, and infected by its polluted water. Chancery and Parliament prevent any change. Its people either dissolve, literally as does Krook, or metaphorically, as does Miss Flite into madness or Richard Carstone into bankruptcy and death by fever. Against this powerful array of negativity, Dickens presents the modest domestic achievement of Bleak House. Yet even the achievement of Bleak House is not entirely unalloyed.

Bleak House exists as a refuge, but it can do little more than offer a place in which one can escape the world; it can not change it, and it is not even immune to the fever that ravages London. Why this is so is not perfectly clear, but Jarndyce's refusal to have anything to do with Chancery may be another less obvious instance of a failure to take up a social responsibility, similar in kind if not degree to the moral abdication of so many other characters. Jarndyce's refusal to confront the past of Bleak House means he cannot completely escape it: perhaps the fee Chancery exacts for allowing Bleak House to exist as a pleasant haven is that the other property in Jarndyce v. Jarndyce, Tom-all-Alone's, must remain under its seal, derelict and decaying.

Jarndyce's situation is echoed by the role of his private sanctuary, the Growlery. It does serve to defuse his rage so that he may continue good deeds elsewhere, but it also prevents that rage from being directed where it is rightly deserved. The result is that Bleak House remains implicated in its tainted past. Perhaps as a sign of this, it contains several disquieting echoes of that past, like the paintings of military couples who recall Honoria Barbary and Captain Hawdon; or a picture of 'the whole process of preparing tea in China, as depicted by Chinese artists' (66), evoking the spirit of Orient which to Dickens symbolised the endless, crippling repetition of the past.[29]

This is significant, for in *Bleak House*, any connection with the past is suspect. Virtually the worst thing Dickens can find to say about the Dedlocks is that the 'family is as old as the hills' (9). London is so trapped in the past, that a dinosaur walking on Holborn Hill would not appear odd. Perhaps the reason for this is that society has so long been paralysed that the present *is* the past, petrified and perpetuated. This is true even of its people, for one of the striking facts about the novel is how few genuine children there are in it. Skimpole is known as 'the Child'; Bart Smallweed is 'a kind of fossil Imp' (275), and his family is one in which 'old men and women there have been, but no child' (287).

Even the idyllic pastoral dream world which had so often served as a fictional balance to the intolerable city for Dickens, could no longer be treated as a serious alternative. This is hardly surprising, for as we have seen, the city of *Bleak House* is swallowing the countryside entire. Mr Vholes is, as he invariably is, correct when he intimates that in this modern world of ours one can no longer ' "take refuge in rural habits" ' (534). The rural escape is one that existed in the past, but is gone forever,

like the 'brook "as clear as crystial" [which] once ran right
down the middle of Holborn' (130) that Snagsby dimly remembers. There is no life but city life. Perhaps like Miss Flite's birds,
those who live in the city that is their prison must die in it: if the
birds were to be freed, we are told, the wild birds would kill
them.[30]

If we wonder, at the close of *Bleak House*, whether there is
any hope for the survival of English society, it is not surprising
that we fail to reach a firm conclusion. In this, we are only
sensing the uncertainty and confusion embedded in the novel.
Certainly, despite the novel's insistence on individual responsibility, in Dickens' mind England's social ills had moved beyond
the point where individual responsibility mattered as much as
the seeming indestructibility of the 'system'. (So far has Dickens
come from *Dombey and Son*, that the word is never used in
Bleak House without a negative connotation.) The spontaneous
combustion of Krook may offer some hope of the future apocalyptic collapse of Chancery and the ancient social system it holds
up; yet Dickens also presents Conversation Kenge at the end of
the novel, 'gently moving his right hand as if it were a silver
trowel, with which to spread the cement of his words on the
structure of the system, and consolidate it for a thousand ages'
(844)[31].

However, *Bleak House* does end with a tone of cautious optimism. This can be accomplished because London and the
system it represents are not really confronted, but simply
abandoned, as Esther and Allan Woodcourt move north toward
the iron country of Rouncewell to establish a 'new' Bleak House
(though it is not entirely new—it is in certain respects a copy of
the old). The commercial and administrative centre of the nation,
the city, and the ancient agricultural centre, Lincolnshire, are
abandoned for the productive and dynamic industrial north.

George Rouncewell's visit to his brother's factory in the
nameless iron city in Chapter lxiii takes on great importance.
This is how he sees the inside of the works:

> ... a great perplexity of iron lying about, in every stage, and
> in a vast variety of shapes; in bars, in wedges, in sheets; in
> tanks, in boilers, in axles, in wheels, in cogs, in cranks, in

rails; twisted and wrenched into eccentric and perverse forms, as separate parts of machinery; mountains of it broken up, and rusty in its age; distant furnaces of it glowing and bubbling in its youth; bright fireworks of it showering about, under the blows of the steam hammer; red-hot iron, white-hot iron, cold-black iron; an iron taste, an iron smell, and a Babel of iron sounds. (846)

The emphasis is on production (though it is clear Dickens had little idea what processes are involved in it). Fire in the factory is used not to destroy, but to create energy, energy which is harnessed to the human will, and used to produce from the raw native elements shaped, ordered and useful objects, parts of machines which will themselves become agents of yet more production. For all this productive activity, Dickens has nothing but strong admiration.

Many of the objects mentioned are related to railways. For *Bleak House* has moved into the heart of the railway universe of *Dombey and Son*, and located it not in London, but in the industrialised counties of the North where iron was being made into rails and locomotives, the agents of motion and progress. Here, Dickens sensed, there was hope for the nation—but it was a hope that did not remain with him for long.

CHAPTER SEVEN

Hard Times: The Industrial City

Dickens' attitude toward industrialism as it appears in *Bleak House* can aptly be described as being in the mode of the 'technological sublime'.[1] The tone of Chapter lxiii, 'Steel and Iron' as we have seen, is respectful and proud, emphasising the tremendous power of the industrial processes going on in the factory. It echoes the tone of a number of generally approving articles on various technological processes that had recently been appearing in *Household Words*, several of which Dickens had co-authored, including 'A Paper-Mill', with Mark Lemon (31 August 1850; *Uncollected Writings*, 137–42), and 'Plate-Glass', with W. H. Wills (1 February 1851; *Uncollected Writings*, 205–15).

Yet the attitude toward industrialism explicit in *Hard Times* could not be further from this, though Dickens was planning the novel only about six months after he had written the concluding, laudatory ironmaster segment of *Bleak House*.[2] Here the industrial system, which encompasses the philosophy of the masters as well as the processes and routine of factory work, is identified as a prime source of social evil, and represented as a root cause of England's collective and individual social and spiritual malaise. The system is placed in direct opposition to emotional and imaginative spontaneity, perhaps even to life itself. The indictment of the industrial system in the novel is thorough and unrelenting.

There is no direct or conclusive evidence that can explain precisely why Dickens changed his views about the mills so completely in such a brief period of time, but very likely the crucial experience had been a short visit to Preston early in February, 1854. Dickens went to observe a dispute between the mill owners and the workers, and wrote about it in *Household Words*, in 'On Strike' (11 February 1854; *MP*, 423–36). Dickens was always far more accurate and reasonable in his attacks on what he did not like than in his praise of what he did, and so his endorsement of Ironmaster Rouncewell and his work no doubt had been made easier by his relative ignorance of factory life and of the social condition of the labourers in the north of England. But now, even a few days of close observation in Preston were enough to quicken his sympathy for the workers and engage his penetrating analytic imagination. For one thing, the place was not what he expected it to be like: 'It is a nasty place', he wrote to Forster, '(I thought it was a model town)'; indeed, it was very dull, and he complained, 'there is very little in the streets to make the town remarkable' (*Life*, II, 122). Dullness was his overriding impression; even the workers' conduct of the strike was restrained and quiet. (The monotony of Coketown is, of course, one of its salient features.) 'On Strike' opens not with the strike but with an account of an argument Dickens had on the train down with an obnoxious and narrow-minded supporter of the masters. I suspect that hearing sentiments not too distant from ones he had himself expressed in print shortly before, now in the mouth of so obstreporous and repugnant a bigot as this unnamed individual must have even further disposed him to reconsider his attitudes toward what he was about to see.

All this being said, it might be expected that the points about to be stressed are the differences between *Bleak House* and *Hard Times*—yet the opposite is my intention. There is a vast difference between Coketown and the iron city of *Bleak House*, but not between Coketown and the earlier novel's London. The vision of the city and the judgement of the urban experience in both works are in fact strikingly similar. Coketown is in a sense a direct extension of fogbound London.

Admittedly, there is little at first glance to link London and Coketown. The details of the northern town are entirely different: it is a community of red brick buildings, industrial smoke, ceaseless monotony, and very little else, not at all like the teeming chaos of London. But points of contact are there. Both, for example, are places habitually without the light of the sun, one darkened by smoke, the other by fog. What little sunlight does illumine Coketown on a bright summer day reveals only 'a dense, formless jumble' that shows 'nothing but masses of darkness' (111). Darkness is so much a part of Coketown that after

the sun sets 'behind the smoke', night does not fall upon it but
rather, 'darkness seemed to rise slowly out of the ground, and
creep upward, upward . . . up to the sky' (122–3).

The red brick, brass-plated buildings of Coketown are physically unlike the buildings of London, but, again, alike at a deeper
level. What they do share is their fundamental unsuitability to
human need: neither provide fit places for people to live. The
unnaturalness of Coketown's buildings is not a result of its age
but its newness. Like the cities in the America of *Martin
Chuzzlewit*, Coketown has been thrown up from scratch to
conform to an abstract principle, but here as well new has paradoxically become old, progress regress, and civilisation savagery,
as this description hints: 'it was a town of unnatural red and
black like the painted face of a savage' (22). None of the buildings
reflects the need that it should fulfil. Consequently all are
interchangeable: 'The jail', we are told, 'might have been the
infirmary, the infirmary might have been the jail, the town-hall
might have been either, or both, or anything else, for anything
that appeared to the contrary in the graces of their construction'
(23).

What Dickens had come to believe, despite his earlier hopes,
was that the industrial city in essence was not different from
the metropolis. Like London, Coketown is a place hostile to
human life, and the embodiment of those dominant social forces
which have become inhumane. *Hard Times* is, then, a conscious
effort by Dickens to generalise the character of his urban
observation. The full title, pointing toward this, is *Hard Times
for These Times*; and Coketown itself, clearly an amalgam of
several northern cities (apparently Oldham, Manchester and
Preston), is meant to be taken as a type for the northern town,
not a specific place. For this reason, Dickens wrote to Peter
Cunningham, the message of *Hard Times* would have 'reference
to the working people all over England' (11 March 1854; NL,
546).

The most important aspect of this new industrial city is its
unnaturalness.[3] Every social and physical feature is exactly the
opposite of what it should be in this 'ugly citadel, where Nature
was as strongly bricked out as killing airs and gases were bricked
in' (63). The 'key-note' of Coketown, as much as the city's

severe workfulness, is this unnaturalness, and the word recurs
with an almost oppressive frequency. Its inhabitants are reduced
to 'an unnatural family, shouldering, and trampling, and
pressing one another to death' (63). (The working people, 'the
Hands', Dickens quips, toying with the current idiom for
factory workers, would have been better off had they been made
'like the lower creatures of the seashore, only hands and stomachs'
[63].) What is even worse is that unlike commercial London,
industrial Coketown is a centre of production, a place where
wealth is generated, but where only those who do no work can
enjoy that wealth, while those who do the work are condemned
to poverty and a living death. (In Stephen Blackpool's dream
[85–6], this is made clear symbolically: his loom is transformed
into his gallows.)

   This unnaturalness is further emphasised by the three recurring images Dickens uses to describe Coketown and its machines:
the Fairy Palace, the serpents and the mad elephants. In them, he
seems to have been groping for ways of expressing how alien
and wrong a place like Coketown was. The Fairy Palace is the
least successful of these, meant to point out how devoid of fancy
the mills really are; they can appear to be Fairy Palaces only to
those wholly ignorant of their interiors or their purposes. The
serpents and elephants, Coketown's totem animals, are also
somewhat inadequate as metaphors for industrial machinery, but
nevertheless express a feeling that the industrial system was both
malevolent (snakes) and out of control (mad elephants).[4]

   This feeling that things are out of control is analogous to the
feeling that permeates *Bleak House*, that London is a kind of
cancerous growth irreversibly enveloping everything around it.
The same can be said of Coketown, whose influence is if anything
more unnatural and corrupting. At the beginning of *Hard Times*,
it extends as far as the Gradgrind house, Stone Lodge, a few miles
out of town, but already the 'neutral ground' between them is
'neither town nor country . . . yet was either spoiled' (11). A few
years later, it stretches fifteen miles further outward, to Bounderby's 'country' house through the agency of 'a railway striding
on many arches over a wild country' scarred 'by [the] fires and
blank shapes' of coalmines and their machinery (167–8). The
monstrous and ruinous spread of Coketown now seems to ac-

celerate: when Sissy and Rachael walk out from Coketown, everything they see in the country around them is spoilt, undermined by the deserted works of abandoned mines, the waste products of the industrial system.

Rural peace is only a cruel 'illusion' for Stephen Blackpool when he leaves Coketown (164–5). When Rachael and Sissy take their peaceful country walk, it is even more of an illusion, for buried in an abandoned shaft, Stephen lies dying beneath their very feet. Later, as Mr Gradgrind journeys at night to find his fugitive son, between Coketown and the port city that is his destination he sees nothing but 'the illimitable flights of steps' and 'wells' of branch railway lines and a nameless, featureless 'swamp' (178). One cannot even properly speak of a spoiled pastoral in Hard Times, for the countryside is not really spoiled —it has simply ceased to exist.

The patterns of imagery that Dickens uses to structure his social ideas within a larger frame of reference are also remarkably similar in both novels. Bleak House opens with fog and rain that can neither produce fertility nor quench the smouldering passion of Lady Dedlock, but yield only mud and uncontrollable floods. The summer that follows raises no crops, but only dries out the land, the city, and their inhabitants, leading to the spontaneous combustion in Krook's shop, and Lady Dedlock's futile self-consuming flight into her past. In Hard Times, this pattern of stunted growth imagery is augmented by the titles of its three parts, 'Sowing', 'Reaping', and 'Garnering'.[5] The novel does not begin with a flood, but with the 'sowing' of its youthful characters, the Gradgrind children, Sissy and Bitzer, in the unnatural soil of Coketown. The needed rain, and analogous mental nourishment in the form of love and fancy, comes too late, unable to prevent the damage of the drought, and another round of tragic fires.

Louisa Gradgrind's life story recapitulates this pattern. As a teenage girl she is crushed by the regimen imposed by her father's educational theory, yet she is not yet wholly dry inside: her face is still brightened by 'a light with nothing to rest upon, a fire with nothing to burn, a starved imagination keeping life in itself somehow' (12). This spark of life is completely extinguished as she matures into a woman and is married to Bounderby. The point is made again just before her near seduction by Harthouse, when she revisits her home to see her dying mother. But the childhood memories awakened in her by this visit are not of the 'garden in the stony ways of this world' as they should be, but only memories 'of the drying up of every spring and fountain in her young heart as it gushed out' (197). Louisa as a woman is completely dried out, with 'a hunger and thirst' (217) that are unquenchable. Even after the rain and the flood, there breaks out within her 'an unwholesome fire' (224) kindled by the viperous Harthouse. (Adding to the irony, the scene where they meet and almost elope is an obvious parody of the temptation of Eve in Eden.) She does not, like Lady Dedlock, consume herself, but the sterile, lonely life Dickens sketches out for her in the novel's last chapter is hardly much of an improvement.

II

I have tried to suggest that in *Hard Times* Dickens extended his analysis of the contemporary city to the industrial north, and though in doing so he located a different source of urban social malaise, the particulars of the indictment of city life remained substantially as they had been in *Bleak House*. It is not often that the continuities of *Hard Times* with Dickens' other works are stressed, but nevertheless they are substantial, and are present not only in relation to the earlier novels but to those that follow as well.

For one thing, the curious moral identity of people and places which Dickens was now stressing and exploring is far more explicit in *Hard Times* than *Bleak House*. As early as *Dombey and Son*, Dickens was consciously making connections between dwelling and dweller, as he did with Dombey and his cold, aristocratic town house. But when, in *Hard Times*, he calls Gradgrind's Stone Lodge 'calculated' (10), an interesting grammatical ambiguity has entered into the description: is the word simply an adjective, or a past participle? The word not only describes a present characteristic, but past action. It was itself calculated, and is the product (and venue) of calculations. The activity it represents explains the nature of the people (Louisa and her brother) who are its 'products'. This relationship holds equally for the multitude's dwellings in Coketown, whose chimneys were 'built in an immense variety of stunted and crooked shapes, as though every house put out a sign of the kind of people who might be expected to be born in it' (63). From this statement to the world of *Little Dorrit*, where a house will collapse under the pressure of moral iniquity committed within its walls, it is but a very short step.

Hard Times looks towards *Little Dorrit* in another striking way. In *Bleak House*, the greatest risks of urban life are essentially various extreme forms of dissolution of the self—madness, dissipation, and/or gradual death. In all these cases, though the danger is to the self, the cause is outside in the world of events and things: it is the relentlessness of the pressure of a cruel reality which breaks the self down. The risks are still the same in the world of *Hard Times*, but the causal agent is no longer external. The agent has moved inside and appears not as the pressure of circumstance but as a disease of the will. Mrs Gradgrind fades into a transparency of life; Sissy's father apparently wills himself away to 'save' her from the Circus; even as a young girl, Louisa is sick of life, sighing that, ' "I was tired . . . I don't know of what—of everything, I think" ' (13).

The key character in understanding this atrophy of the will is Stephen Blackpool, to whom everything in life has become a muddle. The personal muddle centres around his drunkard, whorish wife, from whom he is unable to procure a divorce. His plight was hardly unique—under the current laws, divorce was available only to those wealthy and influential enough to arrange sponsorship and passage of a private parliamentary bill.[6] It is impossible not to see Stephen's situation as in part a fantastic analogue of Dickens' own marital distress. The feeling that he had that he was trapped in his marriage to Catherine, and slowly suffocating in it, exploded only later in 1856–7, but there had been signs of distress for many years previous. (Indeed, Dickens later dated the troubles from the late 1830s.) What is true is that while his despair was growing, he showed few open signs of it yet, even to himself.[7] The directness of the translation of his own disturbed marriage into his fiction argues that he probably was unaware of the parallels: he had repressed the anxiety deeply enough to force it to seek unconscious outlets of expression.

But in Stephen, and many other of the novel's characters, the part of Dickens' character which, before his separation from his wife in 1858, felt only despair and lacked the will to act in any capacity already can be seen. Present in Stephen and Louisa is the germ of the character of Arthur Clennam, whose chilling lament will be, 'I have no will.'

CHAPTER EIGHT

Little Dorrit: People like Houses

More than in any of his earlier novels, the centre of attention in *Little Dorrit* is upon London. Like most of Dickens' novels from *Martin Chuzzlewit* on, it includes locations in other countries and other parts of England, using material culled from his own travels. But no matter how distant these locations are, the narrative and the many characters of the novel are drawn back to London as if by a magnet, from places as far away as China and the Great St Bernard Alpine pass. *Little Dorrit* is unique not only in its insistence upon London, but in the monolithic character of the city it presents. Each time it is described it is exactly the same, painted by Dickens with more consistency here than in any other of his works. We can say of *Little Dorrit* most truthfully that it is 'about' London, as much as it is about any one thing or person. Indeed, in its own labyrinthine complexity, the novel resembles nothing so much as the labyrinthine city in which it is set.

Whenever the city is described, certain words and images recur. Words like 'wilderness', 'grave', 'dark', 'smoke' and 'labyrinth', and images like the desert, the tomb, the unnatural forest or garden, and of course the prison, are used over and over again. This ceaseless repetition builds up a vocabulary which carries deeper and deeper resonances, so that complex effects can be attained with striking economy by the use of a few key words or phrases, potent far out of proportion to their verbal weight.

One passage which illustrates this, though it is by no means brief, occurs about two-thirds of the way through the novel, at a moment when the development of plot and character are temporarily suspended. Arthur Clennam is now at an impasse in his attempts to trace the runaway Tattycoram, to convey Doyce's invention through the Circumlocution Office, and to penetrate the mystery in which he senses his mother is involved. He decides guiltily to fulfil his filial duty and visit his mother. This is the account of the walk to her house:

> It [the house] always affected his imagination as wrathful, mysterious, and sad; and his imagination was sufficiently impressible to see the whole neighbourhood under some dark tinge of its dark shadow. As he went along, upon a dreary night, the dim streets by which he went, seemed all depositories of oppressive secrets. The deserted counting-houses, with their secrets of books and papers . . . ; the banking-houses, with their secrets of books and strong rooms and wills . . . .; the secrets of all the dispersed grinders in the vast mill . . . ; he could have fancied that these things, in hiding, imparted a heaviness to the air. The shadow thickening and thickening as he approached its source, he thought of the secrets of the lonely church-vaults, where the people who had hoarded and secreted in iron coffers were in their turn similarly hoarded, not yet at rest from doing harm; and then of the secrets of the river, as it rolled its turbid tide between two frowning wildernesses of secrets, extending, thick and dense, for many miles, and warding off the free air and the free country swept by winds and wings of birds. (542)

The key word of this passage is obviously 'secret', and its reiteration draws for us the picture of a city oppressed by a boundless multiplicity of unknown and unknowable secrets. Their oppressiveness becomes literal and palpable, thickening the air. This heaviness is associated with the heaviness of the tomb, as Arthur passes a churchyard in which people are secreted, buried now as they once had buried their secrets. From the tomb Arthur's mind next jumps to the putrescent, waste laden river, literally and metaphorically a river of death, and the very heart of the moribund city through which it passes.

This passage is, to be sure, placed by the narrator in Arthur's consciousness, and so it may be argued this is solely his (Arthur's) view of the city. Yet many times in the novel other passages with similar messages are attributed to other characters, many of them more limited in their perceptions of the world than Arthur. If, then, so many characters arrive at the same view of London, the strength of that view is dramatically increased: how, the reader asks, could all of them be wrong? In this way, the view of London grows organically out of the narrative, and never seems imposed by the narrator. In essence, that view is of London as a hostile and alien environment in which life is virtually no longer possible. Its leitmotifs are an overriding atmosphere of suffocation and oppression, the surrounding wildernesses of buildings, and the dark and dank, mysterious river running through it. It is a view of London as a tomb.[1]

As in *Bleak House*, the novel's overall image of city is built not only of general descriptions like that quoted above, but of detailed portraits of individual houses, each of which reflects and elaborates the general pattern. The survey of dwelling places in this novel is equally comprehensive as was that of *Bleak House*: it ranges from the grand Merdle establishment to the gutters of Covent Garden. But even more than in that earlier novel, Dickens is concerned almost exclusively with where characters live, ignoring almost entirely how they spend their time out of their houses, or how they earn the money to rent them. (Throughout the novel there is a peculiarly distrustful attitude towards earning and having money. Hardly anyone 'works'; that is, engages in activity which produces wealth rather than in activity which merely transfers existing money from one pocket to another. Cavaletto and Doyce are the two major exceptions. Money in *Little Dorrit* seems so deeply involved with moral taint that even to have it is a sign of guilt. As in the passage quoted above, it is often linked with death, the earth, and even excrement; as when Mrs General asks about her defunct husband's bank deposits of 'dust and ashes' [447]. These associations were to be explored by Dickens in much more detail several years later in *Our Mutual Friend*.)

For example, at the higher reaches of the novel's cross-section of society is the house of the head Circumlocutive Barnacle in Mews Street, one of 'two or three small airless houses' in 'a hideous little street of dead wall, stables and dung-hills' (109). This is, one should note, an extremely desirable and expensive house. Even Hampton Court Palace, where Mrs Gowan and other select pensioners of the Crown live, is allowed to be no more than a 'dreary red-brick dungeon' (311). There is Mr Casby's house, located in a street 'which had run itself out of breath' almost before it had been built, amidst 'a wilderness patched with unfruitful gardens' (144). Lower down the social ladder is Bleeding Heart Yard, a nearly derelict ruin, set down in a 'maze of shabby streets' (135), whose inhabitants are quite literally bled dry to meet the extortionate rents charged by Casby, the landlord.[2] But those who live in the Yard are still more fortunate than those who have no home but the streets, 'homeless people, lying coiled up in nooks' on the streets (174).

With so many examples like this already before us, the groundwork is amply laid for a passage such as this description of elegant Mayfair which occurs near the end of Book I:

> It was now summer-time; a grey, hot, dusty evening. They rode to the top of Oxford Street, and there alighting, dived in among the great streets of melancholy stateliness, and the little streets that try to be as stately and succeed in being more melancholy, of which there is a labyrinth near Park Lane. Wildernesses of corner houses, with barbarous old porticoes and appurtenances; horrors that came into existence under some wrong-headed person in some wrong-headed time, still demanding the blind admiration of all ensuing generations and determined to do so until they tumbled down; frowned upon the twilight. Parasite little tenements, with the cramp in their whole frame, from the dwarf hall-door on the giant model of His Grace's in the Square to the squeezed window of the boudoir commanding the dunghills in the Mews, made the evening doleful. Rickety dwellings of undoubted fashion, but of a capacity to hold nothing comfortably except a dismal smell, looked like the last result of the great mansions breeding in-and-in; and, where their little supplementary bows and balconies were supported on thin iron columns, seemed to be scrofulously resting upon crutches. (324)

Effect is piled on effect with tremendous, unrelenting power. The cumulative result is to turn the buildings of London into 'a brick and mortar funeral' (325), and the entire city into its own funerary monument.

Not even Mr Merdle, the great and powerful financier, can escape the dismal city, living as he does in an expensive but very grim terrace house on Harley Street. This is how the street is depicted:

> Like unexceptionable Society, the opposing rows of houses in Harley Street were very grim with one another. Indeed, the mansions and their inhabitants were so much alike in that respect, that the people were often to be found drawn up on opposite sides of dinner-tables, in the shade of their own loftiness, staring at the other side of the way with the dulness of the houses. (246)

The fact of the similarity of houses and occupants is noted here as a small but pointed joke, but it is characteristic of Dickens' fictional method that a theme so urgent in the novel should appear so casually. 'People like houses they inhabit' had been Dickens' note for this chapter in his number plan,[3] and so they are. As we have seen, this relation first appeared in *Dombey and Son* and was explored in greater depth in *Bleak House*, and in *Hard Times*. In those novels, the relation had developed into a tool for exploring the way that the social system was manifest in the lives of individuals. In *Little Dorrit* the equation again takes a central place in the novel's structure, but with new and profound reverberations of meaning.

II

The relation of identity between dweller and dwelling is most clearly exhibited in the case of Mrs Clennam and her house. Along with the Marshalsea, this house is one of the two magnetic poles of London, attracting to it almost all of the novel's important characters, and determining their fates within its walls. To Arthur, it is the very centre of the city's gloom, and in a literal sense this is true, for in its very walls are hidden the papers which have kept secret the existence of a legacy which would have freed William Dorrit and his family from the Marshalsea. Further back in the remote past, Mrs Clennam had perpetrated the novel's other major deed of evil, stealing Arthur from his natural mother, thereby ruining his life, her life and her husband's life.[4]

When the novel turns to London from Marseilles, with

Dickens' much celebrated portrait of 'a Sunday evening in London, gloomy, close and stale' (28), the climax of the description of the city is the picture of the old house down by the river:

> An old brick house, so dingy as to be all but black, standing by itself within a gateway. Before it, a square court-yard where a shrub or two and a patch of grass were as rank (which is saying much) as the iron railings enclosing them were rusty; behind it, a jumble of roots. It was a double house, with long, narrow, heavily-framed windows. Many years ago, it had had it in its mind to slide down sideways; it had been propped up, however, and was leaning on some half-dozen gigantic crutches; which . . . weather-stained, smoke-blackened, and overgrown with weeds, appeared in these latter days to be no very sure reliance. (31)

This more than half ruined house, yet another in the long series of tumbledown variant refractions of the Blacking Warehouse, is as terrifying as its original. The image of the house on crutches is of a house about to die, and the aura of death is even more tangible inside. Over the door is 'a projecting canopy in carved work, of festooned jack-towels and children's heads with water on the brain, designed after a once-popular monumental pattern' (31)—in other words, a tombstone. The tomb motif predominates: there is a cellar 'like a sort of coffin in compartments'; a staircase 'panelled off into spaces like so many mourning tablets'; 'a black bier-like sofa' with a bolster 'like the block at a State execution'; and throughout the smell of black dye (33).[5]

In such a house one is hardly surprised to find that the butler (if Flintwinch can so be described) has 'a wierd appearance of having hanged himself at one time or other, and of having gone about ever since, halter and all' (37). Clearly, if people are like their houses, and their houses are tombs, they must be (as Frederick Dorrit is), 'dead without being aware of it' (236). By extension, the entire city is a necropolis, inhabited by the dead, as these references hint: Flora is described as 'a mummer . . . at her own funeral' (150); Fanny complains that to be in her fashionable house is like 'lying in a well' (693); and when Little Dorrit asks the prostitute in Covent Garden what she is doing, she answers bluntly, ' "Killing myself" ' (175). Indeed, not only

London but the world is a tomb. Calais is described as nothing
but 'an unsightly marine cemetary' (653); the hostel at the Great
St Bernard is crammed full of frozen corpses; and Italy is a
country where there is 'nothing to do but die' (465).

At the centre of this dead world is the old house, and at the
centre of the old house, dressed always in black 'as if attired for
execution' (353), sits Mrs Clennam, paralysed from the waist
down by her mysterious affliction, and so literally half dead. And
at the core of the conception of her identity is her stern Evangelical religion. In the novel, her religion is indicted as the root
cause of her life-denying and evil activities.

Her fierce Christianity is based firstly upon the firm conviction
of her own election to grace. This conviction, of the certitude of
her salvation, ensures that all her actions are justified and morally
righteous. Thus, she can excuse her persecution of Arthur's
natural mother by saying, ' "If I threatened her, then and afterwards, with the terrors [of damnation] that encompassed her,
did I not hold them in my right hand?" ' (777) This is the
activity in which she is engaged when we first see her, 'sternly
fiercely, wrathfully—praying that her enemies . . . might be
utterly exterminated' (35).

Yet more revealing are her relations with her husband. E. P.
Thompson has commented that Methodism and Evangelicalism
were 'permeated with teaching as to the sinfulness of sexuality'
yet had an obsessional . . . concern with sexuality' that revealed
itself both in constant preaching about the evils of the flesh, and
in the perverted eroticism of the Church services.[6] Dickens seems
to have been well aware of this aspect of Evangelical fervour; he
has Blandois aptly describe Mrs Clennam as ' "without love" '
and ' "cold as the stone" ', yet also ' "raging as the fire" ' (772),
burning with a passion only too obviously sexual in origin. Even
after forty years, her jealousy of her husband's lover is so
extreme it arouses in her violent rage. She can never forgive him
having taken ' "a guilty creature in my place" ' (775). The result
has been a marriage entirely without sex, as she intimates when
she states, ' "Arthur's father and I have lived no further apart,
with half the globe between us, than when we were together in
this house." ' (777). It is not difficult to see that what she denied
him is what she herself had desired most.

Most significant of Mrs Clennam's beliefs are those about childhood, the horrific results of which are visible in the stunted character of her adopted son. In strict accordance with accepted Evangelical practice, Arthur's birth was taken as presumptive evidence of his moral iniquity. As Mrs Sherwood, authoress of a popular Methodist child rearing guide, wrote: 'All children are by nature evil.... Pious and prudent parents must check their naughty passions in any way they have in their power....'[7] Since Arthur was a bastard, his soul was in even greater peril, and so Mrs Clennam's task was made more urgent by the need ' "to reclaim the otherwise pre-destined and lost boy; to give him the reputation of an honest origin; to bring him up in fear and trembling" ' (777).

This is what she does, as Arthur remembers well and often. Walking through London on a Sunday reminds Arthur of 'the dreary Sunday of his childhood', passed reading tracts damning him to perdition (29). Reentering his home, his first childhood memory is of a closet, 'of which he had been many a time the sole contents in days of punishment' (33). Yet one feels quite strongly that this cruel physical punishment of solitary confinement is hardly worth noting in comparison with the mental tortures routinely inflicted upon him. He had been allowed no toys, no playmates, and later no opportunity for romantic involvement. Equally involved in this routine deprivation is the house itself. Arthur's old garret room is described as 'even uglier and grimmer than the rest':

> Its moveables were ugly old chairs with worn-out seats, and ugly old chairs without any seats; a threadbare patternless carpet, a maimed table, a crippled wardrobe, a lean set of fire-irons like the skeleton of a set deceased, a washing-stand that looked as if it had stood for ages in a hail of dirty soapsuds, and a bedstead with four bare atomies [sic—anatomies?] of posts, each terminating in a spike, as if for the dismal accommodation of lodgers who might prefer to impale themselves. (37–8)

The view from the window is of 'the old blasted and blackened forest of chimneys, and the old red glare in the sky which had seemed to him once upon a time but a nightly reflection of the fiery environment that was presented to his childhood fancy in

all directions' (38)—in other words, hell. With such a back-
ground, one need not wonder that Arthur at the age of forty
is a mental cripple, lacking in 'will'. The wilful child has been
transformed by systematic brutality into the will-less man.[8]

However, it is not possible to ascribe responsibility for these
crimes solely to Mrs Clennam. Dickens previously had attacked
Evangelical abuse against life and childhood through the Murd-
stones in David Copperfield, but their motivation is simple greed,
and Dickens does not allow us any further insight into their
behaviour.[9] They can be despised and condemned, and quickly
forgotten. With Mrs Clennam this is not the case. We are told
a number of things about her that complicate our response. For
one thing, her suffering, though it be hysterical in its origins, is
genuine, and for many years she has been unable to walk, and
confined to a single room.

Even more germane is her long confession to Blandois in Book
II, Chapter xxx, 'Closing In', which is an explanation for all of
her actions. She pointedly refers to her own childhood:

> 'You do not know what it is . . . to be brought up strictly. I
> was so brought up. Mine were days of wholesome repression,
> punishment, and fear. The corruption of our hearts, the evil
> of our ways, the curse that is upon us, the terrors that sur-
> round us—these were the themes of my childhood. They
> formed my character, and filled me with an abhorrence of
> evil-doers.' (774)

This chilling evocation of her own childhood needs no explanation. From it, it is clear that the very same weapons of fear that
were used against the child Arthur to make him what he became
had been used to mould the character of his mother during her
childhood. What she did to him was not an isolated crime whose
responsibility neatly can be apportioned to her, but part of a
cycle of psychic and physical deprivation, an endless cycle in
which inadequate parents produce maimed children who themselves become, in turn, inadequate parents. Each successive
generation is doomed, even before it is born.

The emphasis Dickens places on the religious aspects of the
explanation of the novel's plot by Mrs Clennam, coming as it
does at the climax of the novel, suggests that he intended

Evangelical Christianity in general to be seen as one of the key crippling social forces in England at the present time. The broad, panoramic sketch of the labyrinthine city and its condemned inmates on a Sunday evening which opens the novel is, after all, a direct attack on Sabbitarian zeal. The extreme suitability of Evangelical belief to sharp business practices is also noted. One might, perhaps, hesistate to claim (as one critic has) that 'the attack on puritanism and its commercial ethic . . . stands right at the heart of the whole definition of contemporary society.'[10] But this is at least implied by Dickens' observations of the way in which Evangelical fervour had permeated all forms and areas of social life, not only serving to cast a gloomy pall over the nation, but neatly coinciding with and acting as a rationale for commercial greed and exploitation. In this, Dickens strikingly anticipated the modern historical judgment, first formulated by Elie Halévy, that Methodism and the broadly based Evangelical movement it generated, were among the primary forces shaping every aspect of social life in Victorian England.[11] In the novel, this perception is what links Mrs Clennam to the novel's other social villains.

III

Further evidencing her central role in the novel, Mrs Clennam can be seen to be representative of the other evil characters. Her crimes, in essence, are crimes against the free expression of human will, whether it be in the form of childhood play, in the erotic form of romantic or sexual love, or in the form of any manifestation of spontaneity or creative imagination. To her mind all these are sinful, and in her battle to crush them she is linked to the many other individual and corporate villains of the novel. (Similarly, the good characters are all defenders of the free, untramelled will. Little Dorrit's goodness, for example, is linked to artistic and religious imagination: 'Shall we speak of the inspiration of a poet or a priest', Dickens asks, 'and not of the heart impelled by love and self-devotion to the lowliest work in the lowliest way of life!' [71])

The Circumlocution Office, for example, is dedicated to stifling and suppressing all political change and innovation; it crushes by its intractability the nation's political imagination, as it does Doyce's 'invention'; and drains the will and resources of the body politic through waste, inefficiency and nepotistic patronage. In the realm of Society, Mrs General, who is the symbolic representative of the prevailing attitudes toward social relations and the question of class, performs a similar function. She is referred to as a vampirish 'Ghoule in gloves' (612), alluding to the way in which she seeks to drain the life out of interpersonal contact, and also to her efforts to insure that 'human imagination should be chilled to stone' (610). In other social spheres, other characters do much the same. Gowan, for example, practices in his painting a sterile mockery of the creative arts which degrades the national taste, and which base art drives the good from the public eye. Casby is another like figure: earlier, he had helped to prevent the marriage of Arthur to Flora, and as has been mentioned above, bleeds the life out of his poor tenants in Bleeding Heart Yard.

One of the most important social villains is Mr Merdle, who though he may be personally insignificant, stands at the pinnacle of a financial system based on the brutal exploitation of the lower and middle classes of society. The Merdle system is a form of social madness, which is explicitly compared to an epidemic disease: 'Bred at first, as many physical diseases are, in the wickedness of men, and then disseminated in their ignorance, these epidemics, after a period, get communicated to those who are neither ignorant nor wicked' (582). This disease leads countless innocent individuals to 'invest' their faith in the belief that through Merdle their life savings can be converted into huge fortunes. In a system where money has become the universal social indicator, able to buy anything from a family coat of arms to a seat in Parliament, their folly can be excused. But not that of their exploiters: a financial system based on speculation no longer has any relation to actual production, but merely drains the pockets of the classes who do work to fill those of the rich who do not. In this way the economic lifeblood of the nation is drained and wasted. That Merdle dies by slitting his wrists and thus draining his own blood is cruel but fitting retribution for his crimes in ruining tens of thousands of others along with himself.

The house of Merdle proves rotten to the core and collapses of
its own weight, having proved no more secure than will the old
house of Mrs Clennam. Seen in this light, the old house takes on
added significance, for in so far as it is the central example of
all the literal and figurative rotten houses of the novel, it is the
objective correlative of the diseased will of society. The house is
an analogue of the social structure, and like the house, the social
edifice is a decaying relic of the past, propped up by its many
crutches, having long outlived its usefulness. The narrator tells
us as much, for when Little Dorrit sees destitute young children
in Covent Garden living like rats, he warns, 'Look to the rats
young and old, all ye Barnacles, for before God they are eating
away our foundations, and will bring the roofs on our heads!'
(166) Society is a structure which, again like the old house, will
produce and go on producing maimed citizens in a ceaseless
vicious cycle of deprivation, as long as it stands.

Yet even more terrifying than this is the suggestion that the
system is propped up and sustained by those who suffer most
from it. Many characters, like the prostitute Little Dorrit meets,
are busy destroying themselves, but unlike her, unaware of what
they are doing. As a psychiatrist examining the novel purely
from a clinical viewpoint has written, '*Little Dorrit* gives a
cross-section of diversified types of psychic masochism.'[12] Believing all the while that they are engaged in normal, healthy
social behaviour, character after character is involved in brutal
self-directed aggression.

Clennam is one of the greatest practitioners of the art. He
believes himself to be prematurely old and used up, and so no
longer able to experience romantic love. This is not the case, and
after his brief attraction to Pet Meagles he wilfully denies himself the curative and life-giving love of Little Dorrit until it is
almost too late for him, simultaneously and unwittingly causing
her needless pain. Other characters are engaged in like activity:
Edmund Sparkler, falling in love with the hateful and bitter
Fanny Dorrit, places 'a heavy set of fetters' on himself (502);
while Fanny's own flight toward destruction is wholly 'self-
willed' (596). Similarly, Pet Meagles, in her fatal attachment to
Gowan, is 'self-deceived' (336). Indeed, while Little Dorrit's
subservience to her family is presented as a noble act of sacrifice,

it is not much different in its debilitating effects on her. The book is peopled by 'a collection of voluntary human sacrifices' (512).

More mystifying are those characters who are aware they are destroying themselves, yet still take delight in doing so. Tatty-coram runs away from the Meagles family to live in mutual agony with Miss Wade, yet when Arthur asks her to return to them, she cries, ' "I'd tear myself to pieces first!" ' (329) By staying with Miss Wade, she does just that. Miss Wade herself is a prime example. Like Dostoevsky's underground man, whom she greatly resembles, she is fully aware of her malady, but takes pleasure in placing herself in relations with other people that exacerbate it, and show her to worst advantage. Some critics have felt uneasy about Miss Wade, but Dickens felt that her confession, 'The History of a Self-Tormentor', was essential to the story; he even went out of his way to insert it as an interpolated tale through an improbable manipulation of plot (she calls Arthur to Calais for no reason but to give him the manuscript). When Forster advised Dickens this was too clumsy, he defended it by raising the example of Fielding, and pronounced that 'the blood of the book circulate[s]' through it (*Life*, II, 185). Dickens was aware that Miss Wade is only an extreme sufferer from what he saw to be the general social malaise.

It is this wilful self-destructive activity which also makes the prisons of the novel as difficult to escape as they are. Mrs Clenham's self-imposed incarceration in the old house is more crippling than any physical malady, made even more so because she does understand in some sense that she is paying with her paralysis for the crimes she has committed against the Dorrits. From the start of the novel, Arthur Clennam seems determined to orphan and bankrupt himself to rid himself of the guilt his family and fortune carry in his eyes. That he does both, and ends in the Marshalsea, is as much his own responsibility as that of Merdle or society. William Dorrit is the most touching of these many self-jailors, for the twenty-four years of his imprisonment have not changed his firm trust in the very social values and institutions which once had bankrupted him, financially and morally. Thus, he is doomed to carry his prison with him wherever he goes.

The terrifying message of *Little Dorrit* is that the crutch which props up the decrepit social structure is our own continuing, self-deluding belief in the system. As in Dante's *Inferno*, it is impossible to escape 'the prison of this lower world' (763) because that which we desire above all is the particular form of our own punishment and imprisonment.

IV

The unmitigated atmosphere of despair which pervades *Little Dorrit* is so intense that one is compelled to ask why this is so. Certainly, from the late 1840s on, Dickens' fictional social criticism had been growing more severe in tone and more radical in its thrust. *Bleak House* is in its way as thorough a critique of contemporary society as *Little Dorrit*, but even in that novel there is an optimistic ending. In *Hard Times*, which refutes the specifics of that optimism, there is nevertheless in the Circus a strong symbol and focus for the forces affirming the power of love, compassion, fellow-feeling and the spontaneous creative imagination. In *Little Dorrit* there is only the tiny, passive figure of Amy Dorrit herself, whose quiet devotion to her crippled family, and later her crippled husband, accomplish almost nothing in the face of the overwhelming social powers arrayed against her.

Dickens' journalism from the years 1853 and 1854 onward reveals the same underlying tone of despair. The journalism of the early years of *Household Words* is characterised by attacks on specific abuses, such as poor water supply, poor sanitation, and above all poor housing, and by suggestions or demands for specific reforms, new laws and new programmes for Parliament and the nation to adopt. The articles written during the gestation of *Little Dorrit* show even by their titles alone the change in emphasis to a more general attack on Government and the nation's institutions: they include a three part series called 'The Thousand and One Humbugs' (21 April, 28 April, 5 May 1855; *MP*, 516–36), which tells in vicious satiric fable form of the many ways the governing classes rob the people; 'The Toady Tree' (26 May 1855; *MP*, 536–41), which catalogues innocent but self-destructive support for the class system among the unprivileged classes; and 'The Great Baby' (4 August 1855; MP, 533–9), which discusses examples of the way in which Government treats the People as a great, ignorant infant.[13]

Behind these articles is apparent Dickens' loss of faith in the ability of Parliament to govern the nation, or for that matter the ability of the nation to govern itself under present conditions. To be sure, since his days in the Gallery of the House of Commons Dickens had never thought much of Parliament, but for all his jocular disdain for the legislature (and his refusal several times to stand for certain election), he was never so extreme in his views as to conceive of the English nation without it. Now he did. When Austin Layard had begun his campaign for administrative reform early in the Spring of 1855, Dickens offered to work with him, almost the only time in his career he engaged in practical political activity. But he retained doubts about the enterprise; in April 1855 he had written to Layard, 'There is nothing so galling and so alarming to me as the alienation of the people from their own public affairs' (10 April 1855; NL, II, 651). He went on to compare England's condition to that of France immediately before the Revolution. The spectre of revolution continued to haunt Dickens during the next five years. The riots in Hyde Park over the strict Sabbitarian measures of Lord Robert Grosvenor's Sunday Trading Bill then before Parliament seemed a certain portent to him. 'I am sorry for what occurred in Hyde Park,' he wrote to Miss Coutts, 'but it is an illustration of . . . the extraordinary ignorance on the part of those who make the laws, of what is behind us, and what is ever ready to break in if it is too long despised' (27 June 1855; MS., PML). That same evening (27 June 1855) he gave a long and dramatic speech for Layard's Administrative Reform Association, but this involvement with it soon ceased. As he had feared, the group could not break through the nation's apathetic attitude toward government. As long as this was the case, he no longer saw any hope for progress through a change in the ballot extending suffrage, as he wrote to Macready that autumn (4 October 1855; NL, II, 695).

The events of those years seemed to Dickens to be proving him right. The revelations in *The Times* of the Crimean fiasco during the winter of 1854–5 had revealed just how corrupt and mismanaged the conduct of the nation's business was. The dissolution

of Chadwick's General Board of Health late in 1854 in effect
had been an admission that the sanitary reform of the metropolis
so far had failed. The Thames which Dickens in *Little Dorrit*
called with no exaggeration an open sewer was more so than
ever before, and more visibly: the smell became so offensive
during the summers of 1855–8 that several times Parliament was
compelled to interrupt its sessions so members could escape the
stench. In 1857, he was telling the Earl of Carlisle[14] that he was
now 'a grievous Radical, and [thought] the political signs of the
times to be just about as bad as the spirit of the people will admit
of their being' (15 April 1857; NL, II, 844).

For all the ominous signs, one cannot but sense that Dickens'
analysis of the state of the nation was incorrect. In retrospect, it
is perhaps easier for us than Dickens to see as the outstanding
feature of political life in the mid and late 1850s its stability. Yet
no better symbol for the nation's steadfast adherence to its faith
in ancient institutions could have been found than the Prime
Minister Lord Palmerston, at seventy-one in 1855 himself seeming almost as old as those very institutions, and very much alive
despite persistent worries about his age. The governing structure
of the nation was far more resilient than Dickens expected, and
it was even at that moment at last laying the groundwork for
effective sanitary reform, and taking measures which led to the
establishment of the modern Civil Service administration. The
revolutionary upsurge Dickens feared was imminent was never a
real possibility, and no great signs of general popular unrest were
to emerge until the mid 1860s, in the years immediately preceding the second great Reform Bill.

Thinking back to Dickens' sane appraisal of the impossibility
of insurrection amidst the general hysteria preceding the last
Chartist demonstration in 1848, it is all the more obvious how
far from being in touch with the condition of the nation he now
was. In the end, his despair must be attributed more to personal
circumstances than to an objective reading of the social health
of England at mid-century. His despair came from within; as
Lionel Trilling wrote in his excellent Introduction to the novel
(in the *Oxford Illustrated Dickens* edition): 'We may say of
Dickens that at the time of *Little Dorrit* he was at a crisis of the
will which is expressed in the characters and forces of the novel,

in the extremity of its bitterness against the social will, in its vision of peace and selflessness' (xiv).

The source of this malaise of the will, which could lead Dickens to put so much of himself into the will-less Arthur Clennam, is complex but clearly centres around his growing dissatisfaction with his marriage. Though Forster dates the critical tension in the Dickens marriage from about 1850, and 'an unsettled feeling greatly in excess of what was usual' from the summer of 1853 (*Life*, II, 193), a more immediate cause was a chance reunion with Maria Beadnell, his first great love, whom he had not seen in twenty years. She appears in the novel as Flora, as giddy and romantic as ever, but now at forty, fat and ridiculous.

One can only speculate why in the first instance Dickens' 'usual' restlessness and frenetic nervous energy should have intensified steadily over these years. But I suspect that the later meeting with Maria, and thinking of the time he had courted her before he had become successful and famous, tended to increase the contrast between the happy, ideal marriage he had always expected and the pleasant but ordinary one he had. 'Why is it,' he wrote to Forster, 'that . . . a sense comes always crushing on me now, when I fall into low spirits, as of one happiness I have missed in life, and one friend and companion I have never made?' (*Life*, II, 197) Yet it would be wrong to see this as only a marital crisis. Despite his fame, his fortune, as well as his family, Dickens felt that in some vague sense his whole life was a failure: increasingly he could find no rest from his mental anguish save exercise in walking and in work. For Dickens, just as walking meant a thirty mile hike, work meant gruelling over-work. But it was, as he wrote to Forster, 'Much better to die, doing', than to allow himself to be idle and suffer the pain of his deep depression (*Life*, II, 196).

As always in times of great stress, the memories of his child-hood ordeal in London returned forcefully to Dickens. These memories surfaced in many ways in *Little Dorrit*. The two polar locations of the novel, the old house and the Marshalsea, are cognate images of the Blacking Warehouse and the prison where John Dickens had been incarcerated for debt. Though the crazy tumbledown warehouse overlooking the river is considerably changed in the book, the prison is not. For the very first time (markedly unlike *David Copperfield*, where the Marshalsea had been turned into the King's Bench prison), Dickens dealt openly and directly with the crushing pain of his father's imprisonment for debt. The character of Little Dorrit, an adult in years but a tiny child in outside form, is in a way autobiographical, representing the stunted part of Dickens' psyche which had never outgrown the terrors of Hungerford Stairs and the debtors prison in the Borough, even after thirty years.[15]

The despair that permeates *Little Dorrit* is largely the despair of a man who felt that at the pinnacle of his career and fame, he was still burdened by the memories—to him often more real than the present time—of the terror he had felt as a child. Those memories seemed a prison he could not escape, just as the child must have felt he could never escape his drudgery and poverty. In the face of this burden of the past, Dickens resigned the struggle of his entire life to overcome it. He no longer had the will to drive himself to his usual superhuman efforts. Feeling trapped also in a hateful marriage just as securely and completely as by his own past, Dickens abandoned—albeit temporarily—all hope of active engagement in life.

V

As the memories of London returned, so did those that invariably accompanied them, of the happy years immediately preceding them in the Kentish countryside. They emerge in the novel as a set of allusions to and evocations of a pastoral world located in the London hinterlands. And it is often tantalisingly suggested that in this pastoral an escape from the city and death is to be found.

Many characters nurture fond dreams of the peaceful countryside. Little Dorrit's fondest childhood memories, as were Dickens' own, are of the country, 'the meadows or green lanes' (70) where the old turnkey of the Marshalsea had taken her on Sunday afternoons. A rural childhood seems to be quite sought after in the novel. Even the vile Casby has hanging in his parlour a portrait of himself at age ten, 'disguised with a hay-making rake ... and sitting (on one of his own legs) upon a bank of violets, moved to precocious contemplation by the spire of a village church' (145). John Chivery regards a few vestiges of garden near the Marshalsea as 'a very Arbour' (212). The Plornish family maintains 'a little fiction . . . in the wall [of their sitting room] being painted to represent the exterior of a thatched cottage' aptly named 'Happy Cottage' (573–4).

The most notable attributes of all these dreams are peace and quiet, and nowhere are they more completely manifest than in the Meagles' cottage at Twickenham. It is far from London's din, suitably old (though partly remodelled to fit the family's needs), and even better, near 'the peaceful river' (191). However, the power of this pastoral retreat is not very great. It certainly cannot actively combat the influence of the city, for Tattycoram and Pet are both lured from it to their destruction. Its passive, restorative powers are equally illusory, for it is here Clennam mistakenly decides he has become 'Nobody', and resigns from his own emotional life.

In truth, the attraction of the countryside is the hope of attaining 'insensibility' (200). In this, it is in essence hardly different from the prison against which it is opposed. When Amy Dorrit is born in the Marshalsea, the attending physician attempts to reassure Mr Dorrit that her birth in such a place is no disadvantage. He explains how pleasant it truly is:

'A little more elbow-room is all we want here. We are quiet here; we don't get badgered here; there's no knocker here, sir, to be hammered at by creditors. . . . It's freedom, sir, it's freedom! . . . I don't know that I have ever pursued it [my profession] under such quiet circumstances, as here this day. Elsewhere, people are restless, worried, hurried about, anxious. . . . Nothing of the kind here, sir. We have done all that—we know the worst of it; we have got to the bottom, we can't fall, and what have we found? Peace.' (63)

Unfortunately, we know that the peace and quiet of the Marshalsea is a form of living death, but one step away from the grave—'a living grave', Little Dorrit calls it (231).

The two great scenes on the Iron Bridge, as Southwark Bridge was known, are another evocation of the pastoral amidst the city, for there it is 'as quiet after the roaring streets, as though it had been open country' (96). Here, too, the peace is only an illusion, for it is the place where Arthur in his blindness wounds Little Dorrit by persisting in thinking of her only as a child and not a woman. Peace in any form can only be had at the expense of life.[16] Similarly, escape to another country, for example to the pure, clean Alps of Switzerland where travellers feel as if they have 'entered on a new existence', is again only a 'delusion' (452). Mrs Clennam's self-incarnation in the quiet of her room is a kindred delusion, in that she believes in it she can shut out the world. This vain attempt only increases the shock of 'the overwhelming rush of the reality' of the city streets (787), when she is forced to emerge into them from her seclusion.

Running through the evocation of the pastoral dream at Twickenham is the river, the very embodiment of those seductive virtues of peace and quiet. But it is so only far upstream; by the time it has passed through the city it has become a deadly sewer, defiling everything it touches. At the other end is the ocean, representing here as always in Dickens, dissolution and eternity. This course of the river is a paradigm of human life: we are innocent in childhood, corrupted and defiled in maturity, and end in death. And despite the overtly Christian significance loaded upon Little Dorrit, death in this world does not offer much to hope for. Redemption has receded so far almost as to be impossible; Dickens writes that 'so deep a hush was on the sea, that it scarcely whispered of the time when it shall give up as dead' (14), the Day of Judgment and the Resurrection. In this life there is only the possibility elaborated by Doyce's (and Dickens') dictum that, ' "You hold your life on the condition that to the last you shall struggle hard for it" ' (189), The struggle, and one's duty, are all one can ever have.

The unbearable gloom and despair of *Little Dorrit* led Shaw to exclaim that, 'as soon as the Englishman realised that *Little Dorrit* was true there would be a revolution.'[17] Indeed, if it were, a revolution would be the only way to end the endless destructive cycle of the social machine. Virtually the only hope left in the novel is that of final Apocalypse, dimply foreshadowed by the collapse of the old house. Society may collapse under its own weight or through Divine intervention—but in the here and now, human action is powerless to alter it. Arthur and Little Dorrit may marry, yet the 'bricks and bars' of the Marshalsea will continue to bear 'uniformly the same dead crop' (815) as always. They will nurse each other's wounded spirits, take care of the mental cripple Maggie and moral cripple Tip, and so lead a 'modest life of usefulness and happiness' (826). But when they go 'down' into the world it is as ministering angels in a literal Hell of 'roaring streets', with no effect upon the 'arrogant and the froward and the vain, fretted and chafed' (826) damned souls who inhabit it.

CHAPTER NINE

A Tale of Two Cities, *The Uncommercial Traveller* and *Great Expectations*: Paradise Revisited

The despairing tone of resignation with which *Little Dorrit* closes leaves unanswered the question of how the battered individual can achieve regeneration. The two novels that followed *Little Dorrit*, *A Tale of Two Cities* and *Great Expectations*, and Dickens' occasional writings in *The Uncommercial Traveller* between them, centre around this problem. Initially, Dickens explored the question of individual regeneration in two parts: first, as a struggle by victims of a morally corrupting and apparently unchaneable social system to reintigrate their shattered selves and lead something like normal lives; and second, as a struggle by characters who are themselves in some way morally culpable to atone for their actions, usually through an act of self-sacrifice. In *A Tale of Two Cities*, these two facets of the central problem are studied through two characters, Charles Darnay and Sidney Carton, who are in more senses than one *alter egos*. In *Great Expectations*, they are explored through a single character, Pip.

Certainly this question, how the individual is to be made whole and healthy again, is never far from one's attention in *Little Dorrit*, but the later emphasis on atonement, which must be entirely a personal action, and the consequent turning away from engagement in (and the possibility of changing) the social world, is a striking development. By comparing Arthur Clennam and Pip this development is more clearly revealed: both are dogged by a sense of guilt, but only Pip has something to be guilty about. Clennam is primarily a victim, but Pip is victim and victimiser both. At the close of the novels, Arthur is saved by the actions of others, but Pip is the sole architect of his own salvation.

This movement away from the purely social toward the purely personal is mirrored in a change in the quality of the actualisation of the world at large in *Great Expectations*. *Little Dorrit* is set in the 1820s, but clearly invokes contemporary England in the 1850s. The later novel is also set in the 1820s, but if anything Dickens seems intent on keeping it there, constantly having Pip note that various social problems of that time no longer exist. There is no institutional abuse to compare with the Circumlocution Office, which is Dickens' last sustained and specific novelistic political attack.[1] Newgate is the type of the social institutions of *Great Expectations*, but it is not seen as an institution which can be improved, or even swept away, but rather as an unchanging part of the landscape of the world of the novel, as much so as the marshes are. The movement these novels take, then, is from the problems of people who live in England in the 1850s to the problems of people who live in any human society at all.[2]

Paralleling this movement is another, even more complex process of reassessment, involving Dickens' deepest and most cherished belief, in the ideal and idyllic nature of the years he had spent as a child in Chatham and the Kent countryside. Even in the middle novels, from *Barnaby Rudge* to *Dombey and Son*, and more so in the later novels, especially *Bleak House* and *Little Dorrit*, where the pastoral in any real sense is rejected by Dickens, the pastoral image rooted in his personal myth of a rural childhood Golden Age had continued to hold a special kind of power over his imagination. The picture he had retained of his life during those early years, almost magical in its effect, was always attractive enough to need thorough consideration before it could yet again be rejected, though its rejection was always certain.

But as Dickens explored the ways in which his fictional characters were themselves responsible for their personal failures, he began to consider his own life in the same way. Was the acute sense of failure he felt—and we have seen that he felt he had failed in much more than his marriage—also of his own making? Dickens had been long accustomed to trace the formation of his character back to his ordeal at Warren's Blacking; as Forster put it, 'to find, at extreme points in his life, the explanation of himself in these early trials' (*Life*, 1, 34). The severe stress and anxiety he was experiencing now was such an 'extreme' point in his life, and it was to that early time he was increasingly drawn over the next few years. As he wrote to Forster in 1862, with more than a touch of sadness, 'something of the character' of himself as a child had 'reappeared in the last five years. The never-to-be-forgotten misery of that old time bred a certain shrinking sensitiveness . . . that I have found come back in the never-to-be-forgotten misery of this later time' (*Life*, 1, 35). During that period he struggled to find the roots of his own identity, even further back than the Blacking Warehouse, in the time of that cherished myth before it. It was a difficult and agonising search, but one he could not fail to pursue—and considering his persistence in the face of the pain it generated, one that can be called nothing less than heroic.

II

A Tale of Two Cities

These fictional developments clearly are related to the emotional distress and events of the final years of Dickens' marriage, and to its collapse in May 1858. As Dickens proceeded toward the completion of *Little Dorrit* in the spring of 1857, he grew more anxious, for now even his customary therapeutic activity of writing would be gone, at least for the time being. Having written a play the previous year with Wilkie Collins, *The Frozen Deep*,[3] and thrown himself into an 'amateur' production of it in January, had done little good, providing only temporary distraction. A new note of urgency entered his already unhealthy state of mind. This can be sensed from a letter to a close friend written later that year:

> [My art] leaves me—the most restless of created beings. I am the modern embodiment of the old Enchanters, whose familiars tore them to pieces. I weary of rest, and have no satisfaction but in fatigue. Realities and idealities are always comparing themselves before me, and I don't like the Realities except when they are unobtainable—then I like them of all things.[4]

Philip Collins has summarised the more general effects of what he calls this 'erotic crisis': 'It is clear that his emotional turmoil of the mid-1850s, which preceded *The Frozen Deep* and his meeting Ellen Ternan, had led to more self-scrutiny, self-dramatising, and projecting himself into possible emotional situations —and this affected his art.'[5] Beginning in mid 1857, with the start of Dickens' serious career as a public reader, his self-dramatisation gained yet another considerable impetus.[6] This projection of himself directly into his fiction is most apparent in *A Tale of Two Cities*, which though it was written in 1859, often appears to be more of a crude personal psychodrama reenacting the events of 1857–8 than a polished work of art. But the phenomenon is already evident in *The Frozen Deep*.

In it, Dickens designed for himself the role of Richard Wardour, a middle-aged man who nobly sacrifices his life to bring together the young woman he loves (named Lucy) and his youthful rival for her hand. With very little elaboration, all the themes of the later novel are present in the play: a man who thinks of himself as prematurely old and emotionally worn out, yet with latent demonic power, who is recalled to his better nature by a much younger woman, and who achieves nobility by sacrificing his life in favour of his competitor for her love. The connections between the play and the novel were sufficiently clear to Dickens for him to write, in the Preface to *A Tale of Two Cities*, that it had been while acting in it he had 'first conceived the main idea of this story' (xiii).

In the summer of 1857 it was decided that the original acting company should revive *The Frozen Deep* as a benefit for the widow of Douglass Jerrold (he had just died). Two of the performances, scheduled for late August, were to be given in a very large theatre, and it was necessary to replace the lady amateurs in the cast with professionals, whose voices would carry better. The actresses eventually recruited were a Mrs Ternan and her two daughters, Ellen Lawless and Maria, both young, pretty, and as it developed, very receptive to Dickens' personal charm and considerable stage power. (Maria, to his great delight, shed real tears at a rehearsal of the scene of Wardour's death.) With such ample imaginative preparation, art and life came together easily enough. Though he did not for some time admit it, it is clear from passages in *The Lazy Tour of Two Idle Apprentices*, a loose account of a journey to the north-east he wrote with Collins the following month for *House-hold Words*, he was already infatuated (if not hopelessly in love) with Ellen Ternan.

Throughout the winter and into the spring, he felt more and more desperate, for his marriage was not only the hateful trap it had always been, but also a bar to any relationship with the young actress. With Ellen before him as a crushing reminder of what might be, the situation became yet more trying. 'The domestic unhappiness remains so strong upon me that I can't write, and (waking) can't rest, one minute', he wrote to Collins (21 March 1858; NL, III, 14). But then a way out appeared in a quarrel with Catherine over a bracelet he had ordered for Ellen, which a jeweller unwittingly sent to Mrs Dickens. The series of events that followed led to a complete break and by mid-May, they were officially separated. In June, Dickens publically announced his separation in *Household Words*, as if to declare finally and irrevocably that he was entirely a free man. It felt to him as if he were starting life all over again.

These are the events which are retold and reconstructed in *A Tale of Two Cities*, serialised in Dickens' new magazine *All the Year Round* from 30 April to 26 November 1859. Dickens admitted as much in the Preface to the book, writing: 'Throughout its execution, it has had complete possession of me; I have so far verified what is done and suffered in these pages, as that I have done and suffered it all myself' (xiii). Virtually every male character in the novel acts out some part of Dickens' retrospective view of his own part in the purely personal key events of 1857–8, Dr Manette being Dickens recalled to life, Carton the worn-out, Clennam-like Dickens who gives up his life, and Charles Darnay (who shares his author's initials) who wins Lucie Manette and his wife.[7]

This material, which can be summed up under the phrase 'Recalled to Life', a title Dickens considered for the novel, is symbolic of the optimism Dickens felt about his future once freed from his marriage. But despite this, the theme of resurrection never functions as anything more than a clumsy, ineffective graft onto the real stuff of the novel, which on a deep level remains just as pessimistic as *Little Dorrit* had been. (This tension, between a deep structure of pessimism and superficial layer of optimism, may well account for A *Tale of Two Cities* being the least satisfactory of Dickens' mature novels.)

This is also evident in Dickens' treatment of the city in the novel. Dickens could not—in his profoundest imagination—ever conceive of meaningful life being lived anywhere outside of the city, but for years now life in the city had appeared equally impossible. And rather than being a place in which one can be recalled to life, the city in A *Tale*—an entity including London and Paris—clearly is in every way as barren and life-denying a place as that of *Little Dorrit*. The key descriptive phrases for it are 'lifeless desert' and 'wilderness' (85). Both cities are inhabited by masses of people devoid of individual identities but who appear collectively and upon the slightest provocation, as a vicious, bloodthirsty mob, described as that 'much dreaded monster' (149). What is most horrifying to Dickens about the Revolutionary Paris he creates is that it is a city ruled entirely by the crowd, where even life itself is subject to its capricious whim.

Balancing this is a persistent strain of perverse pastoral imagery, which by its open association with death makes explicit the hidden meaning of the pastoral in *Little Dorrit*. Indeed, a perverted pastoral image opens the novel, with Death figured as a 'Farmer' (2); for emphasis, Death's pasture, the French countryside, is later described as 'a ruined country, yielding nothing but desolation' (216). The whole Earth is but one 'great grindstone' (250). Jerry Cruncher, who steals fresh corpses from cemetaries, describes himself as an ' "Agricultooral character" ' (291).

If all this is so, it comes as little surprise that Dr Manette's house in Soho, pictured as a pastoral 'harbour from the raging streets' (86), is singularly ineffective in protecting its inhabitants from the crowd, the Revolution, and the guillotine. Like Amy Dorrit, Lucie Manette is a pastoral figure (one might even say figurine), who makes people think of 'imaginary beds of flowers' (65), but she has little power in the world outside. Though she does rescue her father from prison, eventually he relapses into madness. And in the end, only Carton's death can save her lover. If A *Tale of Two Cities* carries a message of hope, it is certainly not embodied in this sham pastoral.

Life is no more easy in the world of this novel than in that of *Little Dorrit*. Dickens even goes so far as to say that all of us have secret urges to die 'hidden in our breasts', thus accounting for the curious attraction (he believed) many people had to dying by guillotine during the Terror (267–8). If life is at all possible in the novel, it is only in another world. Walking through London, Sidney Carton has a vision of another city: 'In the fair city of his vision, there were airy galleries from which the loves and graces looked upon him, gardens in which the fruits of life hung ripening, waters of hope that sparkled in his sight.' Attractive as this is, it is only a 'mirage', and after a 'moment . . . it was gone' (85). The only way Carton can reach this other, visionary city is to die—it is a prevision of Heaven. And if Carton, after his death, is going to 'a far, far better rest' than he has ever known (358), we have only his word, and Dickens' insistent wish to believe in it, that it will be so.

This melodramatic and superficial solution to the question of how the individual was to be reborn into life in the city of *this* world did not long satisfy Dickens, and it is also the central problem of his next novel, *Great Expectations*. But before writing that book, he made a journey back into his past, a literal and figurative pilgrimage to Chatham and the Kent countryside. This was to influence profoundly both the novel and his life.

III

The Uncommercial Traveller[8]

A Tale of Two Cities had been appearing as the inaugural serial novel in *All the Year Round*, which had replaced *Household Words* in the spring of 1859. Dickens had quarreled with his publisher, Bradbury and Evans, over a matter arising out of the complicated circumstances surrounding the breakup of his marriage, and he chose to finish off *Household Words* to sever all connection with them. Dickens attempted to organise the new venture so that he should have absolute and total control over it, and so the periodical was owned entirely by Dickens and his closest business and professional associate, W. H. Wills. He also would no longer have Bradbury and Evans bring out his novels. His new publisher, once again Chapman and Hall, would act only as agents for its distribution. This plan guaranteed that no one or nothing whatsoever could interfere with Dickens' conduct of the periodical. The new novel ensured the magazine's success, with a circulation at once three times that of its predecessor. As soon as the novel was concluded, Dickens launched a series of occasional essays called 'The Uncommercial Traveller'. The origins of the series, however, are to be found much earlier than 1859 or 1860, for they were a reincarnation of one of his original periodical ideas.

Dickens' ideas about periodical literature had from the very start of his career been cast in the mould of the great eighteenth century journals which made up so large a part of his childhood reading: Addison and Steele's *Tatler* and *Spectator*, Johnson's *Idler*, and Goldsmith's *Citizen of the World* and *Bee*.[9] From that time on, the elegant, personal discursive and highly entertaining essay style of the *Bee* and the others was for Dickens the journalistic style he longed to recreate. Its association with the rose coloured memories of Chatham made its hold on him that much stronger.

Dickens' many periodical ventures—beginning with some of his sketches in the early 1830s, followed by *Bentley's Miscellany, Master Humphrey's Clock, Household Words,* and several more along the way that had never got past the planning stage—were all to varying degrees revivals of these models. As revivals, all had failed, for Dickens never wrote anything like that material for very long. But he never abandoned the idea as long as he could attach the blame for those failures elsewhere—to circumstance, like the pressure of too many writing commitments, or to other parties, like meddling publishers. With 'The Uncommercial Traveller', appearing in a journal with which no outsider could interfere, he could do so at last.

The immediate inspiration for the series was probably the work Dickens had done in November 1859, preparing a speech for a benefit dinner for the Commercial Traveller's Schools on 22 December.[10] For one thing, thinking about unfortunate children who were being given an excellent education must have reminded him of his own disrupted schooling, broken up by the move to London. But also while thinking about his speech, Dickens told the gathering, he had 'considered whether anything could be done with the word Travellers; and I thought whether any fanciful analogy could be drawn between those travellers who diffuse the luxuries and necessities of existence' and other varieties of travellers, actual and metaphorical (*Speeches*, 290). This playful consideration of the word quickly bore fruit, and from this speculation to the Uncommercial, and his actual and metaphorical rambling less than two months later, was but a short step.

The first of the papers, about a shipwreck, was prefaced by a brief note setting the tone and plan of the series: 'Literally speaking, I am always wandering here and there from my rooms in Covent-garden, London—now about the city streets: now about the country bye-roads—seeing many little things, and some great things, which, because they interest me, I think may interest others' (2). The element binding the pieces together was to be simply the mind of the Uncommercial, and despite the modest qualifiers ('I think may interest others'), Dickens, by now the experienced public reader in direct communication with a genuinely national audience, never doubted it would work.[11] From the very start, the witty, urbane, and humane tone of the persona of the Uncommercial is confident and consistent. 'Business is business,' he summed up simply in his first essay, 'and I start' (AYR, 28 January 1860; omitted in subsequent editions).

The essays are organised solely around Dickens' preoccupations as he travelled through town and country. The subjects vary—from the opening shipwreck to the closing piece about an Italian political prisoner. Yet one surprising preoccupation almost all exhibit is with death and human corpses. The opening piece is quite literally full of them, describing the actions of the country curate who retrieved the bodies of the drowned travellers. In it Dickens expresses great admiration for this man who had 'most tenderly and thoroughly devoted himself to the dead' (6). Had he himself lost a loved one in the wreck, Dickens muses, knowing the body had been so well tended would almost have made up for the bereavement. In another paper, even so distant a subject as complaints about the poor provision for food in railway stations (a perennial complaint of commercial travellers) leads to an inappropriately lighthearted consideration of drownings in the Surrey Canal ('Refreshment for Travellers', 52–3).

In 'Travelling Abroad', a *mélange* of memories of Continental travel, the Uncommercial notes that whenever he is in Paris, he is 'dragged by invisible force into the Morgue' (64).[12] Dust in a deserted City Church seems, to the Uncommercial, to consist of 'decay of dead citizens in the vaults below' ('City of London Churches', 86). The churches themselves 'remain like the tombs of the old citizens who lie beneath them and around them, Monuments of another age' (93), perhaps like those dead citizens, about to crumble into dust.

As in *A Tale of Two Cities*, Dickens does attempt to counterbalance this almost overwhelmingly morbid gloom. In 'The Shipwreck', as in the novel, it is with an image of the Resurrection. But though he claims he now will never think of death without also thinking of the Resurrection, it is the 'open grave ... the type of Death' (10), which in fact dominates his travels.

There is something of a change in emphasis, however, which begins in 'Travelling Abroad', the seventh essay (7 April 1860). Setting out for Dover in this imaginary journey, the Uncommercial encounters a child identified at first only as 'a very queer small boy' (61). The boy, rather precocious, tells a story: his father used to take him for walks to look at a great house on Gad's Hill near Chatham, saying if the boy worked hard, one day he might own it. Of course, what is remarkable about this incident is that the boy is Charles Dickens, aged no more than nine or ten, the father John Dickens, and the house the one Dickens had purchased in 1856, making the prophecy come true.

Gad's Hill Place had been inherited by an acquaintance of Dickens, and he had heard of it being for sale only by chance through Wills. After negotiations about the price, Dickens purchased it, as it happened on a Friday, his 'lucky' day: this became one of his favourite coincidences. At first, Dickens intended to use the house exclusively as a summer home, and he paid little attention to it. He even toyed with the idea of renting it out. He began staying there more often during the final months of his marriage, but only in the early months of 1860 did he make the decision to live there permanently. He had already begun extensive improvements to the house and grounds, and by March was writing of it with obvious pride as 'the admiration of Rochester' (To Miss Coutts, 13 March 1860; NL, III, 153). In

October, Tavistock House, his London home, was sold, and, apart from the *All the Year Round* offices where he stayed in town, Dickens had no permanent residence in London from this time.[13] The decision was an important one: for nearly forty years Dickens had been a Londoner, yet continued to think of his true home as Chatham. Now, he was back 'home' at last.

And once the parallel fictional 'return' to Chatham had been begun in the Uncommercial series, it was inevitable that it too would be accomplished. It developed into a journey in time as well as space, which in a way it really was. In 'Shy Neighbourhoods' (AYR, 26 May 1860), Dickens describes getting out of bed one morning at two to go for a thirty mile walk. He had actually done this several times, in fact walking all the way from Tavistock House to Gad's Hill; in the essay, however, he remains in London. The next paper, 'Tramps' (16 June 1860), which he remarks was set off by 'the chance use of the word "Tramp"' (104) in the previous one, describes the wanderings of miscellaneous Tramps, taking the Dover Road again and actually ending in a meadow near Gad's Hill. Finally, two weeks later, the Uncommercial arrives home at 'Dullborough Town' (30 June 1860), a composite portrait of Chatham and Rochester, where he can at last get down to 'rambling about the scenes among which my earliest days were passed' (117).

The experience of revisiting 'home' after so many years was profoundly unsettling. Discussing old times with a childhood companion he meets by chance in Dullborough was like speaking 'of our old selves as though our old selves were dead and gone, and indeed they were' (125). 'Paradise re-visited'[14] is a phrase he later used which gives an idea of what he had expected to find; but the town had changed and he had changed, and both were somewhat the worse for wear. The painfulness of the journey into the past and of this realisation were great, and perhaps Dickens hesitated to continue; it was just at this time, on 3 September 1860, that he burned his accumulated correspondence of twenty years in a great bonfire at Gad's Hill. Still, there was really no way of avoiding completing the journey, and in the piece 'Nurse's Stories' (8 September 1860), originally entitled 'Associations of Childhood', a floodgate of Dickens' earliest childhood memories was released.

This cluster of memories of Chatham was at the core of Dickens' innermost self-image, and if now they seemed a lesser constellation than he had been accustomed to think of them as, the realisation involved a dramatic access of self-knowledge. Was he, therefore, also a different kind of person than he had liked to think himself? Had his entire life been different from the way he had come to view it? If so, this experience necessitated as well reassessing the role of the Blacking Warehouse in his personal myth of the formation of his character, and changing his conviction that experience alone had been the source of all his life-long secret guilt and suffering. The paper that followed 'Dullborough Town', 'Night Walks' (AYR, 21 July 1860), is in fact an exploration of guilt, a nightmare tour of London in 'the real desert region of the night' (135).[15] The city is the scene of a nightmare reality, peopled by 'savages' (134), and by the spectres of 'enormous hosts of dead . . . [who] if they were raised while the living slept, there would not be the space of a pin's point in all the streets and ways for the living to come out into' (133).

At the very centre of the city is Newgate. Dickens pauses as he passes it, first to touch the prison walls, imagining the thoughts of those incarcerated within them asleep in their cells, and then 'to linger by that wicked little Debtors' Door' (recall that John Dickens once had been a debtor in another prison) where 'many hundreds of wretched creatures of both sexes— many quite innocent' had been hanged (130). This horrific vision of Newgate was a memory Dickens once wrote he had 'never outgrown' ('Where We Stopped Growing', HW, 1 January 1853; MP, 363). Fear of the prison had been one of his very first associations with London. Its reappearance here is crucial, because it represents a memory of guilt and criminality that predates the experiences in the Blacking Warehouse, one almost contemporaneous with those of Chatham and Kent.

Dickens was not yet fully conscious of the significance of these memories, but that they had stirred his imagination at the deepest level is certain, for the two dominating images of *Great Expectations*, the prison and the marshes, spring directly from them. In a sense, the novel only continues the journey back where the Uncommercial had left off. And if the literary value of the occasional essays of *The Uncommercial Traveller* is slight, it is worth remembering that they laid the groundwork for that great novel which followed them.

IV

Great Expectations

When *Great Expectations* began appearing in *All the Year Round* in December 1860, Dickens' critics responded almost unanimously by hailing it as a return to his earlier, Pickwickian style. (Critics had said much the same thing about *The Uncommercial Traveller*.[16]) Judging by *Great Expectations'* phenomenal sales record, Dickens' reading public felt the same. The critics were, in a sense, right; it was, as we have seen, a return of sorts, having been stimulated by Dickens' recollective journeys to Chatham and the world of his childhood memories in *The Uncommercial Traveller*. Indeed, Forster believed that the idea of the novel was intended at first for an Uncommercial essay, and that Dickens had written in response to his (Forster's) suggestion that he should 'let himself loose upon some single humorous conception, in the vein of his youthful achievements in that way' (*Life*, II, 284). This must have been early in September, probably just after Dickens had finished 'Nurse's Stories', but almost at once he decided that the idea the suggestion had generated was good enough to form the basis of a full length, twenty part novel. But his concern for the prospects of *All the Year Round*, suddenly beginning to suffer from its current serial, Charles Lever's rambling *A Day's Ride*, forced a change of plans at the end of the month: it would be written instead as a weekly serial to save the magazine.[17]

The original impulse, however, remained intact through the permutation of form, and Dickens' core of childhood memories continued to inspire him as he wrote.[18] From its very beginning, the novel evokes with astonishing directness Dickens' personal 'beginning' in Chatham. The time is also the 'beginning' for Dickens' first-person character, virtually the instant of Pip's birth, when he first becomes aware 'of the identity of things' (1) and of himself. The seminal event, as it were, is Magwitch rising up from behind a tombstone, imagined as an Oedipal tyrant (after all he is destined to be Pip's true father) whose power stretches beyond the grave in which Pip's biological father lies.[19]

Once risen, Magwitch tells Pip to steal food for him, and threatens him rather graphically with being eaten alive if he does not. What is more, an omniscient, omnipresent young demon friend of Magwitch is there to ensure that Pip's every move will be known and reported, and his heart and liver torn out and eaten should he fail to do what Magwitch demands. Pip steals the food under this dread compulsion, an extenuating circumstance which exonerates him, as far as we are concerned, from any blame. Nevertheless, it is this theft which becomes the focus of Pip's feelings of guilt, and Pip, as one critic has remarked, must have 'one of the guiltiest consciences in literature'.[20] His guilt clearly is not based on anything he has done, but is from the beginning of his consciousness an integral part of his identity. Far more effectively than any imaginary young man, Pip's guilt will be a lifelong constant companion eating away at his innards. (What Pip *is* guilty of is not stealing food, but betraying Joe's love, Biddy's devotion, and his own better nature.)

Pip, though he is felt even here to be a well rounded, consistent and coherent persona, is at the same time a recognisable projection of his author, and especially so at this point. This experience, the source of Pip's guilt and the cause of his suffering (and furthermore, his most carefully hidden secret), is clearly analogous to the experience that held the same place in Dickens' image of his past, the ordeal at Warren's Blacking. What we are witnessing in the novel, however, is a remarkable rearrangement of the key events of Dickens' vision of his childhood, because it places the guilt, the suffering and the ordeal at a point in time before Dickens' journey to London and the actual time of the Blacking Warehouse.[21] The sequence of events is now radically different; his London ordeal at Warren's Blacking was no longer the source of his personal guilt. That source had been relocated back in the idyllic time of Chatham, which until now had been for him the assumed centre of all good in his character. The implication is unmistakable: the queer, small boy in Chatham had been suffering even before he was packed off like a mere parcel of goods in a coach to London.

Through this intense retrospective effort, Dickens was engaged in overturning and reconstructing an image of his past and his identity, a cherished and supportive personal myth which had sustained him throughout his adult life. The emotional pain was devastating, and as he began writing evidently caused a recurrence of the crippling pain in his side that had always accompanied a resurgence of memories of Warren's Blacking, ever since he had suffered the pain in the Warehouse itself.[22]

Yet, as much as Pip is a cypher for Dickens at this point in the narrative, it is important to recall that he was conceived too as a representative, modern Everyman. That the opening scene enacts, along with Dickens' private drama, a version of the primal Oedipal scene, suggests the broad mythic terms in which Dickens was thinking about Pip from the very start.

The latent message of this incident, both personal and general, is that guilt—Dickens', Pip's, everyone's— is something which precedes experience. Dickens had been guilty before London; even his own sons, who had all the advantages he had not, were tainted by some shadow, too, already beginning to disappoint him by their lack of initiative and seriousness. Guilt is simply part of the condition of existing at all in this world. Nothing need be done to incur it: it is just there. Pip, too, at first is obviously innocent of substantive wrongdoing, but his innocence is no protection against the burden of guilt he must carry. Other people, like Mrs Joe, Pumblechook, and Miss Havisham, help reinforce his sense of guilt, and channel it in certain, socially approved directions; but as his meeting Magwitch is the first conscious experience of his life, their later actions cannot be said to have caused his guilt. At times, Pip's life from this point on seems like nothing so much as a search for crimes he feels he ought to have committed to justify the guilt he already has.

The locale in which this happens is equally important as the event. It consists of a Kentish village and nearby market town compounded out of Dickens' memories of and recent revisits to Chatham, Rochester, and the surrounding area, and it serves as one of the loadstones of the novel. The other, of course, is London, and the novel is almost evenly divided between the two. Before discussing them, however, it will be helpful to consider the third important geographical location in the world of the novel, the marshes.

To call them a geographical entity of the same order as the

village or London is in fact somewhat misleading, because they are never particularised in the same detailed, explicit way. (I doubt a consistent map of them could be drawn from the information Dickens gives.) More than a 'real' place, they are a kind of moral litmus paper, a testing ground where the moral nature of every character can be seen as what it really is. They are not in any way a source of evil and corruption, as are Satis House and Newgate. People act on the marshes only as they do elsewhere, but they do so more openly. The violent confrontation of Pip and Orlick on the marshes is the most dramatic example of this. Every part of their inner lives comes out: Orlick's insanely jealous hatred for Pip, and Pip's equally groundless hatred for Orlick, Orlick's murder of Mrs Joe, and Pip's guilty conscience over the same event. In the sense that their actions and careers mirror each other, these two are *alter egos*, but here on the marshes, it is the essential contrast in their moral natures that becomes obvious—Pip is basically good and Orlick is basically evil. Other examples can be found, including the first scene set on the marshes, the chase of the escaped convicts. Here Magwitch, a villainous ogre only a few pages earlier in the churchyard, reveals his inner goodness by shielding Pip from any blame for the theft of the food. And Compeyson, though he is almost murdered, appears as the cowardly degenerate he really is.

The village of the novel, by contrast, is presented as a recognisably real place, made of memories and pieces of real places to be sure, but at the same time a type for the quiet country village that would have suggested home to anyone who had been born in one. It is one of Dickens' most satisfyingly accurate renditions of rural life, and it is as representative of a shared national heritage as Pip is representative of a common national character. Together with the neighbouring town, it is presented as a complete microcosm of country society, with a church, various merchants, a claque of local dignitaries, and most importantly, the prison hulks and Satis House. Clearly, then, Pip's childhood is not spent in an idyllic fairyland, but in a place where all of the unpleasant and corrupting institutions and influences of society are already present.

It is worth looking more closely at the hulks and Satis House. The hulks need little description: they are prisons, and particularly vile ones, all the more so for their actually having existed. (That they no longer did exist in 1860 is surely beside the point.) Satis House, on the other hand, is the physical and economic centre of the village, as Miss Havisham occupies the place of squireen. But despite Pip's high opinion of it, it is presented in a way that presses home its virtual identity with the hulks. It is a ruin, 'which was of old brick, and dismal, and had a great many iron bars to it. Some of the windows had been walled up; of those that remained, all the lower were rustily barred', as is the gate (50). And to press home the analogy, Miss Havisham lives in the house as if she were a convict sentenced to it for life.

Nevertheless, this house becomes the focus of Pip's desires to rise in the world. Even though Estella lives in the house, it is clear Pip needs little additional prompting from her to make it so. The desires can be seen as clearly to precede the visit, too, for why else had Pip attempted to become a scholar before it? During his first visit, Estella explains that the name 'Satis' means. ' "that whoever had this house, could want nothing else" '. She adds tartly, ' "They must have been easily satisfied in those days, I should think" ' (51). Pip ignores the implicit warning, and Satis House comes to represent all that Pip wants in life—wealth. status and Estella. He firmly believes he will marry Estella and come into possession of the house simultaneously. This appears to Pip the only way to erase his secret shame and guilt. As much an integral part of him as his guilt, then, is the urge to escape it, and Satis House is what he thinks he must have to do it. (Estella is not as important to Pip as the house itself—she simply completes it. When Dickens worked up the novel into a reading, he left out the Estella plot altogether.)[23]

To make the emptiness of Pip's desires even more graphic, Satis House has a ruined garden, a grim, ironic parody of the supposed pastoral qualities of the village. This garden, 'over-grown with tangled weeds' (58), and 'a rank ruin of cabbage-stalks' (74), is in truth not a garden at all but a 'wilderness' (83). It accurately mirrors the House, in which no emotions are nurtured but the convoluted, stunted and poisonous. Pip is as blind to the garden as he is to the House; to him the weeds look like 'precious flowers' (255). There are several gardens in the novel, but one that produces a crop fully as miserable as this, and to which we are probably meant to connect it, is Newgate. Wemmick walks through the prison 'much as a gardener might walk among his plants', treating each prisoner like a young 'shoot' (246).[24] The ruined garden is in this sense an image of society as a whole, which grows from the 'pips' of human beings only the stunted weeds of the criminal and the guilty.

This link between Satis House and Newgate demonstrates that London in *Great Expectations* has no monopoly of corruption and evil. After the first section (fully one third) of the book which is set in the country, the action shifts for a time to London, but everything we see in the metropolis is in essence no different from its Chatham analogue, merely larger and more exaggerated. The dehumanisation enforced by the hulks—Magwitch has the habits of an animal, not a man—is no different from that of Newgate in London. No sooner is Pip in the city than he comes to Smithfield Market and the 'filth and fat and blood and foam' attendant upon the slaughter of animals (155); and immediately afterward he comes to Newgate, where four persons are to be hanged the next morning. The slaughter of men like animals in the city is an image Dickens had used before in *Oliver Twist*, but here is only an amplification of one already placed in the Kentish countryside.

It is not long before we realise that the entire city is like the prison—both are places which systematically incarcerate and dehumanise their inhabitants. It is not only Newgate which does this. Barnard's Inn, Pip's London residence, looks to him 'like a flat burying-ground' whose houses contain a mixture of 'dilapidated blind and curtain, crippled flower-pot, cracked glass, dusty decay, and miserable makeshift' (162). When he opens a window, it slams shut and almost decapitates him like a guillotine. (' "Ah!" ' Wemmick says of the Inn with deadpan accuracy, ' "the retirement reminds you of the country" ' [163].) The city, as Pip succinctly puts it, is 'ugly, crooked, narrow, and dirty' (153). Jaggers' office, another stifling place, is located in Little Britain, with obvious connections to Great Britain intended. One is hardly surprised to hear Wemmick's remark in the office that hanging ' "is quite the natural end here, I assure you" ' (189).

There is, however, one character who successfully manages to exist in London, and more than just exist, even flourish, and that is Wemmick.[25] Wemmick's role in the novel is a large one, and it cannot be said to be wholly justified by his relatively minor contribution to the plot. Wemmick's role is rather symbolic: his lifestyle is meant to represent the way in which life in the overgrown jungle of the city—and by implication, life in the world—can be sustained.

The solution with which Wemmick solves the problem is 'compartmentalisation'.[26] He leads a double life, part in the City, and part at home in his little fortified cottage. The two are kept as far apart as possible; as Wemmick tells Pip, ' "the office is one thing, and private life is another" ' (197). As did Inspector Bucket in *Bleak House*, Wemmick must deal with a world in which guilt and criminality exist, and where prisons and gibbets are ineradicable fixtures of the landscape. One must accommodate oneself to them, as Wemmick does, but at the same time he can maintain the 'Castle' in Walworth, where one can '[brush] the Newgate cobwebs away' (197).[27] Significantly, unlike that of Satis House, Wemmick's garden though dimunative is a true 'bower'. The Castle is, all in all, in the words of the Aged P., ' "a pretty pleasurable ground" ' (196). Here Wemmick manages to provide shelter not only for himself, but also for his father, and eventually Miss Skiffins, his bride.

Wemmick's strategy for urban living is essentially that of modern suburban man, and it may not be entirely coincidental that the period in which this part of the novel is set, ca. 1825–30, was the time of one of London's great suburban explosions. London had had its suburbs even in Elizabethan times, when the Strand was lined with great homes whose gardens ran down to the river. Now, thanks to mass building techniques, the residential charm of suburbia had become available to the middle and lower middle classes as well. Every day at midcentury as many as two hundred thousand individuals commuted into the City on foot or by omnibus from the near suburbs, like Pentonville, Camden Town (where Dickens had lived), or Marylebone. Long before the coming of the commuter railways in the 1860s, or even of the omnibus in 1828, London was a commuting city. When the novel was begun, in 1860, there was another major turning point in the development of the city: in that year, Parliament began requiring that every major railway proposal include a provision for specially cheap workmen's fares to extend to the labouring classes the benefits of the cheap and wholesome housing of suburbia. (Though no new lines with such fares opened until 1864, many already in operation instituted them before that date.)[28] This suburban explosion, creating social and geographical patterns that still dominate the urban scene, is presaged in Wemmick's Castle.

This is not to say that Wemmick's suburban compromise allows him to be as unblemished as an angel in the world of the novel. Like Inpector Bucket again, he is a realist but not a moralist. But in *Great Expectations*, living in a state of untarnished innocence is possible only for those characters who are completely disengaged from the city and the world, and who have no contact with or power in them, like Joe and Biddy (and presumably Pip Junior). One must be aware that Wemmick's Castle is made possible only by the business connections with Newgate which he tries to keep distant from it, and by the 'portable property' he acquires from his condemned clients. Taking money from a soon-to-be-dead convict is not pleasant, but it is eminently practical: the man or woman is guilty, and if not will hang in any event, thereby forfeiting the goods if someone doesn't take them (as happens to Magwitch's fortune). Why not Wemmick, then, especially if he can use the proceeds to preserve his family life in Walworth?

What Wemmick understands is that life must be a compromise, a recognition of the distance between the real and the ideal, and expectation and fulfilment. This simple statement is the kernel of wisdom at the heart of the novel, and if it seems so much more powerful in the novel than it does abstracted here, it is because Dickens conveys it with great tact, profound generosity and humble understanding. The understanding was intensely personal; while Wemmick may at times seem too smug a mouthpiece for his author's sentiments, still we never doubt the veracity of the message itself, because Dickens' emotions are so fully engaged in Pip's struggle to discover it for himself.

As we have seen, the opening of the novel, the scene of Pip's meeting with Magwitch, was in part the expression of Dickens' efforts to reorganise his personal myth of his past. As the story develops, Pip's further adventures continue Dickens' personal quest. For example, both go off to London, but with a difference Dickens had been sent off; in a reversal of this, and of the traditional Dick Whittington fable, Pip's fortune comes from London to seek him. His route to the metropolis is thus a short cut, and he arrives with his wealth and status already assured. Dickens' own intense struggle to attain those same things is not necessary for Pip.

Perhaps this too was part of another painful reassessment. It is as if Dickens, through Pip, were absolving everyone of guilt for his own circumstances by taking the burden of that guilt upon his own shoulders. It is as if he were belatedly forgiving his parents for having dragged him to London. The 'attraction of repulsion' was the phrase Dickens had habitually used to describe how he had felt in London as a child, unconsciously admitting that he had been as much attracted as he was repelled, or indeed attracted by the very repulsion. Now, in the writing of *Great Expectations*, he was coming to grips with this realisation —that then, even as a child, and ever since, he had loved and needed the excitement and stimulation of life in London. There was yet more: the realisation that, had his descent into the city never happened, the wealth and position he had eventually attained also might well never have been his. For his secret shame had been the spur that had driven him to achieve greatness, as Pip had been driven by his to Estella and Satis House.

Painful as this realisation was, it had its compensation, for *Great Expectations* embodies not only the dismantling of the old self-image, but the construction of a new one from the shattered pieces of the old. If the process involved reassessing the meaning of the ordeal in London and at Warren's Blacking, and in doing so placing at least part of their weight of guilt further back in Chatham, at the very same time this was to free Warren's and London of the horrible taint they had always carried. London need no longer be, beneath its surface, a nightmare city, if everything that had made it so had also been in Chatham and Kent. Pip learns this, too: the further he travels in search of his guilt, the closer he returns to his first home. What we are, he discovers, though it takes him half a lifetime of suffering to do it, is what we have always been. (Among the many salient points to be

made about his names, Pip and Pirrip, is that they are palin-
dromes, mirroring the journey of his life which begins and ends
in the same place.) The city, then, was no different from the rest
of the world: it was even like the village home that had seemed
its antithesis. And if this were to tarnish the village, it redeemed
the city.

Thus, freed of a burden of secret guilt that nothing before this
could lift, the city was becoming freely available to Dickens as
fictional material as it had not been at any time since the death
of Mary Hogarth, some twenty-five years before. From that time,
Dickens had struggled at the deepest psychic levels to resolve an
irresolvable tension between a dimly remembered idyllic childhood past in the country, and a tortured existence in the present
in the city. The one could never be re-created, the other could
never be abandoned—but the need to attempt both had been
always insistently there. Now the need had evaporated, for with
the past paradise and the past hell revisited and restructured, the
present could be accepted.

The acceptance involved for Dickens, as for Wemmick, a residential compromise: Dickens could live in the country at Gad's
Hill, and there walk the fields and pastures of his youth, entertain
in the grandest of grand manners, and even play the bountiful
squire to the local yeomanry by organising games and fêtes.
However, at any moment of the night or day, an hour's train
ride would deliver him to the heart of London, where from his
rooms over the *All the Year Round* offices in Covent Garden he
could immerse himself in the streets of his imagination, and soak
up like a dry sponge in water the vital energy he needed to sustain
the demanding pace of his life and art. For Dickens, this world
was not, nor could it ever be, the best of all possible worlds, but
he had reached what was for him the best of all possible accom-
modations with it.

With this in mind, it is perhaps less difficult to understand
why Dickens so eagerly adopted Bulwer Lytton's suggestion to
change the original ending of *Great Expectations* where Pip loses
Estella, to the one we now have where he gains her. Having
achieved—after twenty five years of anguished suffering—the
peace he had sought so fervently, should he not allow Pip to
achieve his peace as well?

CHAPTER TEN

Our Mutual Friend: The Changing City

On 31 January 1861 Dickens took a walk from his rooms at the *All the Year Round* Offices off the Strand to Westminster. 'When I got there,' he wrote to a friend,

> the day was so beautifully bright and warm, that I thought I would walk on by Millbank, to see the river. I walked straight on *for three miles* on a splendid broad esplanade overhanging the Thames, with immense factories, railways works, and whatnot erected on it, and with the strangest beginnings and ends of wealthy streets pushing themselves into the very Thames. When I was a rower on that river, it was all broken ground and ditch, with here and there a public-house or two, an old mill, and a tall chimney. I had never seen it in any state of transition, though I suppose myself to know this rather large city as well as anyone in it. . . . (To W. F. de Cerjat, 1 February 1861; NL, III, 209–10; Dickens' italics)

Dickens was describing the embankment of the river between Millbank and Chelsea begun in 1854 by the Government Commissioners of Works and Public Buildings and completed shortly afterwards. The incident seems trivial; and the point Dickens is making is mundane enough, that things are changing so quickly in London one cannot keep up with them. Yet the passage is significant. It marks the conception of the germ of Dickens' next novel, *Our Mutual Friend*. Indeed it so accurately defines the thematic focus of the novel, what Dickens liked to call simply 'the idea' of a book, it seems almost to have been written after the fact.

Like this passage, *Our Mutual Friend* is primarily about change, and not only change as transition, but change as transformation as well. Having argued that *Sketches by Boz*, Dickens' first book, was also about urban change, it may seem redundant to be retelling the point in reference to this, his last completed book, but it is not so. Whereas that earlier work embodied an intuitive perception of the process of change as the essence of urban life, *Our Mutual Friend* reaches the same insight analytically and deliberately, and with a much more explicit, self-conscious expression of that perception.

The 1860s were a time in which a Londoner, even one as knowing about the city as Dickens, might well be impressed with changes in its appearance. Sir John Summerson has written that in that decade, 'London was more excavated, more cut about, more rebuilt and more extended than at any time in its previous history.'[1] The work was almost entirely the doing of the Metropolitan Board of Works, established by Parliament in 1855 primarily to set about creating an effective sewage system, for London. By the mid-1860s a host of projects that would transform the city were in progress or already completed: the four huge main drainage intercepting sewers, Pimlico Bridge and the extension of the southern railways across the Thames to the new Victoria Station, further railway extensions across the river to Charing Cross and Cannon Street, the huge Victoria Embankment, Victoria Street, Garrick Street, Queen Victoria Street, Holborn Viaduct, and the new dead meat market at Smithfield (these last two belatedly built by the City Corporation). Even London's underground railways were under construction by 1864. It would have taken a much less perspicacious observer than Dickens to decide that change was the keynote of the decade. And that almost all of these projects were constructed by the open cut method, digging rather than tunnelling, only made the disruptions they caused much more noticeable.

What all of these monumental public works have in common is not only that they were great changes in the appearance of the city but that they were, to use the jargon coined to describe them, 'improvements'. They were changes that led to something easily perceived as beneficial, either directly, as by relieving sanitary problems, or indirectly, as by speeding the flow of people and goods through the city. Clearly, once all this construction were completed, the city would be a better place in which to live than it had been at any time in living memory.

But change, one should note, can be personal as well as social. Seeing London change so quickly that even *he* had been caught unaware, might well have made Dickens reflect that he too was changing, and not necessarily for the better—in other words, he was growing old. For one thing, under the strain of the public readings, his health already was deteriorating. He was beginning to seem mortal. In 1863, hearing of the death of his friend Augustus Egg, Dickens wrote to Wilkie Collins recalling when they had all acted together in *The Frozen Deep*, and then thought of the many friends and relations in that production also now dead: 'My brother Alfred, Luard [sic], Arthur [Smith], Albert, [Henry] Austin, [Augustus] Egg. Even among the audience Prince Albert and poor [Frank] Stone!' (22 April 1863; NL, III, 349) With so many friends and associates dead, and with so many of his children now grown and already several scattered across the globe, it was only natural Dickens should be concerned with thoughts of his own death.

Change, and by inevitable association, death, mark the central foci of Dickens' creative imagination in *Our Mutual Friend*, which he actually may have begun as early as the date of that letter in 1861, though certainly he did so by 1862. That he was preoccupied with such thoughts at the time he was writing, and that they might naturally appear in the novel as a result, is not remarkable. What is truly remarkable is that their appearance is neither incidental nor casual, but wholly organic. The novel is not only a catalogue of change, but a celebration of it, and of the city as the most impressive embodiment of change. However, Dickens did not only note the constructive change in the river in that letter, but recalled what the area had been like before the change. It had been a kind of wasteland, and it was from this waste that the splendid new bank had been created. The novel takes up this note as well, and explores the many meanings of the word waste: as noun, e.g. rubbish, pollution, misuse; as verb, to destroy, to consume, to misuse; and as object, things and people that have been wasted. Each variety of waste is transformed in the novel, and it is this constructive change that is celebrated. *Our Mutual Friend* becomes a study of how perhaps even that most fearful and final change, death, can be overcome and rendered if not harmless, at least constructive.

II

The passage about change from Dickens' letter quoted above is also remarkably apposite to *Our Mutual Friend* in that it centres around London's river. The Thames was named by Swinburne the novel's true protagonist, and there can be no doubt that Dickens intended that it, together with the dust mounds, should dominate the physical setting and organisational structure of it. However, one must doubt whether Dickens was entirely successful with this device of the river, since generations of critics and readers have never quite been able to agree precisely of what it is a symbol, or if it is one at all.

Dickens' lamentable soft spot for water imagery no doubt predisposed him toward concentrating upon it once he had thought of using it. And waterside material was the very first he seems to have contemplated using in *Our Mutual Friend*, perhaps having got the idea for a riverside story as early as in the mid-1850s.[2] Dickens habitually employed the sea (and water in general) as a symbol for death, and here, as in *Little Dorrit*, he used the river as a metaphor for life: born upstream in pastoral innocence, 'unpolluted by the defilements that lie in wait for it on its course,' (504) it flows on through the city, and 'stretch[es] away to the great ocean, Death' (71). References to life being like the river recur constantly. And while he was completing the opening numbers of OMF, in early 1864, he read a poem of Bulwer Lytton's in *The Atheneum* called 'The Boatman'. The verse is awful, but as it vaguely describes a river journey that proves to be towards death, Dickens wrote he was 'deeply impressed' by it; he added, 'The lines are always running in my head, as the river runs with me' (To Bulwer Lytton, 15 March 1864; NL, III, 384).

Yet this explanation, undeniably correct on the surface, is unsatisfactory, as every reader of the novel has felt. The river seems to be and to represent so much more than what is present in this hackneyed analogy that we must begin to look for explanations beyond Dickens' conscious intentions.[3] The role of the river in *Our Mutual Friend* must be found embedded in the structure of the text.

The novel opens 'with two figures' in a small boat, 'floated on the Thames' (1). The narrative focuses on the two figures and their mysterious, unnamed task. The conceit of the mystery is merely rhetorical, because we are quickly made to realise they are fishing for drowned corpses. The text is extremely reticent about the river itself, withholding all details of physical description. What we do see is the man lean into the river, and emerge with his arms 'wet and dirty' and with money in his hand (3). From this brief incident three associations are born: the river and death, the river and dirt, and the river and money.

Each of these associations is nurtured and developed, singly and in concert. That with dirt, and human corruption, for example, is reemphasised and extended in Chapter iii, when Eugene and Mortimer go down to the waterside:

> ... down by where accumulated scum of humanity seemed to be washed from higher grounds like so much moral sewage, and to be pausing until its own weight forced it over the bank and sunk it in the river. (21)

Later, linking dirt to death, Dickens gives the river,

> ... a thirst for sucking [men] under. And everything so vaunted the spoiling influences of water—discoloured copper, rotten wood, honey-combed stone, green dank deposit—that the after-consequences of being crushed, sucked under, and drawn down, looked as ugly to the imagination as the main event. (172)

Gaffer Hexam and Rogue Riderhood reappear from time to time engaged in their profession, scavenging drowned corpses to steal the contents of their pockets, and claim rewards for the bodies. So rather than being an analogue of human life as Dickens is at pains to impress upon us, the river is actually presented as a combination sewer and graveyard, and the natural element of the lowest kind of human character.

The Harmon dust mounds, immense rubbish heaps, form the other main feature of *Our Mutual Friend*'s London cityscape, and are introduced in Chapter ii. Critics recently have been arguing whether or not the mounds contained human and/or animal fecal matter, with the intention of establishing whether Dickens did or did not understand Freud's later formulation of the psychic relation between human waste and money. Dickens of course doesn't say outright, and indeed says little at all about the contents of the mounds. Nor could he have—considerations of delicacy prevented him from saying very much about their contents, but in any case he had no need to be explicit because his audience knew quite well of what they would be likely to consist. Dickens has Mortimer describe them as a ' ". . . geological formation [of] Dust. Coal-dust, vegetable-dust, bone-dust, crockery-dust, rough dust, and sifted dust—all manner of Dust" ' (13).[4] Clearly, what matters here is not specifically what made up the dust but that it *is* dust—in other words, waste, the accumulated detritus of urban life. More explicitly, the mounds are connected with a different kind of human waste: their possession inspires old Harmon to become a miser and turn his house and grounds into Harmony Jail. As a result, his wife, his daughter and his son-in-law have died, and his son has been exiled from England. His miserliness then, causes the literal waste of human lives.

However, this is all set squarely in the past. Harmon is now dead, and new tenants, the Boffins, formerly his employees, have taken over the Jail, renaming it Boffin's Bower. Their immediate action is to turn the mounds into money, for there was in Victorian London immense wealth to be made from dust. Actually, the mounds are in the present time surprisingly neutral in character. There is very little of the expected dirt and filth or unpleasant physical qualities of the mounds actually in the novel: moreover, there is even a pleasant little 'lattice-work Arbour' at the top of one of the mounds (57), erected there by Boffin. The mounds are collections of waste but what they are in the novel are vehicles which transform the waste directly into wealth.

This role, as agents of productive transformation, is the most important given the mounds in the novel. The river is another such agent, though with some important differences. The river is in its defiled condition also such a collection of waste. But as Gaffer Hexam tells Lizzie, it is ' "your living! As if it wasn't meat and drink to you!" ' (3); this, when he has just pulled money up from out of it to demonstrate his point. The river acts as an agent of transformation in other direct ways, for example by generating by water wheel the power that runs the paper mill upstream in which Lizzie later works, or by acting as the highway which brings into the city the coal and other vital goods which give it the energy it needs to keep alive and moving.

What all of these transformations have in common is that they involve the direct or indirect production of wealth. This is hardly accidental, for the novel is as much about money as anything else. To note that Dickens was writing a novel about money at the same time Karl Marx was writing a work of economic philosophy about money should not be taken as an attempt to make Dickens into a closet communist. It is rather to point out that at roughly the same moment in time, from two very different vantage points, two profound and perceptive social thinkers had come to the same understanding—that now money was the agent which governed the transformation of the physical world into the human world. Things, i.e. raw nature, are transformed into useful objects by human nature, and the utility added is expressed in terms of added value—in this way, wealth is generated. In contemporary English society, as both Marx and Dickens realised, wealth need no longer have been held in land, or goods, or human chattels, but in money alone.

Money, usually in its most pure form of gold, is used in *Our Mutual Friend* to buy a great many things, such as houses, horses and carriages, clothing and even learning. But it can also buy shares, seats in Parliament, social position, orphan children, wives, and even human life itself. Dickens understood, as Marx did, that gold, '. . . is not money, and . . . when other commodities express their prices in gold, this gold is but the money-form of those commodities themselves.'[5] Money, then, is not so much a thing of value in itself as much as a kind of shorthand notation for other commodities, which we have seen can include people and human relationships as well as mere things. What gold can do that the commodities cannot is act as a medium of exchange by which one thing can, in effect, be converted into another.

There are two abuses of gold which Dickens focuses upon in *Our Mutual Friend*. The first is avariciousness, the seeking of gold for its own sake. Boffin, like Harmon before him, becomes prey to this temptation (or seems to), and there are other miserly characters in the book, fictional and actual, who do the same.

The reason why this is wrong is relatively transparent, and is revealed explicitly in this authorial comment on Fledgeby: 'Why money should be so precious to an Ass too dull and mean to exchange it for any other satisfaction, is strange' (271–2). The point being made is that money is something to be used, not hoarded. A miser might as well be a dead man, and as Gaffer Hexam aptly remarks, ' "Has a dead man any use for money?" ' (4) If it represents the value added to natural goods by human labour, then failure to use it implies a tremendous waste of productive energy.

A more serious abuse of gold is that it can be misused as well as not used at all. This is the key problem for the main characters in the novel, who are the stewards or inheritors of great wealth. The novel shows us how money misused can make a Harmony Jail or, used properly, a Boffin's Bower. This is the dilemma facing Harmon, Bella and the Boffins. But the novel goes a step further than the predicament of individual characters to ask how all the Harmony Jails that already exist can be transformed into Boffin's Bowers. By implication, this is to ask how all the accumulated, wasteful and oppressive structures of society can be transformed into a new and vital social system.

III

Transformation is an idea which surfaces again and again in *Our Mutual Friend*, and at every level of discourse, comic or serious. The Veneering butler, for example, is introduced as 'a gloomy Analytical Chemist', offering wine with a look that intimates he knows what the so-called wine is really made of (10), and he is known for the rest of the novel simply as the Analytical Chemist. The city's financial houses after closing in the evening are rather drily referred to as 'money-mills' which have just 'left off grinding for the day' (603). Mr Venus' shop presents a scene containing 'a muddle of objects, vaguely resembling pieces of leather and dry stick, but among which nothing is resolvable into anything distinct, save [a] candle ... and two preserved frogs fighting a small-sword duel' (77).[6] Aside from the final comic detail, the 'muddle' of objects in Mr Venus' shop is yet another kind of waste, of animal carcasses and human bones,

for he is a taxidermist and articulator of skeletons for medical
students.

The macabre comedy with which Dickens renders Venus and
his trade may distract us from the nature of his work, but that
work does suggest something of a more serious import. Venus
takes the final and irreducible waste products of human life,
bones, even the bones of different bodies, and reassembles them
into whole skeletons. This is in part a parody of a resurrection,
for Venus' specimens are still dead, even if reconstituted. But I
think it is not carrying the sense of his work too far to consider
that if the skeletons help students become doctors who can
practise medicine on the living, then he does in a very indirect
way transform death into life.

Another, far more important collection of waste with the
same potential for transformation are the dust mounds. When
they are first mentioned in the novel, at the Veneering dinner
party, Mortimer casually remarks that the owner of them had
directed ' "himself to be buried with certain eccentric ceremonies
and precautions against his coming to life, with which I need
not bore you" ' (15), but this disquieting hint that the mounds
can have resurrectory effects is allowed to pass unnoticed. And
if the mounds are not as obviously an agent of the conversion of
death into life, they are at least of waste into wealth, which is
equally significant. The mechanism by which this occurs is never
dwelt upon nor does it matter: all we need to know is what we
are told, that the mounds are rubbish and when they are eventually carted off, they fetch several tens of thousands of pounds
in cash.

The mounds make rubbish into gold, but the gold is itself a far
more powerful agent of transformation. It is, as was noted above,
the medium by which one commodity can be transformed into
another. Unfortunately, gold can buy more than only physical
commodities. The Veneerings, for example, can use money (and
money they don't even have!) to buy status, important friends,
influence and for £5000, a seat in the House of Commons as well.
The Boffins discover much the same thing; though they are
ignorant working people, their tremendous wealth makes them
sought after even by dukes and duchesses. The Boffins discover
more than this—that life itself is to be bought and sold. The

Milveys, acting for them, searching for an orphan suitable for them to adopt, discover an orphan market, which fluctuates as wildly as any shares on the Exchange; and they learn as well, that 'the uniform principle at the root of all of these various operations was bargain and sale' (196).

The ability to buy and sell people is at once the most corrupt and corrupting of the powers of money. What money does in buying another person is transform that person into an object, a thing to be owned, used, and then disposed of, exactly as Twemlow is seen by the Veneerings, 'an innocent piece of dinner-furniture' (6). Such a relationship is a contemporary variant on the ancient one of master and slave—i.e. wage slavery. It is the relation, for example, of Riah to Fledgeby, or of Wilfer to Veneering, or for that matter of Wegg to Boffin. ' "You can't buy human flesh and blood in this country, sir; not alive, you can't"' says Wegg to Venus (297), but as usual he is dead wrong. Wegg's constant complaint is that he is treated like a slave by his employer, but he hopes to reverse the role and place Boffin 'in a state of abject moral *bondage and slavery* until the time when [he] should see fit to permit him *to purchase his freedom*' (498; italics mine).

Bella, whose surname 'Wilfer' suggests both the fact that she has been left as a bequest in a will and her own wilful nature which causes her to rebel against this fate, at first believes in this power of money. It is the way to escape the miserable life she sees at home. Harmon, making polite conversation, asks her if a book she holds is about love; she answers, ' "Oh dear no, or I shouldn't be reading it. It's more about money than anything else"' (205). Money is from the first her only interest. Later she intimates to her father she will allow herself to be bought in marriage: ' "I have made up my mind that I must have money, Pa. I feel that I can't beg it, borrow it, or steal it; and so I have resolved that I must marry it"' (320).

Bella is redeemed in part by seeing Boffin's parody of her own beliefs acted out before her. Watching Boffin pushing about Harmon, as his clerk, she thinks:

'Can he be so base as to sell his very nature for two hundred a year? ... But why not? It's a mere question of price with others besides him. I suppose I would sell mine, if I could get enough for it.' (472)[7]

But as Bella falls in love with Harmon, the inconsistency and foolishness of her position is gradually revealed to her, beginning in the scene where she discusses love with Lizzie Hexam. Lizzie asks her, ' "Does a woman's heart that—that has that weakness in it . . . seek to gain anything?" '(527) The question is rhetorical, and the only answer can be no, for love and greed are wholly incompatible. Love requires surrender to another person for no return but mutual trust, a notion on which the laws of market exchange can have no bearing. Bella eventually *gives* herself utterly and freely to Harmon, an act which seals the transformation of the mercenary spoilt child into the selfless mature woman.

Boffin's change for the worse illustrates another aspect of the misuse of wealth, indeed the contradiction at the very heart of the nature of wealth. Money changes a man by enabling him to demonstrate his power over the world by possessing things and other people. But there is a catch, for, as Boffin remarks, ' "we must be equal to the change" ' (464); one must become ' "acquainted with the duties of property" ' (462). One must behave in a manner suitable to one's property: possessions make demands, and so gain power over their nominal owner. Indeed, if one defines oneself in terms of possessions, like the Veneering's friends who 'are only to be spoken of in the very largest figures' (624), then one's identity is at the mercy of one's chattels, human or otherwise. One becomes in some sense a possession of one's possessions, and expressed by them, as Podsnap is by his ornate and base metal table fixtures. And if one's goods are nominally worthless, so too is having power over them. To use money in this manner, then, is to be duped by an empty transformation, and one which further violates the laws that should govern human commerce, in the end benefiting the owner as little as the owned.

These two alternative responses to wealth raise the question of the nature of human transformation in general. It must be admitted first that Dickens is somewhat inconsistent in his representation of the nature of human nature in *Our Mutual Friend*.

For example, the Boffins, Dickens tells us, have led good lives because they 'had guided themselves so far on in their journey of life, by a religious duty and desire to do right', and moreover, had been greatly admired by their wicked employer for it. Dickens goes on: 'And this is the eternal law' (101). It appears, then, as if some people are incorruptably good from birth. Equally clearly, some people are irredeemably bad from birth: no amount of education and middle class respectability can save Bradley Headstone, nor near drowning Rogue Riderhood, from their evil lives and sordid deaths.

On the other hand, there is a middle ground, that occupied by Eugene Wrayburn. Eugene is a moral drifter, neither very good nor very bad, merely a wastrel. He 'did not know what to make of himself' (587), Dickens writes, implying there is yet material from which something might be made. What redeems him is the love of Lizzie Hexam. Eugene toys at length with the idea of making her his mistress, and so simply using her, but he is nearly murdered by Headstone before he can make up his mind. Lizzie rescues him, but does so before realising whom she is rescuing. This is a heroic act of perfect disinterestedness, and more than his immersion in the river, it is her selfless courage and loyal devotion which redeem Eugene, and change him into a moral, productive person. His drowning and resurrection merely seal this transformation.

The river itself is involved in the transformation of both of Eugene and of John Harmon. While this has been read as evidencing symbolic, indeed almost magical, powers of resurrection in the river, it is important to remember that in the novel immersion in the Thames guarantees nothing but a thorough soaking. Rogue Riderhood survives one such bath, but not his second. Dickens did not believe in magic of this sort. If the river is a symbol of life, then near drowning is a figurative immersion in life. It is the strongest life force, love, which is what really works the miraculous sea-change, even, as when Lizzie rescues Eugene, in the face of death.

Love, then, is at least as effective an agent of transformation as gold. But gold's power is limited in that it can only bring about the change of one commodity, one thing, into another, or of a person into a thing. Love can take a reified person and bring that person back to life. This is the secret the knowledge of which above all else signifies election to the community of the saved in *Our Mutual Friend*. This knowledge preserves from permanent harm Lizzie, Jenny Wren and Riah.

The cash nexus and 'love ethic' (to coin an ungainly parallel phrase) are seen as competing systems, often vying like Marlowe's Good and Bad Angels for a single soul. Charley Hexam is one such soul, caught between the values of his education and the love of his sister.[8] The two systems attract certain characteristic rhetorical patterns as well. The cash nexus says one must 'look alive', 'get up in the world', and 'climb' socially. Images associated with it tend to revolve around certain animals, like birds of prey, or cold, unfeeling inanimate objects and materials, such as marble. By contrast the password leading to entry to the kingdom of love is Jenny Wren's cry, ' "Come up and be dead! Come up and be dead!" ' (282) (perhaps echoing St Paul's admonition, to 'reckon ye also yourselves to be dead unto sin, but alive unto God through Jesus Christ our Lord' [Romans, 6:11]). In a certain sense, then, one must be dead to live; that is, be dead to that part of the world which corrupts and eventually destroys the good in human nature.[9] Phrases like 'dragging down', 'falling' and 'drowning', as well as 'turning' or 'changing', are associated with love. Thus, the near drownings of Harmon and Eugene also help to save their lives by showing them that by looking alive they had been immersed and drowning in the cash nexus, and then by teaching them they must die to it to escape it.[10]

The damning paradox embedded in the cash nexus is that looking alive leads only to death. Thus, toward the very end of the novel, there is a shift in the rhetorical pattern: when Headstone drowns himself and Riderhood, his cry is ' "Come down!" ' (802) The end of a life of looking alive, this warns us, is spiritual and emotional death.

To look alive is to place trust in gold, but these characters who are saved learn that love, 'the true golden gold at heart' (772), is the only gold worth having. Once Bella has given herself in love, gold begins to appear around her everywhere, transforming coal-dust into gold-dust, perhaps even inaugurating a new 'golden age' (668). Having this treasure she learns something yet more important about the other gold, that it gives one ' "a great power of doing good to others" ' (680). Once she knows this, she is ready to receive the fortune originally willed to her. Boffin's game of playing the miser illustrates how his stewardship of the Harmon fortune might have prevented this, its proper use. But now, ' "after a long, long rust in the dark" ', old Harmon's fortune ' "was at last beginning to sparkle in the sunlight" ' again (778). (On a larger scale, Parliament in its stewardship of the national fortune is referred to as a national dust heap because it has failed to use the 'enormous treasure at its disposal to relieve the poor' [503].)

When they are first married, the 'Rokesmiths' are allowed to live in a doll's cottage in distant Blackheath, but as soon as Bella has been tested and not found wanting, the 'Harmons' move into Harmony Jail. But the knowledge they have gained, that love can direct the use of wealth toward individually and socially useful ends, is what can finally transform Harmony Jail into Boffin's Bower.

IV

The removal of Bella and Harmon from the suburbs to Harmony Jail has another crucial implication, for it is a return to the city as well. The contrast with the marriages that are made at the close of *Little Dorrit* and of *Great Expectations* could not be greater; both end those novels, whereas this marriage occurs a full thirteen chapters before the end. The Clennams and the Pirrips are crippled survivors who will quietly and passively nurse each other's wounds in isolation and retirement until death ends their struggles. But the union of Bella and Harmon is an entirely different matter, not an end but a beginning.

Their first home in a pleasant garden suburb is allowed to be only a temporary sojourn. The social responsibilities of their 'new' fortune require that they live in London, for it is in London that there is the most need for beneficial social transformation. And as the inheritors of the Harmon fortune, to effect such a transformation is their appointed task in life. Consequently, their transformation of a cold and lifeless jail into a blooming and vital bower indicates that the same may be done for the cold and lifeless city itself.

Early in the novel, Dickens interrupts his description of the dismal Harmony Jail to say this:

> Whatever is built by man for man's occupation, must, like natural creations, fulfil the intentions of its existence, or soon perish. This old house had wasted more from desuetude than it would have wasted from use, twenty years for one. (183)

As with houses, cities—and the London of the novel is admittedly a manmade structure so ill suited to human needs that it has already become a wasteland.

Virtually every description of the city presents the same gloomy prospect. Holloway is 'a tract of suburban Sahara, where tiles and bricks were burnt, bones were boiled, carpets were beat, rubbish was shot, dogs were fought, and dust was heaped by contractors' (33). When Spring comes the city is described as a sawpit, in which, 'The grating wind sawed rather than blew; and as it sawed, the sawdust whirled about the sawpit' (144).[11] The keynotes of these descriptions are decay and sterility; London is a desert where nothing whole or healthy can grow. Its gardens, like 'the mouldy little plantation . . . of Clifford's Inn', produce nothing but 'dry-rot and wet-rot' (97). And not only are the old parts of the city the only decayed ones: the neighbourhood of Bradley Headstone's school, though new, is 'already in ruins' (218). Harmony Jail provides a central image for all of London, the prison: as evening falls, 'The set of humanity outward from the City is as a set of prisoners departing from gaol, and dismal Newgate seems quite as fit a stronghold for the mighty Lord Mayor as his own state-dwelling' (393). London is seen as one great prison—hardly a vision that could be taken as a sign of hopeful optimism. Yet optimism is there.

One of the most dismal of the city's many, many dismal neighbourhoods is the riverside. It is described as a confused interface between land and water; but the water does not make the desert ground fertile, it only turns it into a malignant swamp. Here every single building appears to be disused and rotting away, and even the streets are reduced to 'muddy alleys that might have been deposited by the last ill-savoured tide' (24). Little that can be identified as a purposeful human construction still remains. Yet even here, among the dregs of the moral and

literal sewage of the city there is a place where genuine human community and love can and does flourish. This is the public house named the Six Jolly Fellowship Porters.

The description of this public house establishes it as another in the long series of Dickens' tumbledown waterfront buildings that distantly owe their origins to his memories of Warren's Blacking Warehouse:

> In its whole constitution it had not a straight floor, and hardly a straight line. . . . Externally, it was a narrow lopsided wooden jumble . . . with a crazy wooden verandah impending over the water; indeed the whole house . . . impended over the water, but seemed to have got into the condition of a faint-hearted diver who has paused so long on the brink that he will never go in at all. (61)

As the genial tone will already have indicated, this building is in no way threatening, as such structures usually had been for Dickens. Indeed it is a unique haven in the cruel and rough riverside world. The building's present structure and form have not been altered; on the surface, its past is unchanged. But this crazy, ungainly and uncomfortable structure has been transformed by its proprietor, Miss Abbey Potterson, into a repository of smugness. It is, as Dickens succinctly states, a 'bar to soften the human breast' which positively gushes warmth and good will (62). She has given it new life, and it is now in a 'state of second childhood' (61). (Dickens continues, 'it had an air of being in its own way garrulous about its early life' [61], which makes it difficult not to read this as a personal statement.) Dickens' portrait of the Six Jolly Fellowship Porters shows how completely he had come to accept his buried past at Warren's Blacking, and recognise that it had been so completely transformed by his creative energies that it could now be contemplated calmly and without terror as an important formative incident in the making of the great novelist. The past has been remade and rendered useful.[12]

In the preceding chapter I tried to explain how in his imaginative journey back into his childhood, Dickens had re-examined the myth, to which he had for so many years tenaciously clung, of his 'fall' into London and drudgery. In doing so, he came to

realise that the fall from childhood and innocence into experience
was an inevitable part of human progress into maturity and
adulthood. This myth had always had for Dickens an associated
physical correlative, that of innocence with the country and
misery with the city. The tension between pastoral bliss and
urban blight had been one of the energising forces of Dickens'
creative imagination, though not always with advantageous
results in the fiction. The recasting of the myth led to the de-
fusing of this tension. This is clear from the absence of emotional
excitement in the description of the Six Jolly Fellowship Porters
—the calm tone demonstrates just how completely this had been
accomplished. Even the Blacking Warehouse, the prime symbol
of Dickens' childhood London ordeal, was now neutralised, transformed into the benign Six Jolly Fellowship Porters.

This transformation had more than a personal dimension. For
in revitalising the Blacking Warehouse as a pub, Dickens made
it into a positive symbol of the possibility of creating an environment of life, love and human fellow-feeling within the city. There
is, as we have seen, no sentimental romanticisation of the pub,
nor, for that matter, of the city as a whole. The city is presented
as a dehumanised wasteland, just as the building which houses
the public house is presented as lopsided and tumbledown. But
equally as the ruin can be changed into a cheerful pub, the
ruined city can be changed into a living one.

The story of the dolls' dressmaker emphasises the same
message. Her rooftop garden at Riah's house is not romanticised
either: 'A few boxes of humble flowers and evergreens completed
[it]; and the encompassing wilderness of dowager old chimneys
twirled their cowls and fluttered their smoke, rather as if they
were bridling, and fanning themselves, and looking on in a state
of airy surprise' (279). This garden is in the city and of the city,
but here one can still feel as if one were 'dead', loose the chains
of this world, and experience visions of a world where everything
is 'so peaceful and so thankful' (281), and in doing so achieve
happiness. Here the material transformation has its mirror in a
human transformation: in the garden the crippled Fanny Cleaver
becomes the beautiful and blessed Jenny Wren.

Recalling that passage from Dickens' letter praising the embankment of the river in Westminster which opened this chapter,

one can see that Dickens was confident that constructive changes *could* be effected, not only in his fiction but in the world. The adjective he had used to describe the work he saw in Chelsea then was 'splendid', and I can detect in his response no sorrow at the passing of the old, perhaps more 'romantic', but sordid and filthy river bank. As Dickens finished writing *Our Mutual Friend*, and as every one of its readers would have known, the Victoria Embankment was nearing completion, and a large part of the riverfront the novel describes would soon be no more. This too, Dickens, no doubt, would have seen as splendid. At the very same time, Bazelgette's huge sewage system was being put into operation, and the raw sewage which had for Dickens' entire lifetime polluted the river would be contained, controlled, diverted out to sea, and it was hoped even be used by farmers as fertiliser (and thus made into yet another sort of gold). This too would have struck Dickens as nothing less than 'splendid'. Waste was being made good, physically and actually.

One of Dickens' last essays in *The Uncommercial Traveller* series, 'A Small Star in the East' (AYR, 19 December 1868), embodies precisely the same realistically sober but dogged optimism. It opens with a recollection of Holbein's 'Dance of Death', comparing to it the squalor of East London, where walking human skeletons as horrible as Holbein's are still to be found. The description of this neighbourhood near 'the impure river' (UT, 319) is unsentimental and starkly frank:

> A squalid maze of streets, courts, and alleys of miserable houses let out in single rooms. A wilderness of dirt, rags, and hunger. A mud-desert, chiefly inhabited by a tribe from whom employment has departed, or to whom it comes but fitfully and rarely. (UT, 319)

Dickens explores the insides of these people's dwellings, reporting with no elaboration their impoverishment, hunger, sickness of body and mind, and quiet perseverance in the face of their hellish existence. Thinking of the especial suffering of their children, Dickens succumbs to tears. But toward the end of his walk he comes across the East London Children's Hospital, which he learns is run by a 'gentleman and a lady, a young husband and wife' (327), a doctor and nurse who have given up the chance of a lucrative West End medical practice to serve the poor. The building itself is an old warehouse 'of the roughest nature', yet it has been transformed by their efforts into something 'airy, sweet, and clean' (326). The children inside are treated with kindness and compassion, and given the best medical attention. The couple are even training young working class women from the area to be nurses, instead of needlewomen or prostitutes. The key to their magnificent accomplishment is the simple quality of 'usefulness' (328), a word which, along with several variants, recurs several times. Even in this miserable urban environment, then, human effort properly directed can wring good out of evil.[13]

Our Mutual Friend has too often been seen as a novel about the myth of resurrection, but as 'A Small Star in the East' indicates retrospectively, it is more than this: it is first and foremost a celebration of the real, of the future transformation and imminent resurrection of London. That it would be a difficult task, Dickens surely knew. Much as Dickens' characters in the novel are made to suffer before their rebirths, London would be harrowed before its return to life. Not only would the city be dug up from one end to the other, but workmen would be maimed and killed in the inevitable accidents, and tens of thousands of the jobs and dwellings of working people would be lost as old neighbourhoods were destroyed. But the goal was worth the pain: a city in which a fully realised, rich, varied, productive, and humane life could once more be lived.

Dickens and the City

> London as a place of squalid mystery and terror, of
> the grimly grotesque, of labyrinthine obscurity and
> lurid fascination, is Dickens's own; he taught people
> a certain way of regarding the huge city.
>
> George Gissing

For all its many complexities and virtues, *Our Mutual Friend* is
still a flawed novel, as perceptive readers from Henry James on
have felt, though perhaps often for the wrong reasons. 'It has not
the creative power which crowded its earlier page', Forster remarked (*Life*, II, 295), and as usual his judgment is helpful, if
not quite completely accurate. The book certainly does have
creative power, though more restrained and more deliberately
used than ever before. It was used to structure a novel whose
overall plan was given preeminence over detail: there are virtually no parts that do not reflect and contribute to the pattern
of the whole, no matter how unsuccessful they may be on a local
level. Dickens surely was never more in control of his creative
power than in *Our Mutual Friend*. What Forster did correctly
sense, however, was that the novel was essentially different from
Dickens' previous writings. He had grasped intuitively that
something had happened to Dickens' creative faculty that had
changed the very nature of his fiction.

I have tried to demonstrate that throughout his career, at least
from the time of Mary Hogarth's death, Dickens' deepest creative
and imaginative forces had been invested in a complex psychological and fictional struggle between a mythic vision of pastoral
innocence and a hellish nightmare of urban experience. But in
writing *Great Expectations*, he had begun to overcome this
polarised picture of the world; and in *Our Mutual Friend* the
tension between country and city, and all that was associated
with it in Dickens' mind, which had for so long energised his

fiction, was overcome. The almost Manichean struggle between pastoral good and urban evil is transcended entirely in that novel by a view of the world which admitted the city as it was, which was in essence evil, but which allowed the possibility of the transformation of urban evil into wholly urban good.

The difficulties Dickens experienced beginning work on *Our Mutual Friend* were in all likelihood a reflection of the struggle to accommodate the changing imaginative springs of his fiction; it took him nearly three years from deciding upon a title for the novel in 1861 to begin actually writing it. This gestation period, during which he was thinking yet unable or unwilling to write, was the longest he had yet allowed himself, indicating the added effort that was involved in planning it. The writing proved unusually difficult once begun, too; though Dickens began with a full five monthly numbers in hand, again more than ever before, he quickly was reduced to writing to his monthly deadline. This difficult and slow progress has been seen as a sign of Dickens' failing powers of invention, but a close examination of the novel shows this is far from so: it teems with characters and events. Dickens' struggle to write was rather, I think, a search for new varieties of material. *Our Mutual Friend* is an experimental novel—in it Dickens was exploring techniques which were dramatic departures from anything in his prior writings.

For one thing, Dickens' use of language in the novel is freer and more flexible than ever before. The way that the prose adapts itself in tone and vocabulary to each set of characters is astonishing. For example, the manner in which Dickens forces us to see the Veneering circle as unreal through the style with which he writes about them is far more effective than any moral pronouncement with the same message made by the narrator ever could be. The Veneerings and their circle are denied the same objective status as characters like the Boffins or Eugene and Lizzie. So, those people who have reduced their lives to social abstractions (like the Veneerings), are through the novel's language themselves reduced to abstractions.

This narrative device, which forces the reader to see reality in different ways, is parallelled by Dickens' interest in vision in the novel. *Our Mutual Friend* contains all sorts of visions, from that of the Veneering party in their looking glass, to Betty Higden's vision of the dead, to Jenny Wren's vision of Heaven. Each of these visions is placed in or seen through a particular consciousness, and there are also several remarkable passages of sustained streams of consciousness in the novel in a mode that looks forward to Henry James and James Joyce. The description of Eugene's near murder by Headstone, to point out one of especial interest, is actually made up by Eugene's thoughts just before and at the instant he is struck on the head.

In a curious way, then, the faults of *Our Mutual Friend* are far more those of a first novel than a late one. It has too much exciting material, too many centres of attention, too many modes of apprehension, and even too much overwriting (for example, as the maudlin Betty Higden scenes are overwritten). Dickens' last completed novel is a transitional work, as no doubt would have been more easily seen had several more followed. Of course they did not, and so any analysis of the direction which Dickens was taking as a novelist in the last years of his life must remain speculative. What makes the situation even more complicated is that after 1865, the bulk of Dickens' creative power was poured not into his writing but into the public readings, where he felt he could reach more people more directly, and satisfy himself more as well. Dickens seemed quite aware that in some way he was constitutionally able to write novels *or* read, but not do both at once: thus, he wrote to Thomas Beard in 1862 to say that he was 'wavering' between starting a novel or going on a reading tour of Australia (4 November 1862; NL, III, 314).

Yet the public readings, in turn, became something of an excuse for an even more private drama Dickens enacted with himself in the performance of one particular reading. This was the reading of Nancy's murder by Sykes from *Oliver Twist*, which he had first tried out privately in 1863. But the effect he produced with it was so powerful that he was dissuaded from using such strong material in public; when at last he began reading it regularly before audiences in 1868, he devoted so much of his energy to it that each performance was virtually an attempted suicide, more than once nearly successful.[1] Only when he had retired from the reading platform permanently in 1870— and even his farewell tour had to be ended prematurely because of the grave danger to his health—did Dickens return to writing fiction full time.

However, we can gain some hints about his fictional development late in his career by looking at two of Dickens' last works, the short story, 'George Silverman's Explanation' and the half-completed novel, *Edwin Drood*. 'George Silverman's Explanation' was written (in a few days, according to Forster [*Life*, II, 297]) for the American periodical *Atlantic Monthly* where it appeared in serial form from January to March 1867. It is the story of a poor orphaned waif who becomes a minister, but whose life is ruined because his noble and disinterested actions are always being misinterpreted as evil and self-serving. There are in the story two novel technical innovations: the first is the form of the brief opening 'chapters', which are cast in a surprisingly 'modern' self-conscious narrative mode; and the other, the first person narrative itself, which presents the psychological portrait of a tormented soul entirely from within.[2] However, the development of the tale is far more conventional than its opening. The power of the first few pages is not sustained, and interest falls off rapidly.

The most notable and interesting feature of this story is its focus on the psychology of character. Taken with the part of *Edwin Drood* Dickens had left completed at his death, and the apparently deliberately confusing clues to its ending he scattered while writing it, it appears that Dickens was attempting to write a new kind of psychological fiction centring on the close study of human character. To judge from those two works, and the relevant portions of *Our Mutual Friend*, it is highly probable that his psychological analyses, like those of Dostoevsky, would have been of characters at the extreme edges of human experience—as with the schizophrenic murderer of Edwin Drood, John Jasper. Dickens' plan in *Edwin Drood* was, it seems to have the murderous half of Jasper's character take over the respectable half at the end of the novel, and have it confess his crimes in a long monologue set in a prison cell.

But of course Dickens did not live to finish *Edwin Drood*. After an unusually long day of writing, on 8 June 1870, Dickens began to feel ill. He made light of it, and sat down to dinner with the household. Then, he rose from the table and said he would go to

London at once. Those were the last coherent words he spoke. He collapsed at that moment, mumbled, 'On the floor', and lost consciousness. He died the next day.

II

The implications of this new novelistic career begun in *Our Mutual Friend* are fascinating. For one thing, it suggests that Dickens was moving closer towards a style of fiction which he has always been faulted for *not* writing, that is, one in which the development and exposition of character are given more attention than plot and description. One of the more persuasive recent detractors of Dickens' novelistic talents has claimed that he neglected to provide his characters with 'inner life': 'There is something about Dickens's way of looking at people which is unacceptable by the ordinary standards of serious fiction.'[3] Whatever truth such a charge against Dickens may have in respect of the earlier novels (and I would argue it is still little), it certainly cannot be levelled against either 'George Silverman's Explanation' or *Edwin Drood*, where the analytical study of the leading character's psychology is at the heart of the narratives.

Not wholly unrelated to Dickens' growing interest in character analysis is another development apparent in *Edwin Drood*, that is, the utilisation of physical setting for purely psychological effects. Philip Collins has noted that in *Edwin Drood*, Staple Inn appears several times (Chapters xi, xvii and xxii). Here Dickens describes in turn the chambers within it of Mr Grewgious, Neville Landless and Lieutenant Tartar. Each set of rooms reflects the character and emotional state of its occupant, as indeed do the season, weather and time of day: Tartar's rooms are therefore bright and tidy, and furthermore when we see them it is a warm, sunny summer day. What is unusual about this, as Collins notes, is that Staple Inn (and London itself) is not presented in a consistent manner, but is allowed to vary in tone and appearance considerably to meet exigencies of characterisation. Such manipulation of the physical environment would have been unthinkable in any of the preceding mature novels, where places are invested with tonal qualities independent of the novels' characters. For example, can one imagine Lincoln's Inn in *Bleak House* assuming a benign aspect merely because Esther Summerson is within it?[4]

This change in the character of Dickens' writing about the city is related both to the development of Dickens' attitudes toward the city and the personal past and to his increasing interest in the psychology of character. For one thing, this new attitude toward the city allowed Dickens to write about London locations without necessarily and automatically bringing to the surface deeply buried negative feelings. At the same time, his focusing on psychological portraiture required that physical reality no longer be presented directly by the narrator in his own voice, but rather indirectly through the mirroring consciousnesses of the novel's characters. In this way, the literal physical *milieu* in *Edwin Drood* palpably recedes in importance. The setting, whether it be Cloisterham or Staple Inn, has become more a backdrop to character than an independent fictional entity.

This is itself a startling development, for it implies that toward the close of his writing career the greatest English novelist of the city was ceasing to write city novels. Yet, in a sense, this was precisely what Dickens was doing. However, it is true only in a certain sense. Dickens was no longer writing about the actual city around him as if it were a character, complete with associated feelings, emotions, states of mind and influence over those who come into contact with it. Just how changed his treatment of the city had become can be appreciated by recalling one of the most effective earlier descriptions of the city, that of Smithfield on a market morning in Chapter xxi of *Oliver Twist* (discussed above in Chapter Two). The keynotes of this passage are the confused and excited motion, the crowds of animals and people, the dirt and squalor, but above all the noise, a 'hideous and discordant din that resounded from every corner of the market' (153). It begins with a procession: 'groups of labourers going to their work; then, men and women with fish-baskets on their heads; donkey-carts laden with vegetables; chaise-carts filled with livestock or whole carcasses of meat; milk-women with pails; an unbroken concourse of people' (152), and it closes with a throng that was 'a stunning and bewildering scene, *which quite confounded the senses*' (153; italics mine). This contrasts sharply—

in detail and tone—with the brief, almost casual description of the East End locale of the opium den in *Edwin Drood*: 'a miserable court, specially miserable among many such' (263). No more complete description of it is ever offered us.

The labyrinthine city of *Oliver Twist*, with all its horror, variety, excitement, passion, mystery, danger and vice, clearly is no longer the London we see in *Edwin Drood*. Still, while it has ceased to be equated with the real city, it has not ceased to exist. The nightmare city has become internalised, translated into the tortured, labyrinthine interior space of John Jasper's mind. It is a vision of that strange mind that opens *Edwin Drood*:

> An ancient English Cathedral Town? How can the ancient English Cathedral town be here! The well-known massive grey square tower of its old Cathedral? How can that be here! There is no spike of rusty iron in the air, between the eye and it, from any point of the real prospect. What is the spike that intervenes, and who has set it up? Maybe it is set up by the Sultan's orders for the impaling of a horde of Turkish robbers, one by one. It is so, for cymbals clash, and the Sultan goes by to his palace in long procession. Ten thousand scimitars flash in the sunlight, and thrice ten thousand dancing-girls strew flowers. Then, follow white elephants caparisoned in countless gorgeous colours, and infinite in number and attendants. Still the Cathedral Tower rises in the background, where it cannot be, and still no writhing figure is on the grim spike. Stay! Is the spike so low a thing as the rusty spike on the top of a post of an old bedstead that has tumbled all awry? Some vague period of drowsy laughter must be devoted to the consideration of this possibility.(1)

Here too, as in the London of the earlier novels, is a procession and a din, 'a stunning and bewildering scene, which . . . confounded the senses'—except that it is set not in the city streets but in the interior space of a single soul.

III

In the early decades of the nineteenth century, the city had changed so rapidly and fundamentally that it outdistanced society's ability to apprehend and account for it. As in the description of Smithfield in *Oliver Twist*, typically it struck observers as both mysterious and overwhelming. The great challenge presented by the experience of the nineteenth century city has been formulated as that of radical 'reperception'—a struggle to reeducate the sensibilities to counter a collective loss of faith in traditional ways of seeing and thereby to accommodate the changing social and physical environment.[5] The classic experience in the nineteenth century city was that of alienation, the perception of the city as a threatening and undomesticated otherness. There are many accounts of this experience in literature, perhaps one of the earliest being Wordsworth's shocked realisation in the London of the 1790s, that, 'The face of everyone/That passes by me is a mystery' (*The Prelude*, Book VII, ll. 628–9).

Some time in the 1820s, this frightening experience had become formalised, to a certain extent, in a literary device. This was the image of the city as *terra incognita*, a great unknown territory waiting to be explored. The phrase was used first (to my knowledge) by DeQuincey in 1822 in *Confessions of an English Opium-Eater*, but it was already in common currency by mid-century. Virtually every significant review of *Oliver Twist*, for example, referred to Dickens' illumination of this unknown land, as did Richard Ford in the *Quarterly Review*:

> Life in London, as revealed in the pages of Boz, opens a new world to thousands bred and born in the same city . . . for the one half of mankind lives without knowing how the other half dies. . . .[6]

And while this 'new world' (in another form, one of Disraeli's 'Two Nations') needed to be rediscovered many times over the century, it did eventually become known.

The terrifying mystery of the city was revealed and tamed in many ways: by concerned writers of fiction like Mrs Gaskell; by dedicated journalists, like Henry Mayhew; and by the unflinching and tireless efforts of reporters to Parliamentary Committees and other government bodies, to whose labours Marx acknowledged so great a debt. But beyond any doubt, the greatest work of demystification was that unfolded in the writing and reading

of Dickens' novels: his great accomplishment was to have pene-
trated utterly the inner urban jungle, and made it known to an
entire nation. And his works were, it must not be forgotten, a
truly national enterprise: Dickens' audience over his career
included the vast majority of the English reading public. Cumulative sales of his novels to 1870 numbered in the millions and
a circulation of over 300,000 has been claimed for the final years
of *All the Year Round* in his lifetime. His popularity, if anything,
grew in the years immediately after his death: from 1870 to 1882
Chapman and Hall sold 4,239,000 volumes of his works.[7]
Furthermore, as a reader, in his 472 public appearances, Dickens'
voice and person became known directly to many tens of
thousands. And in countless households, family readings of his
works reduplicated his own great stage performances.

Dickens' influence upon his age cannot, therefore, be measured
within a narrow literary compass. More than a writer, he was
almost a national institution, so much a part of the national
cultural life of England from the 1830s onward that his contemporaries absorbed him whole, as they did the Bible, breathing
in the very rhythms and stuff of his prose and as they did their
first breaths of learning. The city of Dickens in this way became
the possession of an entire nation.

I have noted at the start of this work that Dickens had few
fellows among his literary contemporaries as a novelist of the
city. Initially, there were good reasons for this. As I have tried
to indicate, there opened up over the first half of the century a
tremendous gap between the social actuality of the life of the
majority of town dwellers and the social actuality perceived by
the majority of the literate middle and upper classes. The causes
of this are obscure and mystifying, but the situation did exist
and writers were no more immune to its effects than anyone
else. They were as reluctant or unable to depict what they did
not or refused to know as were, for example, the painters of the
Royal Academy, whose works reveal a similar lack of urban
subject matter.[8]

It is also relevant to note that the nature of the literary
profession and the literary world was changing at mid-century.
The profession was, as were most cultural institutions, less
centred on London than during the previous century, and more

dominated by the provincial middle classes. Its members were likely to have absorbed an anti-metropolitan bias from two sources: from a Nonconformist religious culture which often viewed the metropolis with suspicion as the modern Babylon; and from the two ancient Universities of Oxford and Cambridge, which aside from their considerable pastoral attractions tended to inculcate disdain for the business pursuits associated with the metropolis. In this respect George Eliot is a far more representative literary figure than Dickens. She was never at ease while in London, and only toward the end of her career, in *Middlemarch* (1871–2), wrote a novel endorsing modern city life, and after it with *Daniel Deronda* (1876) a true city novel, thus arriving at the analogous moment in her fiction to that at which Dickens had begun his writing career with *Sketches by Boz*.

All this notwithstanding, it is more difficult to understand the lack of any notable literary successors to Dickens as a city novelist. The leading talents of the next generation had all the advantages of having Dickens' example before them; yet the generation of James and Hardy seems to owe little to Dickens in their choice of material.

Part of the answer to this must be that the anti-urban myth continued to flourish in England long after it had ceased to have any basis in actual experience. 'What was wrong with this "myth" of rural life', writes E. P. Thompson, 'is that it became softened, prettified, protracted and then taken over by city-dwellers as a major point from which to criticise "industrialism"', and so could be used by city-dwellers to avoid any true confrontation of urban society.[9] The city was the unit of society which most closely represented and constituted modern life, and as writers more and more found themselves in opposition to that life, they assumed automatically an anti-city stance. Much as Edwardian industrialists were sinking their fortunes in country estates, later nineteenth and early twentieth century writers turned to the country house rather than the city for their inspiration. Later novelists, for example Forster, Lawrence and Huxley, still regarded urbanised England with distaste, and sought fictional escape in more exotic (but nevertheless recognisably 'country') settings, such as India, Italy, and New Mexico. Indeed, this is a phenomenon of our time, too. The anti-urban myth remains active, relegated to the popular but lively forms of the historical and romantic novel and the 'B' film.

But this persistence of the pastoral mode, debilitating as it was for the literary culture, offers only a partial explanation—after all, Dickens was highly susceptible to it himself. Dickens' unique position in England as a city novelist surely owes something as well to the unique character of his achievement. For in as much as Dickens had made the city 'known', there was no need for anyone to repeat his work. The work of discovery was over: the city of Dickens had entered the consciousness of the age, as it had the mind of John Jasper. As his continental contemporaries, Balzac, Hugo, Gogol, Dostoevsky and Baudelaire, were doing in their own work, Dickens was liberating the city, so that what was unknown and feared could become the possession of all. He was transforming it into a place where, as Conrad wrote in the preface to *The Secret Agent* (1907), 'There was room enough . . . to place any story, depth enough . . . for any passion, variety enough . . . for any setting, darkness enough to bury five millions of lives.' For Conrad, as for the two greatest modern city writers, Joyce and Eliot, the city was not *a* world, but *the* world, and the only world there was. Modern life had become exclusively city life[10].

Gissing, perhaps of all his generation the most appreciative of Dickens' influence, did not exaggerate when he wrote that, 'he taught people a certain way of regarding the huge city.'[11] To read his novels over the thirty some odd years during which they were written was to enter into a profound enterprise: it was to approach more closely one's own reactions to a changing environment, and in doing so, to understand better the world in which one lived. His work constituted an act of exploration that made freely available to the sensibility of his culture its most mystifying and most urgent experience.

From unknown land, to a mine in which all of human experience could be found by one who knew where and how to look: that suggests the literary history of the city in the nineteenth century. In no small part, this had been Dickens' work: he had brought the city forth from its obscurity and mystery, and made known the urban world to those who inhabited it, and to us, who inhabit it still.

APPENDIX I

A Note on George Scharf

Many of the illustrations for this study are the work of George Scharf (1788–1860), and are drawn from the large collection of Scharf's sketch books, drawings and watercolours in the Department of Prints and Drawings of the British Museum.

Scharf was born in Bavaria, and trained as a portraitist in Munich. After travelling widely on the Continent during the Napoleonic Wars, he joined the British Army at Waterloo, and in 1816 came to England. He remained in London for the rest of his life, establishing himself in the 1820s as one of the leading scientific lithographic draughtsmen of the period. During his lifetime he was known almost exclusively for his geological and scientific drawings; among his many eminent clients were Charles Darwin and Richard Owen, the geologist. His eldest son, later Sir George Scharf, was for many years director of the National Portrait Gallery, London.

Almost immediately upon his arrival in England, Scharf began sketching London street scenes and street life, apparently hoping to turn this work to some financial advantage. But aside from occasional commissions from architects, and a successful arrangement with the New London Bridge Committee in 1830–1, to record the demolition of the old bridge and the construction of the new, Scharf derived little profit from his city sketches. Nevertheless, until shortly before his death he continued to record the varied and changing face of the city with great skill and in scrupulously exhaustive detail. In their comprehensiveness and representational accuracy, Scharf's drawings and paintings constitute a unique and uniquely valuable pictorial record of late Georgian and early Victorian London.

APPENDIX II

A Note on Sources and Further Reading

This is a compilation of those general sources I have found most useful in writing this essay, and to which I owe more than could be acknowledged in notes to the text. It is also intended to be a guide to further reading on subjects central to the concerns of this study. In the section below, *The City*, I have concentrated primarily upon works of bibliographical interest.

The City: An excellent introduction to and bibliographic survey of the growth of the systematic sociological study of the city in America and Europe is Don Martindale's introductory remarks in Max Weber, *The City* (London: Heinemann, 1960), 9–62. Still unsurpassed as an outline of the parameters of an urban sociology is Louis Wirth's essay, 'Urbanism as a Way of Life', in *American Journal of Sociology* 44 (1938), 1–24. Paul K. Hatt and Albert J. Reiss, eds., *Cities and Society* (New York: Free Press, 1957), provide a useful collection of articles on urban sociology. The organised study of urban history is a relatively recent development. Two excellent anthologies which offer a representative variety of approaches to the subject are, Oscar Handlin and John Burchard, eds., *The Historian and the City* (Cambridge: M.I.T. and Harvard, 1963), and H. J. Dyos, ed., *The Study of Urban History* (London: Edward Arnold, 1968). This latter collection includes Professor Dyos' historical and bibliographic survey, 'Agenda for Urban History', 1–46, which is of especial interest. Dyos supplements this material in several long review articles in *British Book News*, August and September 1973, and November 1976. Two periodicals contain invaluable information: *Urban History Newsletter* (1963ff.) and *Urban History Yearbook* (1974ff.).

The study of the Victorian city has been more fully documented. Lional Madden's comprehensive research guide, *How to Find Out About the Victorian Period* (Leicester: Leicester, 1970), is worth noting as a general introduction to the literature in the field, and to the study of Victorian England in general. Asa Briggs' *Victorian Cities* (London: Odhams, 1963) is a provocative and thorough survey of the subject; the fullest modern general history of Victorian London is Francis Sheppard, *London, 1808–1870* (London: Secker and Warburg, 1971). A massive and eminently useful collection of material compiled by H. J. Dyos and Michael Wolff, *The Victorian City* (London: Routledge and Kegan Paul, 1973), continues to follow the catholic and interdisciplinary approach pioneered by Lord Briggs by including the work of authors from many different areas of specialisation. Of great value is the journal *Victorian Studies* (1957ff.), especially the exhaustive annual bibliography published in it.

Literature and the City: The only general survey of the development of attitudes toward the city and the country in English literature is by Raymond Williams, *The Country and the City* (London: Chatto and Windus, 1973). His earlier article 'Literature and the City', in *Listener*, 78 (1967), 653–6, is also of some interest. Two descriptive surveys of nineteenth century English literary treatment of the city are worth noting: Asa Briggs, *Victorian Cities* (1963), 57–82; and John Henry Raleigh, 'The Novel and the City: England and America in the Nineteenth Century', *Victorian Studies*, 11 (1968), 291–328. A provocative study of a relevant non-literary text is Steven Marcus, *Engels, Manchester and the Working Class* (New York: Random House, 1974), which contains many helpful generalisations about the nature of town life and Victorian approaches to it. A useful compilation of extracts from many literary and non-literary source materials is B. I. Coleman, ed., *The Idea of the City in the Nineteenth Century* (London: Routledge and Kegan Paul, 1973).

Dickens and the City: The first and still a most useful general study which explores the social dimension of Dickens' writings was Humphry House, *The Dickens World* (London: Oxford, 1942). Donald Fanger pioneered the study of Dickens as an urban writer in *Dostoevsky and Romantic Realism* (Cambridge: Harvard, 1965), 65–100; his essay is a systematic attempt to view the overall development of Dickens' fictional treatment of London, in relation to its European context. Alexander Welsh's provocative work, *The City of Dickens* (Oxford: Clarendon, 1971), offers a synchronic approach to the novels, which sheds in passing a great deal of light on Victorian literature and culture; for a fuller discussion of it, see above, Chapter Two. Philip Collins' essay, 'Dickens and London', in H. J. Dyos and Michael Wolff, eds., *The Victorian City*, 537–58, discerns a broad pattern of development in the life and work, and offers a number of suggestive remarks.

Select Bibliography

This list contains information about those works which have been found most useful in researching and writing this study. It is not intended to be a complete record of all works consulted. In general, articles in periodicals referred to in footnotes above have not been listed here unless they are of especial interest.

Altick, Richard D. *The English Common Reader*. Chicago: University of Chicago Press, 1957.

—. *Victorian People and Ideas*. London: J. M. Dent and Sons, 1974.

Ames, Winslow. *Prince Albert and Victorian Taste*. London: Chapman and Hall, 1967.

Bagehot, Walter. *Literary Studies*. 3 volumes. London: Longmans, Green, 1898.

Besant, Walter, ed. *The Fascination of London*. 12 volumes. London: A. & C. Black, 1902–8.

Best, Geoffrey. *Mid-Victorian Britain, 1851–1875*. London: Weidenfeld and Nicolson, 1971.

Boynton, Percy. *London in English Literature*. Chicago: University of Chicago Press, 1913.

Boys, Thomas Shotter. *Original Views of London As It Is*, 1842. Facsimile edition. London: The Architectural Press, 1926.

Briggs, Asa. *The Age of Improvement, 1784–1867*. London: Longman, 1959.

—. *Victorian Cities*. London: Odhams Press, 1963.

—. *Victorian People*. Expanded edn. New York: Harper and Row, 1963.

Buckley, Jerome Hamilton. *The Triumph of Time*. Cambridge, Massachusetts: Harvard University Press, and London: Oxford University Press, 1967.

Bulwer Lytton, Edward. *Eugene Aram*. London: Henry Colburn and Richard Bentley, 1832.

—. *Paul Clifford*. London: Henry Colburn and Richard Bentley, 1830.

Burn, W. L. *The Age of Equipoise*. London: George Allen and Unwin, 1964.

Butt, John and Tillotson, Kathleen. *Dickens at Work*. London: Methuen, 1957.

Carey, John. *The Violent Effigy*. London: Faber and Faber, 1973.

Cazamian, Louis. *The Social Novel in England 1830–1850.* Trans. by Martin Fido. London: Routledge and Kegan Paul, 1973.

Chesney, Kellow. *The Victorian Underworld.* London: Temple Smith, 1970.

Chesterton, G. K. *Charles Dickens.* Introduction by Steven Marcus. New York: Schocken Books, 1965.

Clark, G. Kitson. *The Making of Victorian England.* London: Methuen, 1962.

Cobbet, William. *Rural Rides.* 2 volumes. London: Dent (Everyman's Library), and New York: Dutton, 1912.

Cole, G. D. H., and Postgate, Raymond. *The Common People, 1746–1946.* Fourth edition. London: Methuen, 1961.

Coleman, B. I., ed. *The Idea of the City in the Nineteenth Century.* London: Routledge and Kegan Paul, 1973.

Collins, Philip. *Dickens and Crime.* Second edition. London: Macmillan, 1964.

—. *Dickens and Education.* London: Macmillan, 1963.

—. 'Dickens's Reading'. *Dickensian,* 60 (1964), 136–51.

Collins, Philip, ed. *Dickens, The Critical Heritage.* London: Routledge and Kegan Paul, 1971.

Conrad, Peter. *The Victorian Treasure-House.* London: Collins, 1973.

Cruse, Amy. *The Victorians and Their Books.* London: George Allen and Unwin, 1935.

DeQuincey, Thomas. *Collected Writings.* Ed. David Masson. Vol. i: Autobiography. Vol. ii: Autobiography and Literary Reminiscences. Vol. iii: London Reminiscences. London: A. & C. Black, 1896–97.

DeVries, Duane. *Dickens's Apprentice Years.* New York: Barnes and Noble, 1976.

Dexter, Walter. 'The London Dickens Knew'. *Dickensian,* 25 (1929), 59, 105, 207, 272, and 26 (1930), 58.

Dickens, Charles. 'Memoranda Book'. MS. Notebook, 1855–70. Berg Collection, New York Public Library.

—. Unpublished Letters to Baroness Burdett Coutts. Pierpont Morgan Library, New York.

—. *The Oxford Illustrated Dickens.* 21 volumes. London: Oxford University Press, 1947–58.

—. *The Clarendon Dickens.* 3 volumes, to date. Oxford: Clarendon Press, 1966ff.

—. *Collected Papers.* 2 volumes. London: Nonesuch Press, 1937.

—. *Miscellaneous Papers.* Ed. B. W. Matz. London: Chapman and Hall, 1908.

—. *The Letters of Charles Dickens.* 3 volumes. Edited by Walter Dexter. London: Nonesuch Press, 1938.

—. *The Pilgrim Edition of the Letters of Charles Dickens.* 3 volumes, to date. Edited by Madeline House, Graham Storey, *et al.* Oxford: Clarendon Press, 1965ff.

—. *Letters From Charles Dickens to Angela Burdett-Coutts 1841–1865.* Ed. Edgar Johnson. London: Jonathan Cape, 1953.

—. *Mr. and Mrs. Charles Dickens: His Letters to Her.* Ed. Walter Dexter. London: Constable and Co., 1935.

—. *The Public Readings.* Ed. Philip Collins. Oxford: Clarendon Press, 1975.

—. *The Speeches of Charles Dickens.* Ed. K. J. Fielding. London: Oxford University Press, 1960.

—. (co-author). *The Uncollected Writings of Charles Dickens: Household Words 1850–1859.* 2 volumes. Ed. Harry F. Stone. London: Allen Lane The Penguin Press, 1969.

—. (Editor). *All the Year Round.* London: 1859–70.

—. (Editor). *Household Words.* London: 1850–9.

Dickens, Henry F. *The Recollections of Sir Henry Dickens, K.C.* London: Heinemann, 1934.

—. *Memories of My Father.* London: Victor Gollancz, 1928.

Dodds, John W. *The Age of Paradox: A Biography of England, 1841–1851.* London: Victor Gollancz, 1953.

Dostoevsky, Fyodor. *Summer Impressions.* Trans. by Karl Fitzlyon. London: John Calder, 1955.

Dupee, F. W. 'The Other Dickens'. *Partisan Review,* 27 (1960), 110–22.

Dyos, H. J. and Wolff, Michael, eds. *The Victorian City: Images and Realities.* 2 volumes. London and Boston: Routledge and Kegan Paul, 1973.

Egan, Pierce. *The Finish to the Adventures of Tom, Jerry, and Logic.* London: Reeves and Turner, 1869.

—. *Life in London, or the Day and Night Scenes of Jerry Hawthorne, Esq. and his Elegant Friend Corinthian Tom in their Rambles and Sprees through the Metropolis.* London: John Camden Hotten, 1869.

Empson, William. *Some Versions of Pastoral.* London: Chatto and Windus, 1935.

Engel, Monroe. *The Maturity of Dickens.* Cambridge, Massachusetts: Harvard University Press, and London: Oxford University Press, 1959.

Engels, Frederick. *The Condition of the Working Class in England.* London: Panther Books, 1972.

Fanger, Donald. *Dostoevsky and Romantic Realism: A Study of Dostoevsky in Relation to Balzac, Dickens and Gogol.* Cambridge, Massachusetts: Harvard University Press, 1965.

Fielding, K. J. *Charles Dickens: A Critical Introduction.* 2nd edition. London: Longmans, Green, 1965.

Finer, S. E. *The Life and Times of Sir Edwin Chadwick.* London: Methuen 1952.

Ford, George H. *Dickens and His Readers.* Princeton, New Jersey: Princeton University Press, and London: Oxford University Press, 1955.

Forster, John. *The Life of Charles Dickens.* Ed. J. W. T. Ley. London: Cecil Palmer, 1928.

—. *The Life of Charles Dickens.* Revised Everyman's Library edition. 2 volumes. Ed. A. J. Hoppé. London: Dent, and New York: Dutton, 1969.

Garis, Robert. *The Dickens Theatre: A Reassessment of the Novels.* London: Oxford University Press, 1965.

Gelfant, Blanche Houseman. *The American City Novel.* Norman: University of Oklahoma, 1954.

George, M. Dorothy. *London Life in the XVIIIth Century.* London: Kegan, Paul, 1925.

Gissing, George. *Charles Dickens: A Critical Study.* London: Blackie and Son, 1898.

—. *Critical Studies of the Works of Charles Dickens.* New York: Greenberg, 1924.

Godwin, George. *Town Swamps and Social Bridges.* Facsimile of 1859 edition. Leicester: Leicester University Press, 1972.

Gomme, G. Laurence. *London in the Reign of Victoria (1837–1897).* London: Blackie and Son, 1898.

Gross, John and Pearson, Gabriel, eds. *Dickens and the Twentieth Century.* London: Routledge and Kegan Paul, 1962.

Halévy, Elie. *England in 1815.* Trans. by E. I. Watkin and D. A. Barker. London: Ernest Benn, 1949.

Hammond, J. L. and Barbara. *The Bleak Age.* West Drayton, Middlesex, and New York: Penguin Books, 1947.

Handlin, Oscar and Burchard, John, eds. *The Historian and The City.* Cambridge, Massachusetts: M.I.T. Press and Harvard University Press, 1963.

Harrison, Brian. *Drink and the Victorians.* London: Faber and Faber, 1971.

Hatt, Paul K. and Reiss, Albert J., eds. *Cities and Society: The Revised Reader in Urban Sociology*. New York: The Free Press, 1957.

Hill, T. W. 'Books that Dickens Read'. *Dickensian*, 45 (1949), 81–90, 201–7.

—. 'Dickens and His "Ugly Duckling"'. *Dickensian*, 46 (1950), 190–6.

—. 'Notes on *Bleak House*'. *Dickensian*, 40 (1943–4), 39–44, 65–70, 135–41.

—. 'Notes on *Little Dorrit*', *Dickensian*, 41 (1945), 196–203, and 42 (1946), 38–44, 82–91.

—. 'Notes on *Sketches by Boz*'. *Dickensian*, 46 (1950), 206–13, 47 (1951), 41–8, 102–7, 210–8, and 48 (1952), 32–7, 90–4.

Hobsbawm, E. J. *Industry and Empire*. Harmondsworth: Penguin Books, 1969.

Hollingsworth, Keith. *The Newgate Novel, 1830–1847*. Detroit: Wayne State University Press, 1963.

Horne, R. H. *A New Spirit of the Age*. Vol. 1. London: Smith, Elder, 1844.

Houghton, Walter E. *The Victorian Frame of Mind, 1830–1870*. New Haven and London: Yale University Press, 1957.

House, Humphry. *The Dickens World*. 2nd edition. London: Oxford University Press, 1942.

Hunt, Leigh. *Leigh Hunt's London Journal*. London: 1834–5.

—. *Political and Occasional Essays*. Ed. L. H. Houtchens and C. W. Houtchens. New York and London: Columbia University Press, 1962.

Hutter, Albert D. 'Psychoanalysis and Biography: Dickens' Experience at Warren's Blacking'. *Hartford Studies in Literature*, 8 (1976).

Irving, William Henry. *John Gay's London*. Cambridge, Massachusetts: Harvard University Press, 1928.

James, Henry. *Essays in London and Elsewhere*. London: J. R. Osgood, McIlvaine, 1893.

James, Louis. *Fiction for the Working Man, 1830–1850*. London: Oxford University Press, 1963.

Johnson, Edgar. *Charles Dickens: His Tragedy and Triumph*. 2 volumes. London: Victor Gollancz, 1953.

Jordan, Robert Furneaux. *Victorian Architecture*. London: Penguin Books, 1966.

Keating, P. J. *The Working Classes in Victorian Fiction*. London: Routledge and Kegan Paul, 1971.

Kermode, Frank. *Modern Essays*. London: Fontana, 1971.

Klingender, Francis D. *Art and the Industrial Revolution*. Edited and revised by Arthur Elton. London: Paladin, 1972.

Knight, Charles, ed. *London*. 6 volumes. London: Knight, 1841–4.

Kris, Ernst. *Psychoanalytic Explorations in Art*. New York: Schocken Books, 1964.

Lamb, Charles. *Miscellaneous Prose, 1798–1834*, Ed. E. V. Lucas. London: Methuen, 1903.

Langton, Robert. *The Childhood and Youth of Charles Dickens*. London: Hutchinson, 1891.

Lansbury, Coral. 'Dickens' Romanticism Domesticated'. *Dickens Studies Newsletter*, 3 (1972), 36–46.

Leavis, F. R. and Q. D. *Dickens the Novelist*. London: Chatto and Windus, 1970.

Lindsay, Jack. *Charles Dickens*. London: Andrew Dakers, 1950.

Mack, Maynard. *The Garden and the City: Retirement and Politics in the Later Poetry of Pope, 1731–1743*. Toronto: University of Toronto Press, and London: Oxford University Press, 1969.

Madden, Lionel. *How to Find Out About the Victorian Period*. New York and Oxford: Pergamon Press, 1970.

Marcus, Steven. *Dickens: From Pickwick to Dombey*. New York: Basic Books, 1965.

—. *Engels, Manchester, and the Working Class*. New York: Random House, 1974.

—. *Representations*. New York: Random House, 1976.

Marx, Leo. *The Machine in the Garden*. New York: Oxford University Press, 1964.

Mayhew, Henry. *The Unknown Mayhew*. Ed. E. P. Thompson and Eileen Yeo. London: Merlin Press, 1971.

Metcalf, Priscilla. *Victorian London*. London: Cassell, 1972.

Miller, J. Hillis. *Charles Dickens: The World of His Novels*. Cambridge, Massachusetts: Harvard University Press, 1958.

Miyoshi, Masao. *The Divided Self*. New York: New York University Press, and London: University of London Press, 1969.

Moers, Ellen. *The Dandy: Brummel to Beerbohm*. London: Secker and Warburg, 1960.

Mumford, Lewis. *The City in History*. London: Secker and Warburg, 1961.

Nisbet, Ada and Nevius, Blake, eds. *Dickens Centennial Essays*. Berkeley and London: University of California Press, 1971.

Oddie, William. *Dickens and Carlyle: The Question of Influence*. London: The Centenary Press, 1972.

Partlow, Robert B. Jr., ed. *Dickens the Craftsman*. Carbondale,

Illinois: Southern Illinois University Press, and London: Feffer and Simons, 1970.

—, ed. *Dickens Studies Annual*. Carbondale, Illinois: Southern Illinois University Press, and London: Feffer and Simons, 1970ff.

Pevsner, Nikolaus. *Some Architectural Writers of the Nineteenth Century*. Oxford: Clarendon Press, 1972.

Pugin, A. W. N. *Contrasts: Or, A Parallel Between the Noble Edifices of the Fourteenth and Fifteenth Centuries, and Similar Buildings of the Present Day; Shewing the Present Decay of Taste*. Facsimile of 1841 edition. Leicester: Leicester University Press, 1969.

—. *An Apology for the Revival of Christian Architecture in England*. Facsimile of 1843 Edition. Oxford: Basil Blackwell, 1969.

Rasmussen, Steen Eiler. *London: The Unique City*. London: Jonathan Cape, 1937.

Reddaway, T. F. 'London in the Nineteenth Century'. *Nineteenth Century*, 145 (1949), 363–74, 147 (1950), 104–18, 118–30, and [as *Twentieth Century*] 151 (1951), 163–77.

Sala, George Augustus. *Twice Round the Clock*. Facsimile of 1859 edition. Leicester: Leicester University Press, 1971.

Seaman, L. C. B. *Life in Victorian London*. London: Batsford, 1973.

Sheppard, Francis. *London, 1808–1870: The Infernal Wen*. London: Secker and Warburg, 1971.

Spears, Monroe K. *Dionysus and the City: Modernism in Twentieth-Century Poetry*. New York and London: Oxford University Press, 1970.

Steegman, John. *Victorian Taste*. Facsimile edition of *Consort of Taste*. London: Nelson, 1970.

Storey, Gladys. *Dickens and Daughter*. London: Frederick Muller, 1939.

Summerson, Sir John. *Georgian London*. Revised edition. London: Barrie and Jenkins, 1970.

—. *The London Building World of the 1860s*. London: Thames and Hudson, 1973.

Sussman, Herbert L. *Victorians and the Machine*. Cambridge, Massachusetts: Harvard University Press, 1968.

Sutherland, John A. *Victorian Novelists and Publishers*. London: Athlone Press, 1976.

Thompson, E. P. *The Making of the English Working Class*. Revised edition. Harmondsworth: Penguin, 1968.

Tillotson, Kathleen. *Novels of the Eighteen-Forties*. Oxford: Clarendon Press, 1954.

Tobias, J. J. *Crime and Industrial Society in the Nineteenth Century.* London: Penguin Books, 1972.

Watt, Ian. *The Rise of the Novel.* London: Chatto and Windus, 1957.

Weber, Max. *The City.* Trans. and edited by Don Martindale and Gertrud Neuwirth. London: Heinemann, 1960.

Weimer, David R. *The City as Metaphor.* New York: Random House, 1966.

Welsh, Alexander. *The City of Dickens.* Oxford: Clarendon Press, 1971.

Williams, Raymond. *The Country and the City.* London: Chatto and Windus, 1973.

—. *Culture and Society, 1780–1950.* London: Chatto and Windus, 1958.

Young, G. M., ed. *Early Victorian England, 1830–1865.* 2 volumes. London: Oxford University Press, 1934.

—. *Victorian England: Portrait of an Age.* 2nd edition. London and New York: Oxford University Press, 1953.

Notes

Introduction. The Genesis of a Myth

1 Figures are from Eric Lampard, 'The Urbanizing World', in H. J. Dyos and Michael Wolff, eds., *The Victorian City* (London and Boston: Routledge and Kegan Paul, 1973), 33 and 41.

2 See Louis Wirth, 'Urbanism as a Way of Life', *American Journal of Sociology*, 44 (1938), 2.

3 This is something of an overstatement: literary studies have done so, but only tentatively, and in fits and starts. Raymond Williams' *The Country and the City* (London: Chatto and Windus, 1973) remains almost alone in what surely must be a huge and rewarding field of enquiry. Alexander Welsh's *The City of Dickens* (Oxford: Clarendon, 1971) is not, despite its title, as much about the city as Victorian attitudes towards death, women and domestic life. Dyos and Wolff, eds., *The Victorian City*, contains several essays on the subject, among them, G. Robert Strange, 'The Frightened Poets', 475–95, and U. C. Knoepfelmacher, 'The Novel Between City and Country', 517–36. Other works include relevant material, though not nominally about the city: an excellent example is Louis James, *Fiction for the Working Man* (London: Oxford, 1963). There are several studies of the city and American literature: Blanche Gelfant, *The American City Novel* (Norman: Oklahoma, 1954); Leo Marx, *The Machine in the Garden* (New York: Oxford, 1964); and David Weimer, *The City as Metaphor* (New York: Random House, 1966). A brief discussion of urbanisation and the eighteenth century novel can be found in Ian Watt, *The Rise of the Novel* (London: Chatto and Windus, 1957), 174–91.

4 *Literary Studies* (London: Longman, Green, 1898), II, 140.

5 For further discussion of Dickens and his contemporaries and the city, see the Epilogue, below.

6 There are several studies which on the whole confirm this view: Humphry House, *The Dickens World* (London: Oxford, 1942); and Philip Collins, *Dickens and Crime* (London: Macmillan, 1964), and *Dickens and Education* (London: Macmillan, 1963).

7 It is worth noting that this 'Warren's Blacking' was *not* the source of the original, celebrated product manufactured by Robert Warren, but a rival firm, established by Robert Warren's distant relation Jonathan but now owned by George Lamert, and managed by James Lamert, who was a Dickens cousin on good terms with the family, and who arranged the job for Charles.

8 Statistics used below are based on information in B. R. Mitchell, *Abstract of British Historical Statistics* (Cambridge: Cambridge, 1962), 6, 20, 24, 26.

9 Eric E. Lampard, 'The Urbanizing World', in H. J. Dyos and Michael Wolff, eds., *The Victorian City*, 12, 13, and *passim*.

10 A large but unknown fraction of these migrants were Irish, almost all from the Irish countryside.

11 For accounts of town life in the early and middle years of the nineteenth century, see R. H. Mottram, 'Town Life and London', in G. M. Young, ed., *Early Victorian England* (London: Oxford, 1934) I, 153–223; J. H. and M. H. Clapham, 'Life in the New Towns', ibid. 225–44; and T. F. Reddaway, 'London in the Nineteenth-Century', *Nineteenth Century* 145 (1949), 363–74, 147 (1950), 104–18, 148 (1950), 118–30, and [as *Twentieth Century*] 151 (1951), 163–77. Also of interest is M. Dorothy George, *London Life in the XVIIIth Century* (London: Kegan Paul, 1925).

12 *Industry and Empire* (Harmondsworth: Penguin, 1969), 87.

13 For classic accounts of this type of experience see Robert Jay Lifton's *History and Human Survival* (New York: Random House, 1970); for an excellent account of the effects on personality of the concentration camps, see Bruno Bettelheim, 'Reflections', *New Yorker*, 62 (2 August 1976), 31–52.

14 This narrative is pieced together from Forster's *Life*, I, 11–33, combining passages he quoted directly from the fragment, and others which are not direct quotations, but whose wording suggests they are almost exact paraphrases with very little beside the pronouns and verb forms altered. For that reason, I have treated it as a continuous narrative in Dickens' own words. (Unfortunately, none of the original manuscript has ever come to light, and presumably was lost along with that of the *Life*.)

15 'Dickens: The Two Scrooges', in *The Wound and the Bow* (1952), 5. A great deal of confusion has been caused by Wilson's use of the word 'trauma': it is borrowed from psychoanalysis, but the usage is not properly psychoanalytic. No formative trauma in the analytic sense could occur as late in life as age eleven or twelve. Five or six would be a more probable age for such an event. Strictly speaking, then, Dickens' experiences were a great shock, but not a trauma.

16 In the discussion which follows, I have drawn freely from Steven Marcus, *Dickens: From Pickwick to Dombey* (1965), 277–92, and 360–78; and a paper delivered at the 1975 Modern Language Association Dickens Seminar by Albert D. Hutter, 'Reconstructive Autobiography: Dickens's Experience at Warren's Blacking', reprinted in *Hartford Studies in Literature* (1976). Also noteworthy is Sylvia Manning, 'Masking and Self-Revelation: Dickens's Three Autobiographies', *Dickens Studies Newsletter*, 7 (1976), 69–75.

17 The telescoping effects increased as Dickens grew older; thus, in a letter to a person seeking biographical information about him in 1838, Dickens remembered having lived in London as an infant, and also more correctly noted his age at returning to London as twelve. See, To J. H. Kuenzel, ? July 1838, PL, I, 423.

18 'The Metropolis on Stage', in H. J. Dyos and Michael Wolff, eds., *The Victorian City*, 216–17; see also 213, and *passim*.

19 *Fiction for the Working Man* (1963), 202, quoting 'An Invitation', by Elija Ridings; see also 117–23.

20 A magnificently illustrated and allusive account of his day in the City is John Greaves, 'Gone Astray', *Dickens Studies Annual*, 3 (1974), 144–61.

21 Quoted by Gladys Storey, *Dickens and Daughter* (London: Muller, 1939) 92. Anonymity seemed to be essential to these perambulations; as Dickens grew older these walks became something of 'a royal progress', according to his son Henry (*Memories of my Father* [London: Heinemann, 1928], 17), which must have made it difficult to find the sort of release he desired. In 1867 he told an interviewer that while walking he often resorted to disguise, or would act like a rent collector, or other person on business, to

avoid attracting notice (See G. D. Carrow, 'An Informal Call on Charles Dickens', reprinted in *Dickensian*, 63 [1967] 112–19).

22 *Dickens's Apprentice Years* (New York: Barnes and Noble, 1976), 1–17.

23 *Dickens: From Pickwick to Dombey*, 381–2.

1. *Sketches by Boz*: Fiction for the Metropolis

1 The text used here is that of the first collected book editions of *SB*—First Series, February 1836 and Second Series, December 1836. Since Dickens altered *SB* substantially in successive editions, this text is closer to the original than that of the Cheap Edition of 1850, which is the basis of modern editions. But for convenience, all page references given are to the Oxford Illustrated Dickens Edition.

2 The most notable of recent critical studies are J. Hillis Miller's seminal lecture, 'The Fiction of Realism: *Sketches by Boz, Oliver Twist,* and Cruickshank's Illustrations', reprinted in Ada Nisbet and Blake Nevius, eds., *Dickens Centennial Essays* (Berkeley and London: California, 1971), 85–153, and Duane DeVries, *Dickens's Apprentice Years* (New York: Barnes and Noble, 1976), to both of which this essay owes much; still invaluable is Kathleen Tillotson's work in her and John Butt's *Dickens at Work* (London: Methuen, 1957), 35–61.

3 The texts of most known reviews were reprinted by Walter Dexter, in 'The Reception of Dickens' First Book', *Dickensian*, 32 (1936), 43–50. See also his 'Contemporary Opinion of Dickens's Earliest Work', *Dickensian*, 31 (1935), 105–8, and 157–8, which extracts earlier critical remarks from periodicals.

4 The total sum paid was £2250, probably including £250 for existing stock; to some extent, it was paying Macrone not to reissue *Sketches* in monthly parts himself, perhaps thereby damaging the sales of *Pickwick*. Even so, the sum was exceptionally large: Dickens estimated he did not earn more than £2500 for *Pickwick* itself (though Chapman and Hall, the publishers, earned £14,000).

5 Butt and Tillotson, *Dickens at Work*, 37. Interestingly, the popular success of Pierce Egan's *Life in London*, issued in parts over 1822–4, is similarly explained by his biographer; see J. C. Reid, *Bucks and Bruisers: Pierce Egan and Regency England* (London: Routledge and Kegan Paul, 1971), 68–9.

6 The population figures are taken from G. L. Gomme, *London* (1837–1897) (London: Blackie, 1898), 30, 127, and differ slightly from those used in the Introduction, above.

7 *Rural Rides* (8 January 1822), Everyman Edition (London: Dent, 1912), I, 65, George Cruikshank's famous plate, 'London Going Out of Town' (1828), depicting an army of bricks and builders' tools laying waste the countryside as they erect rows of shabby terrace houses, embodies the same complaint.

8 The first census was taken in 1801, and several statistical societies were founded in the early 1830s, culminating with the London and Manchester Societies in 1834. The General Register Office was opened in 1837, and the first Government *Statistical Abstract* was published in 1840. See M. J. Cullen, *The Statistical Movement in Early Victorian Britain* (New York: Barnes and Noble, 1975).

9 From the *Weekly True Sun*, 8 September 1833; reprinted in L. H. and C. W. Houtchens, eds., *Leigh Hunt's Political and Occasional Essays* (New

York and London: Columbia, 1962), 283, which contains several of the *Weekly True Sun* pieces.

10 W. E. Trotter, *Selected Illustrated Topography of Thirty Miles Round London* (1839), 'Introduction', n.p.; Charles Knight, *London* (1841–4), i. Compare also passages about London by Wordsworth and Carlyle, both of which move from the urban scene to otherworldly considerations, Wordsworth to nature, or Carlyle to Calvinist ruminations on Judgement; in *The Prelude* (1805 version), Book VII, *passim*, and Carlyle's London Journal for 1831, in J. A. Froude, *Thomas Carlyle* (1882), II, 207.

11 This argument parallels that of Louis James in *Fiction for the Working Man* (London: Oxford, 1964), explaining similarly the rise of a largely urban lower class literature beginning at about the same time.

12 See Lot no. 310 in Sotheby's 1971 Suzannet Sale Catalogue, 117. (I am grateful to Dr Michael Slater for bringing this quotation to my attention.)

13 *Complete Works*, Virginia Edition (New York: Crowell, 1902), IX, 46.

14 See F. G. Kitton, *Charles Dickens by Pen and Pencil* (London: Sabin, Dexter, 1890), 130–1.

15 See J. P. Collier, *An Old Man's Diary* (published by the author 1871–2), IV, 12–14 (entry for 24 July 1833); Collier also tells this story, dated somewhat later, *ca.* 1834: 'He [Dickens] informed me, as we walked through it, that he knew *Hungerford Market* well, laying unusual stress on the first two syllables' (IV, 15). Dickens' punning allusion to the locale of Blacking Warehouse shows that then he could not only use but also joke about his past. (The old market had recently been demolished.)

16 They are: 'A Dinner at Poplar Walk' reprinted as 'Mr Minns and his Cousin', 'Mrs Joseph Porter', 'Horatio Sparkins', 'The Bloomsbury Christening', 'The Boarding-House' [in two parts], and 'Original Papers' [reprinted as 'Sentiment'].

17 See Duane DeVries, *Dickens's Apprentice Years*, 61–5, and Talbot Penner, 'Dickens: An Early Influence', *Dickensian*, 64 (1968), 157–62, on journalistic influences. For an interesting example of Dickens' own journalism see Walter Dexter, 'Dickens's First Contribution to 'The Morning Chronicle'' ', *Dickensian*, 31 (1935), 5–10.

18 Carl E. Schorske, 'The Idea of the City in European Thought: Voltaire to Spengler', in Oscar Handlin and J. Buchard, eds., *The Historian and the City* (Cambridge: M.I.T. and Harvard, 1963), 109. For other discussions of changes in attitudes toward the city, see Schorske, *passim*; Alexander Welsh, *The City of Dickens* (Oxford: Clarendon, 1971), 2–9; Jerome H. Buckley, *The Triumph of Time* (Cambridge: Harvard, and London: Oxford, 1956), 116–53; and Raymond Williams, *The Country and the City* (London: Chatto and Windus, 1973), *passim*.

19 Quoted by Florence Hardy, *The Life of Thomas Hardy* (1933), I, 271. (I am again indebted to Dr Michael Slater for this reference.)

2. *Pickwick Papers*, *Oliver Twist* and *Nicholas Nickleby*: Labyrinthine London

1 Reviews of *PP*'s opening numbers, while not overwhelmingly favourable, do tend to praise those qualities which the new effort had in common with *Sketches*; see Walter Dexter, 'Some Early Reviews of Pickwick', *Dickensian*, 32 (1936), 216–18.

2 For a brilliant discussion of this process see Steven Marcus, 'Language into Structure: Pickwick Revisited', *Daedalus* 101 (1972), 183–202, reprinted in *Representations* (New York: Random House, 1976).

3 [Charles Buller], *Westminster Review* 27, (1837), 196; John Ruskin, *Complete Works*, ed. E. T. Cook and A. Wedderburn (London: Allen and Unwin, and New York: Longmans, Green, 1909), XXXVII, 26.

4 From late in 1836, until the Spring of 1839, Dickens was usually working on at least two of these three novels at the same time; for this, and reasons which will become clear below, it seems valid to discuss them as moments in one unified period of Dickens' career.

5 It was originally called Mudfog when OT was appearing in *Bentley's Miscellany*, after a loose series of comic papers, 'The Mudfog Papers', Dickens had been writing for that magazine. (Mudfog has been taken for a redaction of Chatham.) The relation between OT and the humorous series was merely incidental, and Dickens wisely dropped the name entirely when the novel was issued in book form in November 1838.

6 This word, 'labyrinth', occurs with almost obsessive frequency in the novel, along with related words like 'maze'. It is used like a talisman to evoke the labyrinthine London throughout *Oliver Twist*.

7 But this description of a London rookery, powerful as it is, if anything falls considerably short of what life in such a place must have been like. Descriptions of such places would be sure to shock, and one senses Dickens' uncertainty about how far he could go in fiction before losing his readers. Compare Edwin Chadwick's description of the reactions of his co-workers preparing the report of the Royal Commission on the Health of Towns in 1843 after visits to similar slums: 'Dr Playfair has been knocked up by it and has been seriously ill. Mr Smith has had a little dysentery. Sir Henry De La Beche was obliged at Bristol to stand up at the end of alleys and vomit while Dr Playfair was investigating over-flowing privies. Sir Henry was obliged to give it up'. Quoted by S. E. Finer, *The Life and Times of Sir Edwin Chadwick* (London: Methuen, 1952), 234.

8 No doubt the description of Smithfield's live meat market also falls far short of the actuality; see Francis Sheppard, *London, 1808–1870* (London, Secker and Warburg, 1971), 189–90. The market was an outrage—but an intensely profitable one to the City Corporation—until its closure in 1855. Perhaps because it possessed its own 'attraction of repulsion', Dickens returned to Smithfield often in his fiction and essays.

9 Steven Marcus, *Dickens: From Pickwick to Dombey* (New York: Basic Books, 1965), 72.

10 Cruikshank's illustrations also emphasise this separation of the labyrinth. For example, in the dark world Oliver tends to face the left hand side of the plate; elsewhere, he faces right. Other instances of this effective graphic symbolism are the similar structure of the plates depicting Oliver asking for more gruel, and entering Fagin's den; and that of the burglary where Oliver is discovered in a dark underground cellar literally on the threshold of the door to the light world.

11 There is also in these novels a related fear, of being recognised as one's true self at the wrong time, and that being seen conveys one into the power of the seer. Pickwick must sit for his 'portrait' before the turnkeys at the Fleet, so that they will know him for a prisoner. Oliver terrifies Fagin (for once) by seeing his secret treasure; Fagin emerges in the country only to

see Oliver and then vanish; Fagin himself is surrounded by eyes in the courtroom.

12 *Charles Dickens: The World of His Novels* (Cambridge: Harvard, 1958), 30.

13 See Chs. xxxiii–xxxiv; Fagin and Monks appear outside Oliver's window but disappear without leaving any footprints in the soft earth. Dickens never explains the incident. See Steven Marcus, *Dickens: From Pickwick to Dombey*, 370–5, for an interpretation of its significance.

14 This opposition of the country and the city as places (respectively) of life and death in OT is also discussed in Joseph M. Duffy, 'Another Version of Pastoral: *Oliver Twist, Journal of English Literary History*, 35 (1968), 403–21.

15 To H. G. Adams, 18 January 1840, *PL*, II; the full statement was, '...I have many happy recollections connected with Kent, and am scarcely less interested in it than if I had been a Kentish man bred and born, and had resided in the country all my life.' (Adams was starting a Kentish periodical, and had asked Dickens to contribute to it, which proposal Dickens graciously declined.)

16 The account of it which follows is based largely on Edgar Johnson, *Charles Dickens* (London: Gollancz, 1952), 195–204, and W. J. Carlton, 'The Death of Mary Hogarth', *Dickensian*, 63 (1967), 68–74. I am grateful to Dr Paul Lieberman, MD, for advice and assistance with the discussion of Dickens' reaction to her death which follows.

17 He did miss two later instalments of OT, but only because he was quarrelling with Richard Bentley, and withheld them from *Bentley's Miscellany* to gain an advantage over him.

18 Regression is defined as, 'a reversion in behaviour, thinking, attitudes or identifications to an earlier mental or behavioural level or to an earlier stage of psychosexual development in response to organismic stress' (*Webster's Third International Dictionary*).

19 Steven Marcus, *Dickens: From Pickwick to Dombey*, 133: see also ibid., 132–40, on the psychological significance for Dickens of her death, and on the same subject, Jack Lindsay, *Charles Dickens* (London: Dakers, 1950), 121–3 and 131–5. That Mary Hogarth lived with the family for only a few weeks before her death, and not for the entire period of their marriage (as has often been assumed) only emphasises how much she was for Dickens an ideal creation of his imagination, rather than a real person.

20 As he later wrote, 'but for the mercy of God, I might easily have been, for any care that was taken of me, a little robber or a little vagabond' (Forster, *Life*, I, 25). For the autobiographical elements incorporated into OT, see Steven Marcus, *Dickens: From Pickwick to Dombey*, 358–78.

21 The Blacking Warehouse and tumbledown riverfront buildings form a recurring pattern of imagery in the novels; for a comprehensive discussion of them, see John Cary, *The Violent Effigy* (London: Faber and Faber, 1973), 147ff.

22 Compare to this passage the more direct and less theoretical verse below, which Dickens wrote for the August 1837 issue of *Bentley's Miscellany*:

> I stood by a young girl's grave last night,
> Beautiful, innocent, pure and bright,
> Who, in the bloom of her summer's pride
> And all its loveliness, drooped and died.

(Quoted by W. J. Carlton, 'The Death of Mary Hogarth', *Dickensian* 63 [1967], 73.) Here Dickens is simply stating that she was good and she died;

as time passed, his need to justify her death and his relationship to her increased. The crisis it precipitated continued for several years, as we shall see below.

23 His rising income, of course, also played an important role in extending his summer holidays. In 1839, for example, he was absent from London from the end of April to the beginning of October, about five months.

24 It should be remarked that his worship of her after her death was at least in this respect not entirely exceptional. Tennyson's similar enshrinement of Hallam's memory, witnessed by *In Memoriam* (1850), offers a striking analogue to it, even to the cult of remembrance at a country grave. Tennyson and Dickens were almost the same age at their respective bereavements, and the great, long-lasting shock both experienced seems to have involved each in throwing into question the nature of his own identity. (Dickens, incidentally, had always a very strong liking for Tennyson's verse.)

25 The sentence was a highly possible one, even considering the minor nature of the crime and tender years of the offender. See J. J. Tobias, *Crime and Industrial Society* (London: Penguin, 1972), 88–94, for a discussion of juveniles and the law.

26 In the novel Frank Cheeryble returns from a trip to Germany to study business methods there. Frederick Engels made a similar journey (in reverse) about four years later, with somewhat different results. See Steven Marcus, *Engels, Manchester and the Working Class* (New York: Random House, 1974), 249–52, for a comparison of Dickens' and Engels' responses to Manchester and the factory system.

27 Even the name 'Cheeryble', is a failure, suggesting a combination of 'cheery' and 'able' and thus evidencing a desire to force a significance upon them they simply do not bear out. Doubling them into twins is, I suspect, another attempt to strengthen them by resort to artifice.

3. The *Old Curiosity Shop* and *Barnaby Rudge*: Breakdown and Breakthrough

1 Dickens eventually narrowed the choice of title to two: *Old Humphrey's Clock* and *Master Humphrey's Clock*. It is possible that the initials M.H. were what attracted him to the latter, even though Dickens realised 'Master' was a more ambiguous term than 'Old', in that it could refer to a young boy as well as a man (*Life*, I, 116).

2 Unconscious motives continued to direct the course of OCS. Dickens' remarks about not wishing to murder Little Nell, yet being forced to do so against his will (*Life*, I, 122–3), reveal a similar situation at the close of the novel.

3 Dickens' use of the Curiosity Shop in this manner was no doubt unconscious and he does not make much of it; nevertheless it makes an interesting comparison with Balzac's exploitation of the same device in *La Peau de Chagrin* [*The Skin of a Wild Ass*] (1831).

4 Nell's imminent transformation into a woman is in a sense her real danger, and as the example of Mrs Quilp suggests, her own latent sexuality could be the means of her downfall. For an examination of sexual matters in OCS, see Laurence Senelick, 'Little Nell and the Prurience of Sentimentality', *Dickens Studies*, 3 (1967), 146–59.

5 The interest in the actual past was also revealed in Dickens' asking for George Cattermole as an illustrator for MHC: according to the editors of the *Pilgrim Letters*, 'it was doubtless because of his [Cattermole's] skill in antiquarian and architectural subjects that he [Dickens] made this request' (PL, II, 8n).

6 See E. J. Hobsbawm, *Industry and Empire* (Harmondsworth: Penguin, 1969), 122-3. Feargus O'Connor, one of the most personally popular Chartist leaders, drew much of his support from such a demand for land, and did so in the heavily industrialised Midlands. Such a scheme was not only politically impossible, but if implemented would have been catastrophic in its consequences. Factory workers would not have made good farmers. Mrs Gaskill's *Mary Barton* (1848) provides a more critical analysis of some of the conservative and regressive aspects of early Chartism.

7 Letter to W. H. Harrison, 6 June 1841, *Complete Works* (London: Allen and Unwin, and New York: Longmans, Green, 1909), XXXIV, 26

8 Ibid. 26.

9 See, for example, Jack Lindsay, '*Barnaby Rudge*', in John Gross and Gabriel Pearson, eds., *Dickens and the Twentieth Century* (London: Routledge and Kegan Paul, 1962), 104.

4. *Martin Chuzzlewit: Architecture and Accommodation*

1 He had, no doubt, been reading *The French Revolution* shortly before or while writing BR; 'Chartism' had appeared in 1839, and *Past and Present* in April 1843, as MC was appearing (the first number was published in January 1843).

2 After this chapter had been written, there appeared an essay by Alan R. Burke, 'The House of Chuzzlewit and the Architectural City', *Dickens Studies Annual*, 3 (1974), 14-40, which makes many of the same observations about the architectural dimension of MC. However, its main use of these points is to adumbrate a rather mechanical interpretation of the novel which sees it as anti-urban, and so reaches exactly the opposite conclusion to mine.

3 See Paul Fussell, *The Rhetorical World of Augustan Humanism* (Oxford: Clarendon, 1965), 171-210, for a discussion of architectural imagery in eighteenth-century writing.

4 *Dickens: From Pickwick to Dombey* (New York: Basic Books, 1965), 214.

5 *Charles Dickens* (London: Longmans, Green, 1965), 96. It is difficult to understand how usually perceptive critics like Forster and Chesterton dismissed the American material—as structurally unrelated to the novel— admitting it to be riotously funny, but a red herring nevertheless.

6 This last matter has been overestimated in importance. A careful reading of the letters and Forster's *Life* reveal that Dickens' disillusionment had begun before the full weight of the American reaction to his advocacy of the international copyright had begun to be felt. See Paul B. Davis, 'Dickens and the American Press, 1842', *Dickens Studies*, 4 (1968), 32-77.

7 This struck many English visitors as odd, for in England wood as a building material was already in short supply, as it was not in America.

8 On the theme of corrupted Edens, see Stuart Curran, 'The Lost Paradises of *Martin Chuzzlewit*', *Nineteenth Century Fiction*, 25 (1970), 51-67. See also, for a comprehensive discussion of Dickens' reactions to nature in America,

Coral Lansbury, 'Dickens' Romanticism Domesticated', *Dickens Studies Newsletter*, 3 (1972), 36–46.

9 Quoted by Edgar Johnson, *Charles Dickens* (London: Gollancz, 1953), 409.

10 It is within this larger context of the novel that the view from the roof should be seen; Dorothy Van Ghent's influential essay, 'The Dickens World: A View from Todgers's', *Sewance Review*, 58 (1950), 419–38, makes it serve a general argument about Dickens' vision with little immediate reference to MC.

11 *Dostoevsky and Romantic Realism* (Cambridge: Harvard, 1965), 82; see also Raymond Williams, *The Country and the City* (London: Chatto and Windus, 1973), 154–6, where the same point is developed in slightly more detail.

12 *The Condition of the Working Class in England* (London: Panther, 1972), 58.

5. *Dombey and Son*: The World Metropolis

1 See Michael Slater, 'Carlyle and Jerrold into Dickens: A Study of *The Chimes*', in Ada Nisbet and Blake Nevius, eds., *Dickens Centennial Essays* (Berkeley and London: California, 1971), 184–204, and the same author's Introduction to Volume I of the Penguin *Christmas Books* (1971). On the general issue of Carlylean influence, see Michael Oddie, *Dickens and Carlyle* (London: Centenary, 1972). I agree with Oddie's conclusion that Carlyle's effect on Dickens was to help him move in directions and toward positions he had already instinctively adopted, and not to change fundamentally Dickens' social thinking.

2 Though all of Dickens' novels before this had centred around London, the decision to set DS in the metropolis may not have been automatic. Dickens had spent the better part of the years 1844–6 on the Continent, first of all to save money, but also to gather foreign material to use in his writing.

3 Quoted by E. P. Thompson and Eileen Yeo, eds., *The Unknown Mayhew* (London: Merlin, 1971), 97, 101.

4 Mayhew again provides an apposite remark: 'The mere name of London awakens a thousand trains of varied reflections. Perhaps the first thought that it excites in the mind, paints it as the focus of modern civilization, of the hottest, the most restless activity of the social elements.' (Ibid. 97)

5 Figures from J. W. Dodds, *The Age of Paradox* (London: Gollancz, 1953), 223, 245.

6 From 1841 to 1850, imports increased in value 60 per cent; exports, despite two serious depressions, increased 100 per cent.

7 Quoted by A. P. Stanley, *The Life and Correspondence of Thomas Arnold* (London: Fellowes, 1877) II, 388.

8 It is possible that Dombey would have suggested to readers an implicit comparison with Hudson. But what would have impressed them most were the differences between them. Hudson was a self-made man who controlled a huge railway network (before his collapse in 1854) and was in 1846 clearly the man of the hour, having in the previous year become M.P. for Sunderland. Readers would also have noticed that Dombey and Son was a privately owned concern, and not a new limited liability company, which entities first had become legal in 1844. This corporate form, which meant that a director was not personally responsible for the debts of his company, was what made large scale capital ventures, like railway building, and modern

business as we know it, possible. Dombey is committed to the business practices of the past; thus, when the house 'falls', Dombey is bankrupted along with it.

9 See Steven Marcus, *Dickens: From Pickwick to Dombey* (New York: Basic Books, 1965), 300–13, for a discussion of social change in the novel.

10 For example, see Kathleen Tillotson, *Novels of the Eighteen-Forties* (Oxford: Clarendon, 1954), 200.

11 'The English Dickens and *Dombey and Son*', in Ada Nisbet and Blake Nevius, eds., *Dickens Centennial Essays*, 8.

12 Steven Marcus, *Dickens: From Pickwick to Dombey*, 355.

13 The story was told by one of his sons, Henry, that having told his father he had won a prize at school, he was gravely disappointed that his father made no response, until later that day Dickens broke down in tears to tell him how happy he was. Henry concluded: 'He was curiously reserved; he did not like to show what he really felt' (Henry F. Dickens, *Recollections* [London: Heinemann, 1934], 36).

6. *Bleak House*: Homes for the Homeless

1 Mr Dombey's railway ride in Chapter xx of *DS* probably owes something to Austin's experience.

2 See *Coutts*, 77ff, and Edgar Johnson's valuable commentary on the letters. For the history of the institution, the best account is Dickens' own article, 'Home for Homeless Women', *HW*, 23 April 1853; *MP*, 368–82.

3 *The Bottle*, which Cruikshank conceived shortly after his sudden 'conversion' to the Temperance cause, was a series of eight dramatic plates showing the gradual ruin of a working class family after the insidious 'Bottle' is introduced one night at supper. The series was sold at only one shilling, with the hope it would reach a wide audience. It was extremely successful, inspiring many poets to praise it (Matthew Arnold among them), and in stage versions continued to be popular for over fifty years.

4 The case is made by K. J. Fielding in 'Dickens's Novels and Miss Burdett-Coutts', *Dickensian*, 51 (1955), 31–4. Though certainly just in this contention, I think Fielding underestimates the influence of Urania Cottage in Dickens' sympathetic and generous treatment of Martha, the prostitute, in *DC*.

5 In the discussion below I am indebted to two valuable studies of Victorian critical thought and practice, Richard Stang, *The Theory of the Novel in England, 1850–1870* (New York: Columbia, 1959), and Kenneth Graham, *English Criticism of the Novel, 1865–1900* (Oxford: Clarendon, 1965).

6 See Harry Stone, 'Dickens and the Uses of Literature', *Dickensian*, 69 (1973), 139–47, for a fuller discussion of this question.

7 From the preface to the first edition of the First Series of *SB*.

8 In *Dostoevsky and Romantic Realism* (Cambridge: Harvard, 1965), 13; see also 3–27.

9 See Alexander Welsh, *The City of Dickens* (Oxford: Clarendon, 1971), 16–32, for a discussion of the growing perception of the city as problem in nineteenth-century literature.

10 This part of the entry for 'Fog' in Charles Dickens Junior's *Dickens's Dictionary of London*, Facsimile of 1879 edition (London: Howard Baker, 1972).

11 Quoted from *The Lancet*, July 1855, by G. Laurence Gomme, *London, 1837–1897* (London: Blackie, 1898), 218.

12 I am indebted to K. J. Fielding for suggesting that the East Wind also interrupted the normal operations of shipping in the Port of London and the Thames estuary, thus linking it to the agents of economic stagnation in the novel (Chancery, the Dedlocks, etc.).

13 A great number of the novel's particulars have been linked closely to 'real', that is to say actual, people and events. See John Butt, *Dickens at Work* (London: Methuen, 1957) 176–200, and '*Bleak House* Once More', *Critical Quarterly*, 1 (1959), 302–7; K. J. Fielding and Alec Brice, '*Bleak House* and the Graveyard', in Robert B. Partlow, ed., *Dickens the Craftsman* (Carbondale: Southern Illinois, 1970), 115–39; numerous studies by Trevor Blount, including 'The Graveyard Symbolism of *Bleak House* in the Context of 1850', *Review of English Studies*, N.S. 14 (1963), 370–8, 'The Importance of Place in *Bleak House*', *Dickensian*, 61 (1965), 140–9, and 'Dickens and Mr. Krook's Spontaneous Combustion', *Dickens Studies Annual*, 1 (1970), 183–211; and Anne Smith, 'The Ironmaster in *Bleak House*', *Essays in Criticism*, 21 (1971), 159–69.

14 See K. J. Fielding, 'Dickens's Work with Miss Coutts:—I, Nova Scotia Gardens and What Grew There', *Dickensian*, 61 (1965), 112–19, from which I have drawn freely in the account below. See also, his 'Dickens's Work with Miss Coutts:—II, Casby and the Westminster Landlords'; ibid. 155–60, which discusses a slightly later effort to encourage landlords to improve existing properties.

15 The project lapsed after this because the principal tenant could not be evicted. No further work was done until 1859.

16 The importance of the house image in BH has been noted by two critics, Jack Lindsay, in *Charles Dickens* (London: Dakers, 1950), 24 and 300–2, and Alice Van Buren Kelly, in 'The Bleak Houses of *Bleak House*', *Nineteenth Century Fiction*, 25 (1970), 253–68. I should like to acknowledge in particular my debt to Van Buren Kelly's article, from which I have drawn freely in the following section of this chapter.

17 The brick-field is placed near St Albans, but may have been modelled after the Kensington Potteries, often called London's worst slum, and overrun by the pigs its mainly Irish inhabitants kept.

18 The letter continued in a more practical vein: 'you cannot fail to be struck by the consideration that if large buildings had been erected for the working people instead of the absurd and expensive separate walnut shells in which they live, London would have been about a third of its present size, and every family would have had a country walk, miles nearer their own door' (*Coutts*, 199).

19 For a thorough study of the role of women in the novel, see Ellen Moers, '*Bleak House*: The Agitating Women', *Dickensian*, 69 (1973), 13–24.

20 See J. Hillis Miller, *Charles Dickens: The World of His Novels* (Cambridge: Harvard, 1958), 196, and Q. D. Leavis in F. R. and Q. D. Leavis, *Dickens the Novelist* (London: Chatto and Windus, 1970), 124–5 for discussions of the metaphorical implications of Chancery.

21 Quoted by Robert A. Donovan, 'Structure and Idea in *Bleak House*', *Journal of English Literary History*, 29 (1962), 181.

22 Red tape was the red cotton string used in the nineteenth century to tie bundles of government and legal documents.

23 See G. Kitson Clark, *The Making of Victorian England* (London: Methuen,

1962), 214ff. for a discussion of the political power of the gentry. Trollope's Palliser novels demonstrate this equally well, though from a different moral standpoint than that of Dickens.

24 Priscilla Metcalf, *Victorian London* (London: Cassell, 1972), 41.

25 Esther's other dreams are also important. J. Hillis Miller sees in her dream of being a bead in a flaming necklace a fear of alienation, of becoming an interchangeable thing (*Charles Dickens: The World of His Novels*, 24–5). In a dream account Dickens cut from the proofs, Esther wanders Bleak House with a bundle of keys, trying all the locks with them in vain. This is a similar situation with an element of sexual frustration added, a foreshadowing of the life she would lead as Mrs Jarndyce (Leslie C. Staples, 'Shavings from Dickens's Workshop—*Bleak House*', *Dickensian*, 50 [1954], 189).

26 For a more detailed discussion of the description of *Bleak House*, see Alice Van Buren Kelly, 'The Bleak Houses of *Bleak House*', *Nineteenth Century Fiction*, 25 (1970), 265–7.

27 As Q. D. Leavis notes, this technique of the split character is an antecedent of one more fully developed in GE, with Jaggers and Wemmick; see F. R. and Q. D. Leavis, *Dickens the Novelist*, 139.

28 They are reprinted in RP as, 'The Detective Police', 485–503, 'Three Detective Anecdotes', 504–12, and 'On Duty with Inspector Field', 513–26. They date from 1850–1.

29 Dickens' view of Chinese society (discussed at the end of the previous chapter) as trapped in the past by an outmoded and paralysing social system offers an interesting perspective on BH; see his 'The Chinese Junk', *Examiner*, 24 June 1848; MP, 102–5.

30 For discussions of pastoral imagery in the novel, see Louis Crompton, 'Satire and Symbolism in *Bleak House*', *Nineteenth Century Fiction*, 12 (1958), 284–303; and Robert Barnard, *Imagery and Theme in the Novels of Dickens* (Bergen, Norway: Universitetsforlaget, 1974), 66–9.

31 If one agrees with J. Hillis Miller's conclusion that the source of social evil in BH is 'in the ineradicable human tendency to take the sign for the substance, and in the instinctive habit of interpretation, assimilating others into a private or collective system of meaning' (Introduction, Penguin edition [1969], 33–4), there is no hope for social regeneration. But if one does accept this, it would appear that novelists would be among society's chief villains. Dickens' commitment to the power of the written word makes this interpretation too extreme, well argued as it is.

7. Hard Times: The Industrial City

1 The phrase is used to describe Turner's painting 'Rain, Steam and Speed', by Herbert L. Sussman, in *Victorians and the Machine* (Cambridge: Harvard, 1968), 31. See also ibid. 41–75, for an intelligent and useful discussion of Dickens' changing attitudes toward industrialism throughout his career.

2 That chapter of BH had been written in the summer of 1853, appearing in the concluding double number, XIX–XX, in September 1853; the planning for HT began no later than January, 1854.

3 In the discussion below I have drawn freely upon George Bornstein's

excellent study, 'Miscultivated Field and Corrupted Garden: Imagery in *Hard Times*', *Nineteenth Century Fiction*, 26 (1971), 158–70.

4 It has also been argued that these images reflect the proper, creative response of the narrator to those unpleasant facts; see Monroe Engel, *The Maturity of Dickens* (Cambridge: Harvard, 1959), 195. On the question of creative imagination, see David Sonstroem, 'Fettered Fancy in *Hard Times*', *PMLA*, 84 (1969), 520–9

5 These titles did not appear in the serial version in HW, but were added for the one volume edition later in 1854.

6 The law was changed in 1857, making divorce a civil action. The grounds for divorce, however, were extremely limited, though they would have freed Stephen (if he could had saved enough money to afford the services of counsel and pay court fees).

7 In this fantasy translation, an important feature is that the roles of the spouses are reversed: it is the wife rather than the husband who is the guilty party. When Dickens' marriage collapsed it was he that engineered the break, not Catherine, but he blamed her for it publically, and even charged her with emotional desertion, in having been indifferent to her own children.

8. *Little Dorrit*: People Like Houses

1 In a useful essay, Edwin A. Barrett examines Dickens' use of metaphors of disease in the novel, which tend toward the same effect; see '*Little Dorrit* and the Disease of Modern Life', *Nineteenth Century Fiction*, 25 (1970), 199–215.

2 The origin of the name, perhaps known to Dickens, is in the medieval representation of the five Sorrowful Mysteries of the Rosary, the Virgin's heart pierced by five swords, gushing with blood. See T. W. Hill, 'Notes on *Little Dorrit*', *Dickensian*, 41 (1945), 200. (Later in the novel, when Arthur unintentionally is cruel to Little Dorrit, it is described as if he were thrusting a 'dagger into the faithful heart of his Little Dorrit' [381].)

3 MS., V&A; cited by Paul D. Herring, 'Dickens' Monthly Number Plans for *Little Dorrit*', *Modern Philology*, 64 (1966), 34.

4 For a novel with such an oppressive atmosphere of evil, there are very few actual misdeeds other than these, both set in the past. The only evil act we actually know to occur in the present is Blandois poisoning Pet's dog. And even Blandois' principle past crime, murdering his wife, is not allowed to be a legal certainty.

5 Unnatural imagery also dominates this additional descriptive passage, which Dickens cut from the proofs (for Book I, Ch. xv): 'So disused was the spot, and so long since it had known repair, that the whole seemed to be resolving itself into the city mud and dust, and showers, fogs and winds. The outer surface of the bricks turned to powder under the hands; the painted wood peeled off in layers; the iron railings was in rusty rags. The twigs broke when they were touched, and the patch of grass was little better than green mildew on the ground. What matter of worms... underneath it... that occasionally died on the surface were as black as the twigs, and as brittle, and assumed their forms and crumbled with them and cast their undistinguished mites of rottenness into the general bank.' (Leslie C. Staples, 'Shavings from Dickens's Workshop—*Little Dorrit*', *Dickensian*, 49 [1953], 169–70.)

6 *The Making of the English Working Class* (Harmondsworth: Penguin, 1968), 407.

7 Quoted by Gordon R. Taylor, *The Angel-Makers* (London: Heinemann, 1958), 302.

8 Arthur was born in about 1785, and it appears that Methodist child rearing intensified in severity and rigidness toward the close of the century, the years he was growing up. In constructing the details of his childhood, Dickens was no doubt quite accurate. It is interesting to compare Arthur's childhood with that of Augustus Hare, an eminent Victorian art critic, who was born somewhat later, in 1834. Toward the end of the century, Hare wrote an autobiography in which he outlined his early years, revealing that as a suckling infant he had been adopted by—or rather given to—a maiden aunt who raised him as her own son, and whom all his life he regarded as his 'true' mother. Brought up in accordance with her firm Evangelical beliefs, he was never allowed friends or playmates; had all his toys taken from him at age four; was never allowed to play and once was whipped (with a riding whip) for tumbling in the hay; often was locked in a small room as punishment, and confined there for days on bread and water; and on one particularly gruesome day, was forced to watch his stepmother hang his pet cat in the garden as a lesson he should love no one but her. Perhaps such brutalities against children were far more routine in the nineteenth century than would be comfortable to believe. See the early volumes of his autobiography, *The Story of My Life* (London: George Allen, 1896–1900).

9 Their religion is also not particularly central to the novel, being more in the way of a means of adding horror to their roles as David's tyrannical, Oedipal step-parents.

10 The claim is made by Jack Lindsay, *Charles Dickens* (London: Dakers, 1950), 38.

11 See Halévy's *England in 1815* (London: Benn, 1949), 387–587; and for more recent studies which have upheld this view, though with qualifications, G. M. Young, *Portrait of an Age* (London: Oxford, 1953), *passim*, G. Kitson Clark, *The Making of Victorian England* (London: Methuen, 1962), *passim*, and E. P. Thompson, *The Making of the English Working Class*, 385–440. It should be noted that Dickens was not alone in his interest in Evangelicalism at this time: other novelists who were examining it in the 1850s include Thackeray, in *The Newcomes* (1853–5), shortly before *LD*, and George Eliot, in *Adam Bede* (1859), shortly after it. No doubt, their interest had been stimulated by the long public controversy over the reinstitution of a Catholic hierarchy in England in 1850, and the publication in 1854 of the results of the religious census of 1851, which had revealed one half the population to be dissenters of one sort or another.

12 Edmund Bergler, '*Little Dorrit* and Dickens' Intuitive Knowledge of Psychic Masochism', *American Imago*, 14 (1957), 385.

13 The changing tone of Dickens' political journalism is discussed more fully by John Butt, in 'The Topicality of *Little Dorrit*', *University of Toronto Quarterly*, 29 (1959), 4–7.

14 Carlisle (as Lord Morpeth) had been a sanitary reformer in the late 1840s and early 1850s and during that time became friendly with Dickens. Now he was Palmerston's appointment as Lord-Lieutenant of Ireland.

15 As Angus Easson notes, Dickens' portrait of the prison was based entirely on his childhood memories, and yet was extremely accurate, testifying to

the power of those memories after three decades. See, 'Marshalsea Prisoners: Mr. Dorrit and Mr. Hemans', *Dickens Studies Annual*, 3 (1974), 77–86.

16 A thorough analysis of the Iron Bridge episodes which reaches the same conclusion can be found in Douglas Hewitt, *The Approach to Fiction* (London: Longman, 1972), 113–22.

17 In a speech, 'Charles Dickens and *Little Dorrit*', reprinted in *Dickensian*, 4 (1908), 323.

9. A *Tale of Two Cities*, The *Uncommercial Traveller* and *Great Expectations*: Paradise Revisited

1 Philip Collins notes that Dickens' periodicals, HW and AYR, contain less political satire after about 1856; see 'A Tale of Two Novels', *Dickens Studies Annual*, 2 (1972), 346.

2 Robert Garis justly compares *Great Expectations* to Freud's *Civilization and its Discontents*; see *The Dickens Theatre* (London: Oxford, 1965), 206–7.

3 Though FD is normally attributed to Collins, Dickens worked with him so closely that he should be considered a co-author; in a letter to Collins some time later Dickens called it a joint production (14 October 1862; NL, III, 310). See Robert L. Brennan's thorough introduction to his edition of the working script, *'The Frozen Deep': Under the Management of Mr. Charles Dickens* (Ithaca, N.Y.: Cornell, 1966).

4 Letter to Mrs Watson, 7 December 1857; quoted by Franklin P. Rolfe, 'More Letters to the Watsons', *Dickensian*, 38 (1942), 190.

5 'A Tale of Two Novels', *Dickens Studies Annual*, 2 (1972), 345.

6 He had read intermittently for charity since 1853. The first of several readings in 1857 beginning in June were also for charity; Dickens did not read for his own profit until 29 April 1858.

7 A number of critics of TTC have explored the biographical antecedents of these characters; Philip Collins, 'A Tale of Two Novels', *Dickens Studies Annual*, 2 (1972), 336–51; Jack Lindsay, *Charles Dickens*, (London: Dakers, 1950), 359–69; Leonard Manheim, 'A Tale of Two Characters', *Dickens Studies Annual*, 1 (1970), 225–37; and K. J. Fielding, *Charles Dickens* (London: Longmans, Green, 1965), 189–206. Lucie Manette is obviously inspired by Ellen Ternan, looks like her, and what is more, though she is 17 in the novel, Dickens first put her age as 18, that of Ellen in 1857, altering it only after writing several chapters (MS., V&A). The kind of projection represented by Manette is altogether different, and the account of his illness (191ff.) is an astonishingly accurate self-analysis by Dickens of his own mental condition. Manette's shoemaking is very close indeed to Dickens' shoeblacking; and oddly enough Trollope often made an analogy between writing novels and making shoes, which perhaps he had unconsciously absorbed from TTC (See his *Autobiography* [London and New York: Oxford, 1950], 323–4).

8 This section discusses only the first series of UT, seventeen articles which appeared in AYR from 28 January to 13 October 1860, and which were collected in a one-volume edition in December 1860. A second series followed in 1863, and it was resumed intermittently until Dickens' death. Initially it enjoyed a modest success, selling out two small editions and part of a third by the end of 1861, 3000 copies in all. (I am indebted to Professor Robert L. Patton for assistance in compiling this information.)

9 See Harry Stone's Introduction to his *Uncollected Writings* (London: Allen Lane, 1969), 4–5, and *passim*, from which this account of Dickens and periodical literature up to the founding of AYR in large part is taken.

10 The Schools were charitable, supported by contributors mainly from the travellers themselves, for children of indigent or deceased members of the trade. The connection between the speech and UT was examined by W. H. Drayton, 'The Uncommercial Traveller and the Royal Commercial Travellers' Schools', *Dickensian*, 57 (1961), 118–20, and originally noted by Forster, *Life*, II, 231.

11 The identifying tag 'London' appended to 'Covent-garden' above may also indicate a conscious appeal to a national, rather than his assumed customary metropolitan, audience.

12 The awful pun on dragged (as in dragging the river for a corpse) is probably intentional, as one of the corpses on view is that of a drowned man; a few pages later, the Uncommercial takes a river bath but flees in terror after imagining corpses floating toward him in the Seine.

13 He did rent houses for short periods so his daughters could be in town for the 'season'.

14 The phrase is a running title Dickens made up for the first page of 'Nurse's Stories', apparently for the Charles Dickens Edition, but never used; it is written (in Dickens' hand) at the head of page 115 in a copy of the cheap Edition of 1866 (MS., Berg).

15 The essay may have drawn upon dim memories of a piece in Goldsmith's *Bee*, 'A City NIGHT-PIECE'. In it, Goldsmith walks the city at 2 a.m., feeling its oppressive gloom, and imagining, 'There may come a time when this temporary solitude may be made continual, and the city itself, like its inhabitants, fade away, and leave a desert in its room.'

16 The critic of *The Morning Chronicle* had written of UT, 'the old humour which first shone out so brilliantly in "Pickwick Papers" still exists in all its original force' (10 January 1861). The sentiment was echoed by James Fitzjames Stephen in *Saturday Review*, 11 (23 February 1861), 194–6.

17 The story of Lever's serial and Dickens' response to its dullness is told in John Sutherland, *Victorian Novelists and Publishers* (London: Athlone, and Chicago: Chicago, 1976), 166–87.

18 For a brilliant analysis of how many of those memories surfaced in GE, see Harry Stone's two essays, 'Fire, Hand, and Gate: Dickens' *Great Expectations*', *Kenyon Review* 24 (1962), 662–90, and 'The Genesis of a Novel: *Great Expectations*', in E. W. F. Tomlin, ed., *Charles Dickens* (1969), 109–31. See also Ada Nisbet, 'The Autobiographical Matrix of *Great Expectations*', *Victorian Newsletter*, No. 15 (Spring, 1959), 10–13.

19 In a sense, this event picks up where *David Copperfield* had left off; David recalls being terrified of his father's grave after hearing the story of Lazarus, but Pip actually experiences a nightmarish parental resurrection.

20 Julian Moynahan, 'The Hero's Guilt: The Case of *Great Expectations*', *Essays in Criticism*, 10 (1960), 60.

21 In fact, as Joseph Gold notes, the novel contains a light-hearted joke about the Warehouse, with Joe commenting, when he comes to London and sees it, that 'it don't come up to its likeness' (210), thus indicating the extent to which the subject had become emotionally defused for him; see his *Charles Dickens: Radical Moralist* (Minneapolis: Minnesota, and London: Oxford, 1972), 241.

22 See Jerome Meckier, 'Some Household Words', *Dickensian* 71 (1975), 5–20,

which prints the texts of two recently discovered accounts of Dickens' conversations mentioning the pain, which Meckier convincingly dates from early December, 1860.

23 See *PR*, 305–63.

24 Emphasising the connection, Dickens later notes that Magwitch has returned, as he actually would have, from Botany Bay (314).

25 A case can be made for Jaggers doing so too, but my own guess is that Jaggers' eventual redemption rubs off from Wemmick's, and was not part of Dickens' original design. Jaggers is so repulsive at first that it is difficult to believe he was intended to be a sympathetic character. For such an argument, though, see Anthony Winner, 'Character and Knowledge in Dickens: The Enigma of Jaggers', *Dickens Studies Annual*, 3 (1974), 100–21.

26 The apt phrase is taken from Noel C. Peyrouton's thorough defence of Wemmick's character in 'John Wemmick: Enigma?', *Dickens Studies*, 1 (1964), 39–47.

27 Walworth in the 1820s was, though relatively close to the City, undeveloped marshy land in which a bemoated house would not have been very difficult to construct, and which would have been quite practical as well.

28 See Francis Sheppard, *London, 1808–1870* (London: Secker and Warburg, 1971), 151–5, for a summary discussion of the development of London's suburbs.

10. *Our Mutual Friend*: The Changing City

1 *The London Building World of the 1860s* (London: Thames and Hudson, 1973), 7.

2 The entries in Dickens' 'Memoranda Book' which refer to this material, 'Found drowned' and 'A "long shore" man-woman-child-or-family', occur in a context which suggests they were written in 1855; 'Found drowned' is the title of a bill which appears in the opening number of *Little Dorrit*, which appeared in December 1855. Either the note had stuck in his memory, or he had been looking through the book before beginning *OMF* ('Memoranda Book', MS., Berg).

3 For a fairly representative catalogue of the many possible symbolic meanings that have been given the river, see Monroe Engel, *The Maturity of Dickens* (Cambridge: Harvard, and London: Oxford, 1959), 138–45.

4 From the evidence of Mayhew it does seem incontrovertible that rough dust (i.e. unsorted) usually did contain fecal matter, certainly of horses and dogs if not humans. And in the context in which this topic is introduced, a dinner party, for Dickens to have allowed Mortimer to be more specific than this in his description would have been extremely indecorous and offensive.

5 *Capital* (Chicago: Kerr, 1921), Vol. I, 117. Dickens also extends his analysis to include shares, taking the concept of the abstraction of wealth into gold one step further, into paper (Book I, Ch. x). Compare this to the much discussed passage about the wind blowing London's 'mysterious paper currency' a few chapters later (I, xii).

6 The introduction of frogs is a private joke—an object exactly like this was one of Dickens' favourite desk ornaments.

7 On the same subject Marx wrote: 'Labour power is . . . a commodity which its possessor, the wage-worker, sells to capital. Why does he sell it? In

order to live' (*Selected Works of Marx and Engels* [London: Lawrence and Wishart, 1968], 74).

8 Perhaps Dickens' ambivalence about the value of education in OMF is partly explained by his realisation that learning had become the qualification and preparation for entry into the world dominated by money and commercial values. For an interesting discussion of this and related matters, see Richard D. Altick, 'Education, Print and Paper in *Our Mutual Friend*', in C. de L. Ryals, ed., *Nineteenth-Century Literary Perspectives* (Durham, N.C.: Duke, 1974), 337–54.

9 For a study of Jenny Wren's role in the novel, see Garrett Stewart, *Dickens and the Trials of Imagination* (Cambridge: Harvard, 1974), 198–221.

10 Near drownings, in which someone is thought dead but returns to life, seem to occur often in the fiction of the 1860s, in Tennyson's *Enoch Arden* (1862) for example. Various forms of resurrections, aquatic or otherwise, play important parts in Mrs Humphrey Wood's bestseller, *East Lynne* (1861), and Mrs Gaskell's *Sylvia's Lovers* (1863); the Tichbourne case of the early 1870s was one much publicised instance of an alleged such return to life by a missing spouse.

11 It is definitely not Thompson's Spring, Dickens adds, perhaps inspiring T. S. Eliot's use of the same comparison in *The Waste Land*.

12 The phrase 'in its own way garrulous about its early life' further recalls an incident in the mid-1860s reported by his son Henry F. Dickens, when the writer, Henry and the other children were playing a memory game, and Dickens used in it the phrase 'Warren's Blacking', doing so 'with a strange twinkle in his eye'. None of them realised the significance of the phrase until years later they read about their father's childhood in Forster's biography (*The Recollections of Sir Henry Dickens, K.C.* [London: Heinemann, 1934], 45).

13 This essay is the subject of an interesting analysis by Alexander Welsh in *The City of Dickens* (Oxford: Clarendon, 1971), 13–15, who uses it to illustrate his contention that in the nineteenth century the artist's response to the city changes from satire to serious journalism, and then religious hope. He does not, however, relate it with particularity to Dickens' career.

Epilogue. Dickens and the City

1 See Philip Collins, '*Sikes and Nancy*: Dickens' Last Reading', *Times Literary Supplement*, 11 June 1971, 681–2, and his edition of *The Public Readings* (1975), 465–71, for the history of this particular reading.

2 In an interesting experiment, these chapters were given to an advanced undergraduate class in practical criticism, and after a discussion, the group attempted to date them. The students almost unanimously agreed they were by some unknown modernist writer of the 1920s; the other teacher present thought them by some later nineteenth century follower of Dickens, such as Gissing.

3 Robert Garis, *The Dickens Theatre* (London: Oxford, 1965), 44.

4 Collins makes this observation about ED in 'Dickens and London', in H. J. Dyos and Michael Wolff, eds., *The Victorian City* (London and Boston: Routledge and Kegan Paul, 1973), 544.

5 I have borrowed this concept from Philip Fisher, 'City Matter: City Minds', in J. H. Buckley, ed., *The Worlds of Victorian Fiction* (Cambridge: Harvard,

1975), 371–89. See also Steven Marcus, 'Reading the Illegible', in H. J. Dyos and Michael Wolff, eds., *The Victorian City* (1973), 257–76.

6 *Quarterly Review*, 64 (1839), 87; see also *passim*, 83–102. The notion that London's neighbourhoods were so diverse as to have little in common was current from the eighteenth century. But the sense of urgency and even panic conveyed by the phrase *terra incognita* developed only in the early nineteenth century. See, for example, Dr Johnson's placid advice to Boswell, noting 'the wonderful extent and variety of London, and ... that men of curious enquiry might see in it such modes of life as very few could even imagine. He in particular recommended us to *explore Wapping*, which we resolved to do.' (When Boswell did, in 1782, he was quite disappointed with Wapping, and lamented the 'uniformity' which was overtaking the metropolis!)

7 Figures from Richard D. Altick, *The English Common Reader* (Chicago: Chicago, 1957), 383–4 and 395. See also 379–96 for useful comparative figures.

8 For useful discussions of the ways in which writers repressed their knowledge of the city, see G. Robert Strange, 'The Frightened Poets', in H. J. Dyos and Michael Wolff, eds., *The Victorian City*, 475–95; and U. C. Knoepflmacher, 'The Novel Between City and Country', ibid. 517–36.

9 'A Nice Place to Visit' [Review of Raymond Williams, *The Country and the City*], *New York Review*, 22 (6 January 1975), 35.

10 For a suggestive essay on modernism and the city, see Malcolm Bradbury, 'The Cities of Modernism', in Malcolm Bradbury and James McFarlane, eds., *Modernism 1890–1930* (Harmondsworth: Penguin, 1976), 96–104.

11 *Critical Studies of the Works of Charles Dickens* (New York: Greenberg, 1924), 53.

Index